Cooking the U.P. way

Niru Gupta

Orient Longman

ORIENT LONGMAN LIMITED

Registered Office
3-6-272 Himayatnagar, Hyderabad 500 029 (A.P.), India

Other Offices
Bangalore / Bhopal / Bhubaneshwar / Calcutta / Chandigarh
Chennai / Ernakulam / Guwahati / Hyderabad / Jaipur
Lucknow / Mumbai / New Delhi / Patna

© Niru Gupta 2000

ISBN 81 250 1558 2

Book Design and Typeset by
OSDATA
Hyderabad 500 029

Printed in India at
Orion Printers
Hyderabad 500 004

Published by
Orient Longman Limited
3-6-272 Himayatnagar, Hyderabad 500 029

Contents

Glossary

Indian	English (American)	Indian	English (American)
Adrak	Fresh Ginger	Deghi Mirch	Chilli Powder
Ajwain	Carum/Thymol	Dhania	Coriander
Amchoor	Mango Powder	Dhuli Moong	Husked Green Gram
Amrood	Guava	Dhuli Urad	Husked Black Gram
Anjeer	Figs	Frans bean ke Beej	Haricot beans (Navy beans)
Arbi	Colacosia	Frans Beans	French Beans (String Beans)
Arhar daal	Yellow Lentils	Gajar	Carrots
Badaam	Almond	Genhu	Wheat
Badi Elaichi	Black Cardamom	Ghiya/Lauki	Bottle Gourd/Marrow
Baingan	Aubergine/Brinjal	Guar ki Phalli	Green Beans
Bajra	Millet	Gulgul	Lemon
Bathua	Pigweed	Gur	Jaggery
Besan	Chickpea/gram Flour	Haldi	Turmeric
Bhindi	Ladies' Fingers (Okra)	Hara Pyaaz	Spring Onions (Scallions)
Bund gobhi/		Hari Saunf	Aniseed
Pattagobhi	Cabbage	Heeng	Asafoetida
Channa Daal	Husked Bengal Gram	Imli	Tamarind
Chhilke wali Urad	Split Black Gram	Jaiphal	Nutmeg
Chhoti Elaichi	Green Cardamoms	Jau	Barley
Chote Tamattar	Cherry Tomatoes (Button	Javitri	Mace
	Tomatoes)	Jeera	Cumin
Daal	Lentils (Pulses)	Jhaari	Slotted Spoon
Dahi	Yogurt (Curds)	Jimikand	Yam
Dalchini	Cinnamon	Kabuli Channa	Chickpea

Indian	English (American)	Indian	English (American)
Kachnaar	Bauhinia	Makki ka Atta	Cornmeal
Kaddu/Sitaphal	Pumpkin	Malai	Clotted Cream (Top of the Milk)
Kairi/amiya	Green Mangoes	Matar	Green Peas
Kaju	Cashew Nuts	Methi	Fenugreek
Kala Channa	Whole Bengal Gram (Horse Gram)	Misri	Rock Sugar
Kala Namak	Black Rock Salt	Mooli	Radish
Kala/Shah Jeera	Black Cumin	Moong	Green Gram
Kalonji	Nigella/Onion Seeds	Moong phalli	Groundnuts (Peanuts)
Kamal Kakri/Bhein	Lotus Root	Moti Kutti Lal Mirch	Coarsely Ground Red Pepper
Karaunda	Carissa Carandas	Murgh	Chicken
Karela	Bitter Gourd	Nariyal	Coconut
Kathal	Jackfruit	Nariyal ka burada	Dessicated Coconut
Keema	Mince Meat	Nimbu	Sour Lime
Kesar/Zafran	Saffron	Nimbu ka Sat	Citric Acid
Kewra	Vetiver	Palak	Spinach
Khajoor	Dates	Paneer	Cottage Cheese
Khira	Cucumber	Phitkari	Alum
Khoya	Thickened Milk	Phoolgobhi	Cauliflower
Khurmani	Apricot	Pissi Kali Mirch	Black Pepper Powder
Khus Khus	Poppy seeds	Pissi Lal Mirch	Cayenne Pepper
Kishmish	Raisins	Pudina	Mint
Lahsan	Garlic	Sabut Kali Mirch	Black Peppercorns
Lassi	Buttermilk	Sabut Masoor	Eygptian Lentils
Laung	Cloves	Sabut Urad	Black Gram Whole
Lobhia	Black-eyed Beans	Safed Petha	Ash Gourd/White Pumpkin
Machchli	Fish	Sarson	Mustard Seeds
Maida	Refined Flour	Saunf	Fennel Seeds
Makhana	Lotus Seed	Sem	Broad Beans

Indian	English (American)	Indian	English (American)
Shah/Kala Jeera	Black Cumin	Soojee	Semolina (Cream of Wheat)
Shakarkandi	Sweet Potato	Tawa	Griddle
Simla Mirch/Pahari Mirch	Capsicum/Bell Pepper	Tej patta	Bay leaf
Singhara	Water Chestnuts	Til	Sesame
Sonth	Dry Ginger	Tinda	Round Gourd
		Torai	Rigde Gourd

List of Colour Plates

Page 1
(Left)   Saankhein, Aloo rasedaar, Methi ka parantha, Sookhe matar
(Right)   Zarda, Dahi ki Pakori, Khatta meetha kaddu, Dahi ke aloo, Ghutti hui gobhi, Poori

Page 2
(Left)   Gajar methi, Ghiya malaiwala, Sada parantha, Makhmali kofte
(Right)   Sabut arbi, Chhunke hue sabut matar ki sabzi, Saade chawal, Aalan ka saag

Page 3
(Left)   Dahi, Cachoomber, Maash ki daal, Shahi biryani, Sookhe kofte
(Right)   Fish frie, Phulka, Korma-e-Vakil, Palak ki bhurji

Page 4
(Left)   Pyaaz ka lachcha, Palak gosht, Lassooni kabab, Sabut masoor ki khichdee
(Right)   Surkh murgh, Andaa karee, Moong daal ki khichdee

Page 5
(Left)   Ghiya channe ki daal , Machchli kabab, Raan mussallam
(Right)   Murgh do piaza, Naan, Bhuni kaleji, Frans bean gajar

Page 6
(Left)   Machchli masala, Makhmali murgh, Gobhi dum
(Right)   Nargisi kofta, Methi aloo, Daal gosht, Naan

Page 7
(Left)   Kathal ki sabzi, Murgh mussallam, Keema matar
(Right)   Lal mirch ka benarsi achaar; Hari mirch aur nimbu ka achaar; Kabuli channa aur aam ka achaar; Aam ki chutney; Aam ka achaar I; Aam ka achaar II

Page 8
(Left)   Shahi tukra, Zarda, Kiwaamee sevian, Santre ki kheer, Gulab jamun
(Right)   Aloo matar ki chaat, Gole gappe ki chaat, Mathi, Besan ke laddoo, Badaam ki barfee, Petha, Aloo ki tikki

Photographs credit: Arrt Creations, New Delhi

Introduction

Uttar Pradesh, the erstwhile (pre-Independence) United Provinces is, perhaps, best known as simply U.P. U.P. is one of the largest states in India and through it flow the rivers Ganga and Yamuna. U.P. was the stage for much of India's history, evident today in its many palaces, forts and pilgrim spots sacred to Hindus, Muslims and Buddhists. It's wealth of handicrafts have made the towns of U.P. famous—Lucknow for its chikan (or shadow) work, Agra for stone, mainly marble, sculptures, Varanasi and its environs for carpets and textiles, etc. Most people who live in U.P. are either Hindus who are mostly vegetarian, (some do not eat even garlic and onion) or Muslims who prepare the most delicious meat dishes.

Lukhnavi nazaakat (etiquettes followed by the people of Lucknow) is beyond compare and is now the butt of a well known joke about the excessive politeness of two Lukhnavis spending a life-time saying *pahle aap* (or 'after you') to each other! Urdu, spoken mainly by the Muslims, is one of the sweetest languages—its soft cadences make it polite and a pleasure to listen to. U.P. is known for its laid-back attitude and old-world charm. These give rise to the feeling that while states like Punjab have progressed and prospered, towns like Kanpur and Lucknow have stagnated. A story about Wajid Ali Shah, the extravagant ruler of Awadh, who had time only for dance, music and chess is believed to be symbolic: when he was told that the British were almost at the door, and that he must escape, Wajid Ali Shah, the story goes, was fretting and waiting for his servant to bring him his shoes!

The first thing that strikes you as soon as you move out of Lucknow or Kanpur station is the chaotic traffic and noise. One discovers quickly that these are places where might is certainly right. Large vehicles thunder ahead with the hands of their drivers seemingly fixed to the horns. The smaller vehicles are finally forced to swerve out of the way!

Once the initial shock wears off and you begin looking around, the character of some of the places becomes apparent. This is especially true of Lucknow where a visitor's first stop has to be the huge Bada Imambara built by Asaf-ud-Daulah. Two features of this monument deserve special mention. One is the central hall which is 50 m long and 15 m high, and the other is the *bhoolbhulainya* (or maze) which is on the first floor. People have been known to get lost in it. A guide would help lead the way. I tried to go a short distance myself, but had to yell for help very soon! The Rumi Darwaza, a replica of a gateway in Istanbul, and the Chhota Imambara are both worth visits. Also interest-ing is the La Martiniere School set in beautiful, wooded surroundings. It is thought to have been built by a French Major General who planned to live in it, but died before it was completed. He willed it to the school.

The Kaiser Bagh Palace conjures up images in my mind of the dancers and singers – like Umrao Jaan – dressed in beautiful clothes and jewellery, who entertained the ruler while he sipped wine poured out for him by a *saaki* (a server of wine). The people of Lucknow have been great lovers of dance and music, and several *gharaanas* (schools of music) originated here, in Varanasi and Allahabad. And with this image I get a whiff of *Mughlai* cuisine! Once that happens I have to appease my appetite with the delicacies, which this book is all about!

But before we delve into the main contents of this book, let's have a look at some of the other aspects of the state of U.P. Chikan work is the embroidery Lucknow is famous for, the other types being *murri* (raised) work or *tepchi* which is embroidery done with a single thread. The embroideries of Lucknow have taken India by storm. Today's entrepreneurs have adapted the traditional work to suit modern styles and tastes not only on clothes, but on linen too.

Chinhat near Lucknow is famous for its pottery. Until about thirty years ago there was a distinct difference in the designs of the pottery of Chinhat and Khurja (the other town well known for its pottery, which is close to Aligarh), but they seem very similar now. As the demand for pottery is very high, the potters of Chinhat and Khurja could tap the potential and improve their lot.

Antique collectors, often find bargains such as English crockery, silver, antique Indian jewellery and shawls which belonged to the families of erstwhile nawabs.

The town of Allahabad, at the *sangam* (confluence) of the three holy rivers, the Ganga, Yamuna and Saraswati (believed to flow underground) is considered by the Hindus to be very holy. It is the venue for the *Kumbh mela*, which takes place every twelve years when Hindus take a dip in the holy confluence on a particularly auspicious day. Until recently the Kumbh was poorly organised, and always ended in tragedy—stampedes which resulted in a number of deaths. Now, better facilities are now available, and the crowds are better controlled.

Among other places worthy of mention is a fort built by Emperor Akbar on the banks of the Yamuna at the sangam. The All Saints Cathedral, is also interesting. Some of the memorials there make interesting, if poignant reading. Deaths by cholera and blood poisoning seem to have been common in the colonial period. These epitaphs remind me of those in a cemetry in Mussourie (in the Garhwal Hills of

U.P.), which record deaths in the plains in, for instance Meerut, and state that the grave was shifted to Mussourie at a much later date.

The Hanuman Temple in Allahabad with its unique image of a reclining Hanuman is also worth a visit. Three of India's prime ministers came from Allahabad—Jawaharlal Nehru, Indira Gandhi and Rajiv Gandhi. All three belonged to the same family and their palatial house, called Anand Bhawan, is now a museum, gifted to the country by Indira Gandhi.

Impossible to ignore is Agra—home of the Taj Mahal, one of the wonders of the world. A verbal description of it is insufficient and this marble wonder must be seen to be believed. Agra has several ruins and relics of the Mughal era. The Agra Fort and Fatehpur Sikri are two of the most splendid. But there are several lesser known, secret monuments such as an old house I once visited. At one time it was bound by a river on one side. It had a tunnel running under it, which was an escape route, and reached a point on the road to Delhi!

Today, Agra is a centre for the production of several handicrafts including stone and leather artefacts and carpets.

Varanasi and Haridwar are, of course, considered the most important pilgrimage centres for the Hindus. Varanasi is also known for its large carpet industry but the industry which is synonymous with the city is the textile industry. The finest silks are produced here and bought as part of bridal trousseaux. Music is also central to this holy city, which has been the seat of many gharaanas of music and dance.

The tremendous wealth of the art, history and culture of U.P. has filled many volumes. Here, my attempt has been to place its delicious cuisine which is now famous world-wide, within the context of its birth and development.

As mentioned earlier, the people of U.P. are mainly vegetarian Hindus, and Muslims who prepare delectable meat dishes. The speciality of this Mughlai cuisine, is *Dum Pukht*.

Cooked in sealed vessels, it retains its flavour to the maximum, and is traditionally served in the vessel that it is cooked in, with the seal being broken only at the table. Convention has now given way to practicality, and one rarely does that now, with the same dish sometimes cooked in the oven instead.

U.P. boasts a variety of 'mithais', 'chaats' and 'paans'. To name a few, there is the Daulat ki Chaat as it is known in Delhi, or Nimish in Lucknow and Solah Maze in Agra. This is not a savoury, as the name suggests, but a mithai (sweet) made from the froth of milk, when whipped. The 'malai paan' of Lucknow is, quite literally, malai (thick layer of cream which forms on boiled and cooled milk) used instead of a betel leaf stuffed with a sweet mixture of nuts. Kanpur is famous for its 'boondi ka laddoo'. Although people in Delhi have tried to make such 'laddoos', those from Kanpur stand apart. Like Lucknow and Varanasi, it has a few good mithai shops, which produce what could be called pieces of art, and where the base for most mithais is milk, almonds and pistachios. These preparations are getting more and more innovative over the years.

The popular fruits are peaches, lichees, melons and mangoes. While peaches are grown mostly in the Muzaffarnagar area, lichees are grown in and around Dehra Doon. 'Baghpat ka kharbooja' – melons from Baghpat, which is close to Meerut – are especially famous. This is also the large sugar belt. En route Delhi to Mussourie, one can see sugarcane fields which are harvested between March and May with the tell-tale aroma of gur-making permeating the air. A stop at one of the fields can get you a free taste of the jaggery. On the same route you will pass some sugar factories when the strong acrid smell of mollasses will make you cover your nose!

Mango is another delicacy of this state, the more well known being the 'dasheri', 'langra' and 'chausa', and the small 'safeda' (which cannot be cut). Some years ago I stayed overnight at a mango orchard in Kotra, near Lucknow, and was introduced to a large number of mangoes which I had never heard of before. It was a hot day in June, and we were wading in a pool of cold water from a tube well. While in the pool, we were offered these mangoes with such fascinating names as, 'gulab khas' (which had a subtle flavour of roses), 'samar bahist', 'lab-e-mahshook' and many more. We were told that the way to enjoy them was to let them cool off in the pool first, before biting into the delicious fruit. To round off the day, was a 'nautanki'—musical plays performed in the villages, in which the story is sung to very loud music. An essential part of the nautanki is that all the performers are male. Female roles are also played by men. The language of nautanki is not Hindi, but Purabiya, the typical dialect of the region known in Bombay as the language of the *Bhaiya*. Migrants from U.P. (and Bihar) who came to Bombay in search of a livelihood are known there as Bhaiyas, and they have brought with them the rich tapestry of their culture and cuisine, adding to the great metropolitan melting pot that is Bombay. The Bhaiyas were a part of my childhood and I recall that one of them introduced us children to 'bhang' (*Cannabis*)— or so he told us. But since nothing happened, I suspect he fooled us, or gave us so little that it had no effect on us. Bhang is a very essential part of the Holi celebrations in U.P.

Holi is one of the more important festivals in U.P. No work is done for at least 4–5 days before Holi. Special snacks are made, like Gunjiya and Khasta kachauri and downed with Thandai. Bhang is put into laddoos, pakoras, thandai, and whatever else it can be put into. The novice eventually discovers that bhang has a late reaction with the effect being felt only about 1½ hours to 2 hours later. This is a festival of colour, music and food.

'Paan' too, is an essential part of U.P. culture. Traditional homes have their 'paan daans', and the lady of the house makes the paans and serves them. Amongst collectors' items are also antique silver 'paan daans', which are now being sold off by members of erstwhile royal families. The people of Lucknow, Kanpur, Varanasi and Allahabad are inveterate paan eaters. The 'Benarsi patta' is one of the more popular ones. Paan is eaten all over India, but each region has its different flavours, such as the 'maghai' of Varanasi, and the 'kalkatta meetha patta' of Calcutta. A 'meetha paan' is often thought to refer to the sweet filling inside the leaf. In fact, it refers to the leaf itself which is sweet. The sweet filling is asked for seperately and is known as 'meetha masala'.

I have enjoyed putting this book together immensely, because it has taken me to the homes of various people in U.P., people who have been extremely cooperative, and I am thankful to all of them. Many of the recipes are made traditionally in their homes, and I gratefully acknowledge their sharing these with me in the pages that follow. A glossary of non-English words has been provided. Ghee has been used in most of the recipes, but the health conscious can substitute it with any suitable cooking oil. Similarly, mustard oil can be substituted with any other oil preferred. These are recipes of food cooked in homes and so are easy to follow and prepare, and the list of ingredients is not daunting. Once you can cook from this book, you will find it easier to follow more elaborate recipes. If you are interested in cooking (which you must be if you are reading this), I am sure you will enjoy it as much as much as I have enjoyed writing it! On this note, let's move into the kitchen!

Some Basic Information

The recipes I have put together here have been collected from different homes. In my opinion, these recipes are authentic even though they may differ, subtly, between homes. The cuisine of U.P. can be categorised as:

1. Vegetarian without onions and garlic, which is the food of the Banias and the Jains. I believe that this brings out the flavour of the main ingredient more than the other foods, which tend to get masked with the heaviness characteristic of the use of onions and garlic.
2. Vegetarian with the use of onions and garlic. This has its own distinct flavour and people used to cooking with onions and garlic are so dependant on these two ingredients that they cannot imagine how food can be cooked without them!
3. Rich Mughlai non-vegetarian food—rich in spices as well as fat. Dum Pukht is another method of cooking and involves the food being cooked in its own steam.

Before we start with the recipes, here are a few words about the ingredients we will be using. Besides the description, I have given the weights and measures and a basic temperature chart for general information.

Points to Remember:

1. *Oil* used is vegetable oil, except where specified.
2. *Quantity* caters to 4–6 people in most dishes.
3. *Measures* used are standard, in volume as well as weight.
4. *Use one system of measurement;* do not mix weight and volume.

5. *Amount of salt* to be used is according to taste in most cases.

Frying

To pan- or shallow-fry is to fry food items in a thin layer of oil or ghee in a pan. Items have to be turned over to be fried on both sides.

To deep-fry is to fry something in enough hot oil or ghee so that the item being fried can float freely in it.

Things to remember:

1. Use a big enough pan to allow the oil to bubble. Bubbles develop when wet items are fried.
2. Keep a metal lid handy to smother flames in case the oil or ghee catches fire. Do not use water as it only spreads the fire.
3. Judging the temperature for frying: Fry a 2 cm/1 in cube of bread in the oil/ghee for a minute. If it fries to an even, golden brown in that time, the oil is hot enough. If it gets too dark, the oil is too hot and not hot enough, if it is light. If you have a frying thermometer, the correct temperature is 375°F or 190°C.
4. Oil/ghee should not be allowed to smoke as it spoils it for re-use, over-browns the food and makes a hard crust.
5. A simpler way to judge the temperature of the oil/ghee is to toss in a piece of what has to be fried. If it comes up at once, the oil/ghee is ready; if it sinks, it has not yet reached the required temperature.

6. Some items (like samosas and kachauris) need slow frying. For these the oil/ghee should be heated to 375°F or 190°C, the items put in, turned over, and the heat lowered till they are cooked through.

Double frying is essential for things to be fried crisp. Fry the food to a light colour and when almost done, remove from the oil/ghee. Just before serving, fry in hot oil/ghee once again, till a golden colour. Fry the second time on high heat, and only for a short while.

Oven Temperatures

A general guide is provided to help in the conversion of temperatures. The exact temperatures often vary between different ovens:

	Fahrenheit	Gas Mark	Centigrade
Cool	225–250	0–½	105–120
Very low	250–275	½–1	120–135
Low	275–300	1–2	135–150
Very moderate	300–350	2–3	150–180
Moderate	375	4	190
Moderately hot	400	5	204
Hot	425–450	6–7	218–223

Ingredients Required

The ingredients mentioned here are those used in this book as well as some others which are used in Indian cooking. Convenient quantities for storage are also suggested.

ADRAK: (ginger, 100 g per week) The root of a plant. Used fresh in almost everything and is also scalded, dried, and sold as a powder (sonth). Improves the appetite by reducing flatulence, and is good for the respiratory tract.

AJWAIN: (carum/thymol seeds, 100 g) A very tiny seed of the cumin family. Very pungent and aromatic, it is also used as a substitute for oregano and thyme, where these are not available. It is considered to be a digestive, and the water of this is said to cure some stomach ailments.

AMCHOOR: (mango powder, 250 g) Raw mango slices dried, and then powdered. Used to add sourness to dishes; most popular souring agent amongst the vegetarians in U.P.

ANARDANA: (pomegranate seeds, 100 g) Dried seeds of pomegranate, used to add a sour and tangy flavour; small and dark in colour, these are a little sticky; considered good for digestion.

AATA: (whole wheat flour, 10 kg) Only a rare north Indian home does not have this in store; most breads are made with this, or a combination of this flour and the refined white flour (maida).

BADIS: Nuggets made with split and husked dhuli urad (black gram) as a base; made, dried and stored for use throughout the year combined, with various vegetables and rice; also combined with meat. These can also be bought in the market.

BESAN: (chickpea flour/gram flour, 1 kg) Flour made of chickpeas/roasted gram; used in many main dishes, snacks and sweets.

BROILER: A chicken that is young and reared for only a certain number of weeks, so that it cooks tender very quickly.

CHAWAL: (rice, 2 kg) Rice is of different varieties, and is stored according to taste; the best is Basmati, so called because of its fragrance; Sela Chawal or parboiled rice takes a little longer to cook, and is used by many for pulaos, etc. In south India it is also used for dosas.

CHIRONJI: (sunflower seed) Used very rarely, so better bought when needed; small, round and flatish, brown-beige nut, used in some typical sweets and Mughlai dishes.

COCONUT MILK: To make, grate coconut and place in a blender with water. Blend together at high speed and strain. Put leftover coconut back into blender and repeat process with more water. After second straining, discard coconut. A juicer that takes in the pieces and extracts the milk may also be used. Today cans of coconut milk can also be bought.

COCUM: (100 g) A black fruit, dried and used (like tamarind) as a medium to add tang to a dish. Cocum cooked with water is good for the stomach; used more in the western and southern regions of India.

CORNFLOUR: Refined flour of corn, used mostly as a thickening agent.

DALCHINI: (cinnamon, 50 g) The dried inner bark of a laurel-like tree (the leaves of which are called bay leaves—tej patta); can be bought rolled in sticks several inches long, or ground. Pleasantly aromatic, it is an essential ingredient of garam masala.

DEGHI MIRCH: (chilli powder, 100 g) Used in most recipes, this has a strong colour but is not very hot; gives gravy a good colour.

DHANIA: (coriander seeds, 250 g) Dried yellow-brown seeds of the coriander plant; aromatic and pungent flavour; very light; used very extensively in U.P. The green leaves of this (hara dhania) are very refreshing and are a must for garnishing food in U.P., and the rest of the country.

ELAICHI: (cardamom, 50 g) chhoti elaichi (green cardamom), is a green or off-white coloured pod about ¾ cm in size; enclosed in it are very tiny round aromatic seeds; either the whole pod or only the seeds are used. Used in special dishes as well as desserts. Badi elaichi is the other variety about three times larger, with a rougher, dark brown pod. This also encloses small black aromatic seeds, and is almost always used peeled. The skin of this pod is so strongly aromatic, that sometimes these are used by themselves and discarded after cooking.

FILLET: Slice of meat, fish or chicken, which has all the bones removed before cubing or slicing.

GARAM MASALA: (100 g) A mixture of various spices (p 148–49). Each person has his/her own formula for this masala; regional variations are subtly distinctive. The combination of ingredients is approximately the same, but the proportions vary.

GHEE: (clarified butter, 1 kg) Unsalted butter is cooked and strained. The resulting ghee, is used a lot in U.P., though the cholesterol-conscious are using oil now. See p 150 on how to make ghee. Hydrogenated vegetable oil, called vanaspati is also referred to as ghee and today, is used more than the ghee made from butter, since it is half the price and serves the same purpose.

GULAB JAL: (rose water) Rose flower essence, used in cooking of special main dishes as well as desserts.

GUR: (molasses/jaggery, 500 g) Unrefined sugar, this is available in solid form or as a coarse powder (lal shakkar); used in sweet as well as savoury dishes. Another variety, made of palm juice, is used a lot in eastern India.

HALDI: (turmeric, 250 g) Similar to ginger root when fresh, this takes on a yellow colour when dried. Usually used in powdered form, it gives a yellow colour to the food; has a very mild flavour; is often applied to wounds and sometimes mixed in milk and drunk as a cure for coughs and colds because of its antiseptic and healing properties.

HARI SAUNF: (aniseed, 50 g) Strong in flavour, this is a longish, slightly curved greenish, not too hard seed; used mainly as a digestive after meals.

HARI MIRCH/LAL MIRCH: (green chilli/red chilli) Green and red chilli respectively, of the thinner and hotter (pungent) varieties. The red is used in the dried form, either whole (sabut) or powdered.

HEENG: (asafoetida, 25 g) Available in uneven crystallised lumps, brown in colour. The powdered form is also available; with a very strong flavour, it is one of the most popular ingredients in the vegetarian cuisine of U.P. The crystallised form varies in strength so that one has to use one's judgement. Asafoetida is also known to be a very good digestive.

IMLI: (tamarind, 500 g) A soft brown fruit, with dark brown seeds; the pulp is used to add a sour taste to food.

JAIPHAL: (nutmeg, 1 nut) The kernel of the stone of the pear shaped fruit of the nutmeg tree; the dark brown kernel, slightly oval in shape, looks a little like the betel nut; is strongly aromatic and is sold whole or ground.

JAVITRI: (mace, 50 g) The dried outer flower-like layer of the nutmeg; is sold as chips, blades or powder, and is light orange.

JEERA: (cumin seeds) (250 g) Looks like fennel seeds, but larger and darker in colour; used a lot all over India; seeds are also roasted and ground for use as garnishing, especially in yogurt-based dishes. When eaten raw, helps nausea and flatulence.

KACHRI: A dried fruit, which resembles a miniature melon, used to add sourness to certain dishes and also as a tenderiser for meat; especially popular in Rajasthan.

KADHI PATTA/MEETHA NEEM: (curry leaves, 100 g dried) A very aromatic leaf, used mostly in southern and western India, it has been inducted into north Indian cooking as well; used fresh, but can also be dried and stored.

KALA JEERA: (black cumin seeds, 50 g) Used a lot in Mughlai cooking, cakes and breads; looks like a darker and thinner version of fennel seeds.

KALA NAMAK: (black rock salt, 250 g) A dark, pinkish rock-like crystal, which is powdered and used instead of salt, and has a spicy tangy flavour; is used a lot in chaat; has digestive qualities.

KALONJI: (onion seeds/nigella seeds, 50 g) Very tiny black seeds, used a lot in Bengali cuisine, and in pickles all over the country; also used as garnish for breads like naans.

KASOORI METHI: (fenugreek, 50 g) Dried methi leaves used for flavouring foods when fresh methi is not available.

KESAR/ZAFRAN: (saffron, 10 g) In India this is grown in Kashmir; is a speciality of Spain. It is the thin, dried, deep red stigma of the saffron flower; is used only on festive occasions, mainly because it is extremely expensive.

KEWRA: (vetiver) A flavouring agent extracted from the kewra plant. Used in special Indian cooking, primarily desserts and Mughlai food.

KHOYA: This is, literally, unsweetened condensed milk; used in desserts and in some special main dishes; see p 150 for more information on khoya.

KHUS KHUS/POST KA DANA: (poppy seeds, 50 g) These are off-white, extremely light and small seeds; make a good binding and thickening agent.

LAHSAN: (garlic, 2–3 bulbs per week) A strongly flavoured plant of the lily family; when dry, the root can be split into a dozen or more small segments or cloves; considered to be healthy if eaten raw—especially good for blood pressure and colds.

LAUNG: (cloves, 50 g) The (dried) unopened buds of the clove tree which grows in hot, moist climates; rather like small nail-heads in appearance; contain an oil which has a strong fragrance and a pungent taste; sold whole or ground; used both in sweet and savoury dishes; clove oil is said to be effective when applied to aching teeth.

MAGAZ: (melon seeds, 50 g) Seeds of melons of all kinds, but mainly those of musk melons are dried, peeled and used in the sweet as well as savoury dishes of richer cuisines.

MAIDA: (refined flour, 1 kg) Refined whole wheat flour.

MAKKI KA AATA: (cornmeal, 1 kg) Extremely popular in Punjab; used to make 'makki ki roti' traditionally eaten with 'sarson ka saag'.

MANGAURI: Tiny nuggets made of dhuli moong ki daal (husked green gram) as a base; nuggets are dried and stored for use throughout the year; are combined with various vegetables and rice; very popular in Rajasthan, but used a lot in U.P. too; nuggets can be made at home or bought.

MEETHA SODA: (baking soda, 100 g) Used to add lightness to fried, steamed and sometimes baked dishes.

METHI DANA: (fenugreek seeds, 100 g) This is the small, brown, squarish and very bitter seed of the methi plant; used in small quantities; known also for its medicinal properties, particularly for the control of diabetes.

MOTI KUTTI LAL MIRCH: (coarsely ground red chilli, 100 g) If made of a variety that is not too hot, like Kashmiri mirch or Belgaum mirch, this can be a substitute for paprika; always good to add a little to cheese preparations, as it is thought to make the cheese more easily digestible.

NARIYAL: (coconut) Gets stale quickly, so best not stored unless used often; flesh of the coconut fruit, used either fresh or dried; large brown nut must be cracked open, the water drained and the white flesh eased out with a knife for use.

NARIYAL KA BURADA: (dessicated coconut) Dehydrated, grated coconut that is substituted for the fresh, when not available; quarter cup dessicated can be substituted for 1 cup fresh coconut; buy when required.

PISSI LAL MIRCH: (cayenne pepper, 100 g) A bright red chilli powder; is exceedingly hot, should therefore be used carefully.

POHA/CHIDVA: (500 g) Made from boiled rice which is pressed and dried; used for various snack preparations; available in two varieties—one absolutely flat, which tends to dissolve if soaked; the other type is harder, more rounded, takes a little longer to cook; latter is easier to handle when cooking.

PUDINA: (mint) Can be used fresh or dried; has a very refreshing flavour; is often made into chutney.

RAI/SARSON: (mustard seeds, 100 g) Seeds of the mustard plant; very small, smooth and light; used more in pickles than in everyday cooking in U.P. There are three varieties of mustard seeds: the larger brown (sarson), the very tiny brown (rai), and the husked which is slightly yellow in colour (peeli sarson/rai daal) which must be washed well in plenty of water, dried and stored in an airtight jar.

RATTAN JOT: Bark of a tree used to add colour to food; used mostly as garnish by heating a little ghee or oil and placing a small piece in it for a few seconds, removing rattan jot and pouring only ghee into dish. The rattan jot can be re-used.

SAFED TIL/KALA TIL: (white sesame seeds/black sesame seeds, 50 g) Tiny black seeds shaped like tear drops; off-white when husked; have a nutty flavour; ground and used in richer dishes.

SARSON KA TEL: (mustard oil, 1 kg) Mustard seed oil is used a lot in northeastern and north Indian cooking. Used in U.P. only in special dishes; used a lot in pickles.

SAUNF: (fennel seeds, 100 g) Thicker, lighter coloured version of the 'hari saunf'; is similar to aniseed but not as strongly aromatic; is quite commonly served roasted, after a meal, to help digestion.

SENDA NAMAK: (rock salt) Form of white rock salt, powdered and used instead of salt, when one is fasting.

SEVIAN: (vermicelli) Very fine noodles made of maida (refined flour); best bought as and when required; available in packets and are mostly roasted after drying; cook very quickly.

SONTH: (dry ginger, 100 g) See note on adrak, p 6.

SOOJEE: (semolina 1 kg) Form of whole wheat, ground to consistency of sand.

SOOKHA NARIYAL: (dry coconut, whole) Refers to (the fleshy part of) a whole, dried coconut; is a brown hollow nut, can be cut through with knife, or grated (so is not totally dried up). Can be substituted for fresh coconut (though has a more oily flavour). Three-fourth cup of this coconut grated, could be substituted for 1 cup of fresh coconut.

TEJ PATTA: (bay leaf, 50 g) Aromatic leaf of sweet-bay or laurel tree; has a strong almond flavour; is used a lot in small quantities, with other spices; also an ingredient of garam masala.

TIL KA TEL: (sesame oil) Used a lot in southern and western parts of India; not as much in the north.

VARK: (silver leaf) These are 3½ cm (2 in) or 7 cm (3 in) sheets of beaten silver, so thin that they can only be handled with the help of a piece of paper; without this they break and stick to the fingers; generally used to garnish sweets and some Mughlai dishes; believed to be adulterated today with aluminum, therefore, best avoided if one is unsure of its purity. Refer to p 110 on how to use.

To Store: The ingredients listed above should be stored in airtight jars, to keep them free of insects and mould. It is best not to buy very large quantities for storage, as they loose their flavour, if kept too long. Avoid storing them for more than six months though items with shells last longer. In colder climates the shelf life is naturally longer. This is only a general guide line—you will soon make your own, based on your experience.

Some Equipment Used

Here are some of the typical items used in most homes. Although all except the very inexperienced would be familiar with most items, a short checklist would be useful:

BELAN: Rolling pin; found in all homes.

CHAKLA: A round base made of wood or marble, to roll 'rotis' on. The smooth surface of a table top works just as well.

HAANDI: A vessel with a heavy base, deep and round; broad at the bottom and narrow at the top. Traditionally made of brass or copper; used to cook lentils or for slow cooking. Excellent for dum pukht cooking, where the lid is sealed with dough and food cooked over very low heat. Earthen haandis are also available in which food can be cooked and served. They are popular to set yogurt in.

HAMAAM DASTA: (mortar and pestle) A deep iron or brass cylindrical vessel with a long, rod-like hammer, used to pound ingredients. Today, a food processor is a substitute. Despite this, a small mortar and pestle are handy to use for small quantities, like a teaspoonful of something.

JHAARI: (spatula) A perforated, long-handled, flat spoon, used to deep-fry things.

KADAHI: A brass, steel or now, non-stick, shallow-bottomed pan rather like the Chinese wok. Most Indian homes have at least 2–3 of these in different sizes. It is now possible to buy one with a flat, heavy, double bottom made of stainless steel; good for frying gulab jamuns etc., which need to be cooked over very low heat. I would advise your buying one of cast iron too.

KADCHI: A long-handled deep spoon, like a ladle, only, the handle is at right angles to the spoon end. Serves almost the same purpose as a ladle besides also being useful for spreading batter in a frying pan, with the round base of the spoon.

PARAAT: A shallow bowl with a flat bottom, used to knead dough in. Although any shallow bowl will serve the purpose, it is most comfortable kneading dough in this as the hands have a freer movement.

POORI PRESS: A manual machine to press balls of dough into uniformly flat rounds. Used also for tortillas. Definitely a handy tool, especially when making large numbers.

SIL BATTA: A flat stone, on which ingredients are ground with a smaller stone. In south India, round deep ones are available, with smaller, round ones fitting into the deep cavity. These are especially good for wet grinding. The food processor is a substitute, but there are certain items like Daal ki Pakori, which turn out better when ground on a sil batta. I would suggest this be fixed at the work surface level for convenience.

TANDOOR: A cylindrical clay oven heated with charcoal placed at the bottom. Used a lot in Indian barbecues, breads are also baked in it; a speciality of north India. An oven or grill can be substituted for it, at the expense of the flavour.

TAWA: A round, flat, iron griddle that is placed directly on the flame. Used to make rotis. A thick based frying pan can be substituted for it.

Weights and Measures

It is important to use volume measures with standardised measuring cups and spoons. If using weights, all measures should be in weights. Do not mix the two. It is advisable to invest in these cups and spoons before you start cooking. Here are a few tips to help you get started:

1. all measures are level unless otherwise stated
2. dry ingredients should not be packed in, but should be spooned in and then levelled with a straight edged knife or spatula; the cup should not be shaken or tapped to fit in more
3. moist ingredients should be packed in lightly and then levelled off

In this book a cup refers to a cup of 240 g/8 oz (the ounces/grams are taken to the nearest round figure).

Item	Cups	Spoons	Grams	Ounces
Aata/whole wheat flour	1		150	5
Ajwain/carum/ thymol seeds	1	150	5	
Ajwain/carum/ thymol seeds		1 tsp	3	
Almonds, ground	1		120	4
Almonds, blanched, slivered	1		120	4
Almonds, shelled, whole	1		150	5
Amchoor/mango powder		1 tsp	3	
Amchoor/mango powder	1		150	5
Anardana/pomegranate powder	1		200	7
Anardana/pomegranate powder		1 tsp	4	
Butter/margarine/ oil/ghee	1	16 tbsp	240	8
Castor or granulated sugar	1	16 tbsp	240	8

Item	Cups	Spoons	Grams	Ounces
Coconut, shredded dry	1		50	2
Coconut dessicated	1		90	3
Cornflour	1	16 tbsp	120	4
Cream	1	240	8	
Daals/lentils	1		180	6
Dahi/yogurt	1		200	7
Dhania/coriander seeds, powdered	1		50	2
Dhania/coriander seeds, powdered		1 tsp	1	
Garam masala	1		100	3
Garam masala		1 tsp	2	
Garlic paste	1		270	9
Garlic paste		1 tbsp	15	½
Garlic, peeled	1		100	3½
Garlic peeled		1 tbsp	6	¼
Ghiya/bottle gourd, diced	1		125	4
Ginger, coarsely chopped	1		200	7
Ginger coarsely chopped		1 tbsp	15	½
Ginger paste	1		450	16
Ginger paste		1 tbsp	30	1
Haldi/turmeric		1 tsp	1.5	
Haldi/turmeric	1		80	2
Heeng/asafoetida		1 tbsp	3	
Jeera/cumin seeds		1 tsp	3	
Jeera/cumin seeds	1		150	5
Kabuli channa/chickpeas	1		180	6
Kadhi patta dried/ curry leaves	1		45	1½
Kalonji/onion seeds		1 tsp	1.5	

Item	Cups	Spoons	Grams	Ounces
Kalonji/onion seeds	1		80	2
Keema/minced raw meat, firmly packed	1		250	8
Khajoor/stoned dates, firmly packed	1		240	8
Khus khus/poppy seeds		1 tsp	2	
Khus khus/poppy seeds	1		100	3
Lahsan/garlic dried	1		100	3
Lahsan/garlic fresh		1 tsp	2	
Lal mirch, powdered		1 tsp	1.5	
Lal mirch, powdered	1		80	
Laung/cloves, 8–10 powdered		1 tsp		
Maida/refined flour	1	16 tbsp	120	4
Maida/refined flour	¼	4 tbsp	30	1
Matar/shelled peas (approx 500 g unshelled)	1		160	5
Methi/fenugreek seeds		1 tsp	3	
Methi/fenugreek seeds	1		150	5
Milk	1		200	8
Onions chopped	1		250	8
Palak/spinach, pureed	1		750	12
Paneer cubed	1		150	5
Peanuts, shelled whole	1		120	4
Phool gobi/cauliflower	3		500	
Pissi kali mirch/powdered black pepper		1 tsp	2.5	
Potatoes diced 2 cm, ¾ in	1½		250	8
Raw papita/papaya grated	1		80	2½

Item	Cups	Spoons	Grams	Ounces
Rice, ground	1		180	6
Rice, long grain	1		180	6
Sabut kali mirch/peppercorns		1 tsp	2	
Sabut kali mirch/peppercorns	1		100	3
Sabut lal mirch/whole red chilli	1		25	1
Salt		1 tsp		4
Salt	1		200	7
Sarson/mustard seeds		1 tsp	2.5	
Sarson/mustard seeds	1		120	4
Saunf/fennel seeds		1 tsp	2	
Saunf/fennel seeds	1		100	3
Sonth/dried ginger powder		1 tsp	2	
Sonth/dried ginger powder	1		100	3
Sooji/semolina	1		120	6
Tamarind firmly packed	1		200	7
Til/sesame seeds		1 tsp	2	
Til/sesame seeds	1		100	3
Tomatoes, chopped	1		250	8
Vinegar	1		240	8
Walnuts shelled	1		120	4

Menus

There are some basic accompaniments to all the menus, which are listed separately for you to choose from. Only the main dishes are mentioned in the menus. These are suggestions, and can be interchanged according to taste.

Roti is specified only in certain cases where I would like to suggest a particular combination. The menus are divided into vegetarian and non-vegetarian. Though the individual dishes are those that are made traditionally in the state of Uttar Pradesh, the combination may not be traditional, except where mentioned. I have tried to keep the menus balanced as much as possible. Everyday food normally has only one gravy and one dry dish, but depending on the number of people in a household (for example, a joint family), there may be more of each.

Vegetarian Menus

(Recipes without Onions and Garlic)

The items generally served at lunch, a meal usually called *kacha khaana*, are listed first. This implies Chapati as against Parantha, and usually plain boiled rice instead of a 'pulao'. Dessert too is not mentioned, because it is not made every day. In many homes adding sugar to yogurt, or clotted cream, to be eaten as a dessert substitute, is a common practice.

Though these dishes are prepared without onion and garlic, they can be used too. The basic combination of spices may stay the same, but you may add garlic and onions soon after the tempering which consists of asafoetida and cumin seeds; after this, proceed further once the onions are fried well, that is, when the fat separates.

The common items of an every day lunch:

- Saade Chawal (Boiled Rice) p 104
- Chapati/Phulka p 88
- Dahi (Yogurt) p 99
- Chutney (Relishes) p 133
- Achaar (Pickles) p 137

MENU ONE

- ◆ Arhar ki daal I
- ◆ Chhilke wale aloo
- ◆ Torai ki sabzi

ARHAR KI DAAL I

(Yellow lentils are made in almost all vegetarian homes although of course, the seasonings vary between homes. Here is one of the more popular ways of cooking this lentil.)

INGREDIENTS

1	cup	(180 g) **arhar ki daal (yellow lentils)**
½	tsp	haldi (turmeric)
Salt to taste		
½	tsp	chilli powder
1	tsp	amchoor (mango powder)
1	tsp	jeera (cumin seeds)
⅛	tsp	heeng (asafoetida) — for tempering
1	tbsp	ghee
1	tbsp	chopped hara dhania (coriander leaves), for garnish

METHOD

1. Pick, clean and wash the lentils well, about 2 to 3 times, and place them in a heavy-based pan, along with 4 cups of water, turmeric and salt. Place the pan over high heat, and cover partially.

2. Bring to a boil and simmer till cooked (40–50 minutes). If using a pressure cooker add only 2½ cups of water and cook for 8 minutes.
3. Add the chilli powder and mango powder, mix well and bring to a boil. Heat the ghee in a heavy-based pan and add the asafoetida and cumin seeds. When they begin to splutter, add the lentil mixture, and bring to a boil. Then simmer for about 1 minute.
4. Garnish with fresh coriander leaves and serve hot.

CHHILKE WALE ALOO

(Potatoes chopped fine in their jackets, and cooked with a generous amount of oil and spices. I remember going all the way to the Old Delhi railway station to have these at one time!)

INGREDIENTS

500	g	**potatoes,** washed and scrubbed well
½	cup	(120 g) sarson ka tel (mustard oil)
2	tsp	jeera (cumin seeds)
¼	tsp	heeng (asafoetida)
1	tbsp	finely chopped ginger
½	tsp	garam masala I (p 148)
1	tbsp	dhania (coriander powder)

Salt to taste

1	tsp	chilli powder
½	tsp	haldi (turmeric)
2	tsp	amchoor (mango powder)
1	tbsp	chopped hara dhania (coriander leaves), for garnish

METHOD

1. Chop the potatoes very fine (about ½ in) without removing the skin.
2. Heat the oil in a heavy-based pan; add cumin seeds and asafoetida and then the ginger; saute till the ginger is a light brown.
3. Add the potatoes and saute over high heat till they change colour from translucent to slightly opaque.
4. Lower the heat, add garam masala, coriander powder, salt, chilli, turmeric and mango powders; mix well.
5. Cover and cook over low heat, stirring a few times to avoid scorching, till the potatoes are cooked through. Takes approximately 10–15 minutes. Saute till the potatoes look fried and the oil separates.
6. Serve hot, garnished with chopped coriander leaves.

TORAI KI SABZI

(A variety of snake gourd, sauted with spices. A summer vegetable which seems to be an acquired taste. Snake gourd is available in two varieties. One is smooth while the other has a ridged surface. This recipe can be used for either.)

INGREDIENTS

¾	kg	**torai (ridge gourd)** (8–10 small / 6–8 ridge gourd depending on the size of the vegetable)
2	tbsp	(30 g) ghee
⅛	tsp	heeng (asafoetida)
1	tsp	jeera (cumin seeds)
1	tsp	finely chopped ginger
½	tsp	chilli powder
2	tsp	dhania (coriander powder)

Salt to taste

¼	tsp	garam masala II (p 148)
½	tsp	amchoor (mango powder)

½ tsp   sugar
1 tbsp   chopped hara dhania (coriander leaves), for garnish

METHOD

1. Peel and chop the vegetable into pieces about 1cm thick. Discard hard seeds if any. Place the chopped vegetable in water till ready to use.

2. Heat the ghee in a kadahi and add asafoetida and cumin seeds. As the seeds splutter, add the ginger; saute a little and add the chopped snake gourd; stir-fry over high heat till it looks glossy.

3. Add the chilli powder, coriander powder, salt, garam masala, mango powder and sugar; mix well and lower the heat. Cover and simmer till cooked, stirring a few times to avoid scorching. You may need to add a little water if it sticks to the pan.

4. When soft and cooked through (should press easily with the back of a spoon; takes about 20 minutes), serve garnished with fresh coriander leaves. If excess water remains, dry it by leaving pan uncovered over high heat.

Note: Sliced onions can be added with the ginger and sauted until translucent. Thereafter, the method is the same.

MENU TWO

- Dhuli urad ki daal
- Methi aloo
- Guar ki phali
- Missi roti I or II (p 90)

DHULI URAD KI DAAL

(Husked black gram is one of the more popular daals of U.P., and is had mostly at lunch. It is almost as popular as Arhar ki Daal.)

INGREDIENTS

1 cup   (180 g) **dhuli urad (husked black gram)**
½ tsp   haldi (turmeric)
1 tbsp ginger, finely chopped
Salt to taste
2 tbsp ghee
1 tsp   jeera (cumin seeds)
⅛ tsp   heeng (asafoetida)
1 tsp   dhania (coriander powder)
½ tsp   garam masala II (p 148)
1 tbsp ghee ⎫
1 tsp   chilli powder ⎬ for tempering
2 tbsp chopped hara dhania (coriander leaves), for garnish

METHOD

1. Pick, clean and wash the lentils well, 2 or 3 times; place in a heavy-based pan with 4 cups of water, turmeric, ginger and salt. Place the pan over high heat and cover partially.

2. Bring to a boil and simmer till cooked (40–50 minutes). If using a pressure cooker, add only 3 cups of water, cook for 10 minutes and set aside.

3. Heat ghee in a heavy-based pan; add asafoetida and cumin seeds. When the cumin seeds begin to splutter,

add the powdered coriander and garam masala. Mix well, add the lentils and bring to a boil. Simmer for about 1 minute. Transfer the lentils to a serving bowl.

4. In another, smaller pan, heat 1 tablespoon ghee add the chilli powder and garnish the lentils. Sprinkle the chopped coriander leaves and serve hot.

Note: A variation of this is to stir-fry some chopped garlic, onions and tomatoes in ghee till the fat separates before adding the coriander powder. Thereafter, the method is the same.

METHI ALOO

(A preparation in which potato and fenugreek leaves are sauted together. This is a seasonal dish, as fenugreek leaves are easily available only in winter. This is one vegetable I never tire of.)

INGREDIENTS

500 g   **methi leaves (fenugreek leaves)**, chopped fine
250 g   small **potatoes** washed and scrubbed clean
1   tsp   methi dana (fenugreek seeds)
3–4 sabut lal mirch (whole, dried red chilli)
Salt to taste
½   tsp   chilli powder
2   tsp   dhania (coriander powder)
½   cup   (120 g) sarson ka tel (mustard oil)

METHOD

1. Heat the oil in a kadahi and put the potatoes in. Stir-fry for a few minutes over medium heat, till the potatoes are half cooked.

2. Scoop the potatoes out of the oil and set aside. Increase heat to high for a few seconds, add fenugreek seeds and whole red chilli. Stir a few times and add the chopped fenugreek leaves.

3. Stir-fry till the leaves look slightly glossy, add the half-cooked potatoes, salt, chilli powder and coriander powder. Cook uncovered till the leaves are done (till they look a little shrivelled up, and fried). Serve hot.

GUAR KI PHALI

(A variety of green beans, which are flatter and smaller than Frans/French beans. These beans are very fibrous and are available in the peak of summer in north India. They are rather an acquired taste as they are slightly bitter.)

INGREDIENTS

½   kg   **guar ki phali (green beans)**
2   tbsp   (30 g) ghee
¼   tsp   heeng (asafoetida)
1   tsp   jeera (cumin seeds)
2   tsp   dhania (coriander powder)
½   tsp   chilli powder
Salt to taste
¼   tsp   garam masala I (p 148)
¼   cup   (50 g) dahi (yogurt)

METHOD

1. Wash and string the beans. Cut into halves or thirds.

2. Heat the ghee in a kadahi; add asafoetida and cumin seeds.

3. When the seeds splutter, add the beans and saute till they look a bit glossy. Add coriander powder, chilli powder and salt. Cook uncovered over low heat till tender.

4. Mix the garam masala into the yogurt and add to the beans. Saute for 2–3 minutes and serve.

Menu Three

- Sabut masoor ki daal
- Bharwan bhindi
- Gobhi aloo

SABUT MASOOR KI DAAL

(Egyptian lentils. These are also used to make the famous 'daal moth' of Agra. Tomatoes and finely chopped onions with these make a real treat.)

Ingredients

1 cup (180 g) **sabut masoor (Egyptian lentils)**
Salt to taste
1 tbsp finely chopped ginger
2 tbsp (30 g) oil
1 tsp jeera (cumin seeds)
2 tej pattas (bay leaves)
¼ cup (60 g) grated tomatoes
2–3 green chillies, slit
½ tsp garam masala II (p 148)
2 tsp powder dhania (coriander powder)
1 tsp chilli powder
1 tbsp chopped hara dhania (coriander leaves), for garnish

Method

1. Pick, clean and wash the lentils well. Cook with 6 cups of water, salt and ginger.
2. Cook till the lentils are soft (approx 1 hour). If using a pressure cooker add only 4 cups water and cook for 12 minutes.
3. Heat the oil in a pan; add cumin seeds and bay leaves. When the seeds splutter, add the tomatoes and stir-fry till the fat separates.

4. Add the green chillies, garam masala, coriander and chilli powder and mix well. Add the lentils to this mixture and bring to a boil. Simmer for about 10 minutes. Serve hot, garnished with fresh coriander leaves.

BHARWAN BHINDI

(A preparation of whole ladies' fingers, stuffed with masala. It involves a little more work than just chopping and cooking, but is well worth the extra effort.)

Ingredients

500 g **bhindi (ladies' fingers)** of a uniform size, washed and wiped dry

Mix together for masala:
Salt to taste
½ tsp haldi (turmeric)
1 tsp ginger paste
2 tbsp finely chopped hara dhania (coriander leaves)
1 tsp amchoor (mango powder)/1 tbsp grated raw mango
1 tbsp dhania (coriander) powder
1 tsp chilli powder
1 tsp ajwain (thymol seeds)
1 tsp saunf (fennel seeds)   } roasted and powdered
½ tsp methi dana (fenugreek seeds)
$^1/_8$ tsp heeng (asofetida)
¼ cup (60 g) ghee
3 tsp lemon juice
1 tbsp chopped pudina (mint leaves), for garnish

Method

1. Cut off the top of the ladies' fingers and slit lengthwise on one side. Stuff the masala through the slit.

2. Heat the ghee and add the ladies' fingers to it. Stir-fry over high heat, till they look glossy. Lower the heat to medium, add 1 teaspoon lemon juice and mix well. Leave uncovered and continue to saute over medium heat. Add the lemon juice in two more stages, till vegetable is cooked through. (The lemon juice prevents it from becoming sticky.) The ladies' fingers should retain some of their green colour and their shape.

3. Serve hot, garnished with the mint leaves.

Note: You can fry 1 cup sliced onions, crush and mix them with the masala, if desired.

GOBHI ALOO

(Cauliflower cooked with potatoes.
Fresh cauliflower throughout the year is
something people rarely tire of.)

INGREDIENTS

500 g (3 cups) **phool gobhi (cauliflower),** cut into small flowerets
250 g (2 medium) **potatoes**, cut lengthwise to match the cauliflower
¼ cup (60 g) ghee
1 tsp jeera (cumin seeds)
1 tbsp finely sliced ginger
¼ cup (50 g) dahi (yogurt)
2–3 green chillies, slit
½ tsp chilli powder
¼ tsp haldi (tumeric)
½ tsp garam masala I (p 148)
1 tbsp dhania (coriander powder)
Salt to taste
1 tbsp chopped hara dhania (coriander leaves), for garnish

METHOD

1. Parboil the potatoes and set aside.

2. Heat the ghee in a heavy pan and add cumin seeds. When they splutter, add the ginger. When the ginger begins to brown, add the yogurt, a tablespoon at a time, stirring vigorously till the fat separates between each addition.

3. Add the cauliflower, potatoes and green chillies. Stir-fry the vegetables over high heat for two to three minutes, till they get coated with the ghee. Then add the chilli powder, turmeric, garam masala, coriander powder and salt. Stir a few more times, till well mixed.

4. Lower the heat, cover the pan and let the vegetables cook till tender, stirring 2–3 times. Takes approximately 45 minutes. Serve hot, garnished with chopped coriander leaves.

Menu Four

- Urad and channe ki daal
- Bharwan tinda
- Sem aloo

URAD AND CHANNE KI DAAL

*(A combination of split black gram and
husked Bengal gram. This can also be made
with husked black gram, for variety.)*

Ingredients

$^2/_3$ cup (120 g) **chhilke wali urad (split black gram)**
$^1/_3$ cup (60 g) **channe ki daal (husked Bengal gram)**
Salt to taste
1 tbsp finely chopped ginger
2 tbsp (30 g) ghee
1 tsp jeera (cumin seeds)
¼ tsp heeng (asafoetida)
2–3 coarsely chopped green chillies
2 tsp dhania (coriander powder)
¼ tsp garam masala II (p 148)
½ tsp kali mirch (powdered black pepper)
2 tbsp malai (clotted cream) ⎫
1 tbsp chopped hara dhania (coriander leaves) ⎬ for garnish

Method

1. Pick, clean and wash the lentils. Cook in 6 cups of water, with salt and ginger.

2. Cook lentils till soft (takes approx 1 hour). If using a pressure cooker add only 4 cups of water and cook for 12 minutes.

3. Heat the ghee in a pan; add cumin seeds and asafoetida. When the seeds splutter, add green chillies and saute till slightly discoloured. Add the coriander powder, garam masala and black pepper. Mix well and add the lentil mixture. Bring to boil and then simmer for about 5 minutes. Serve hot, garnished with cream and chopped coriander leaves.

Note: Onions and garlic can be added after the cumin seeds. Stir-fry till fat separates. Add some chopped tomatoes and saute till fat separates again before following the rest of the method described above.

BHARWAN TINDA

(Round gourd stuffed with masala and cooked whole.)

Ingredients

500 g   **tindas (round gourd)** of a uniform size (number depends on the size of each)
¼ cup (60 g) ghee

Mix together:
Salt to taste
1 tsp amchoor (mango powder)
½ tsp haldi (turmeric)
1 tbsp dhania (coriander powder)
1 tsp chilli powder
½ tsp sonth (ginger powder)
¼ tsp heeng (asafoetida)
1 tbsp saunf (fennel seeds) ⎫
½ tsp methi dana (fenugreek seed) ⎬ roasted and powdered
1 tsp jeera (cumin seeds) ⎭
Chopped pudina (mint) leaves, for garnish

Method

1. Wash the round gourd and wipe dry (if left wet, they become slimey and difficult to handle when scraped or

cut). Snip off both ends, and scrape off thick skin if any. In season the vegetable is so tender that you may not need to scrape at all.

2. Make slits (for the filling) like a plus sign from one end, to almost the other end, taking care not to separate the pieces.

3. Stuff the masala filling into the slits in the gourds, as tightly as you can.

4. Heat ghee in a heavy-based kadahi and add the round gourds into it. Add leftover masala if any and stir-fry over high heat till they look glossy. Lower heat and cook covered, till tender. It takes about an hour during which you should check on it a few times, and sprinkle some water if vegetable sticks to the kadahi. Serve hot, garnished with mint leaves.

Note: One cup (100 g) sliced onions, fried and crushed, can be mixed with the masala.

SEM ALOO

*(Broad beans sauted with potatoes. Broad beans
are a dark or light green, depending on the season.
Frans/French/String beans can also be made similarly.)*

INGREDIENTS

500 g	**sem (broad beans)** 4 cups after cutting
300 g	(2 large) **potatoes,** peeled
¼ cup	(60 g) oil
1 tsp	jeera (cumin seeds)
1 tbsp	finely chopped ginger
2 tsp	dhania (coriander powder)
Salt to taste	
½ tsp	haldi (turmeric)

1 tsp	dried amchoor (mango powder)
½ tsp	chilli powder
¼ tsp	garam masala I (p 148)

METHOD

1. Wash, string and cut the beans into small pieces, horizontally. Cut the potatoes into cubes to match the beans.

2. In a kadahi or a heavy-based pan, heat the oil and add cumin seeds. When they splutter, add the chopped ginger and saute till slightly brown.

3. Add the vegetables and saute over high heat till they look glossy.

4. Lower heat and add coriander powder, salt, turmeric, chilli powder and garam masala. Mix well and cook covered over low heat till tender, stirring off and on to ensure that it does not scorch. Takes 20–30 minutes.

5. Add the mango powder, saute for a few minutes more and serve.

MENU FIVE

- Mangauchi
- Bharwan karela I
- Chhilke wale aloo (p 16)
- Rote/Moti roti I (p 89)

MANGAUCHI

(A version of kadhi made with green gram as a base. Introduced to me by my friend Pushpa, this is a certain success. The pakories in this are called dumroo numa because they are shallow fried and take on an interesting shape—rounded on both sides with a dent all around the centre).

INGREDIENTS

Pakories:

1	cup	(180 gm) **dhuli moong (husked green gram)**
1	tbsp	**dhuli urad (husked black gram)** soaked in water for 4–6 hours
½	cup	(120 g) oil

Gravy:

1	cup	(200 g) dahi (yogurt)
⅓	cup	of the ground daals (lentils)
1	tsp	turmeric
1	tsp	chilli powder

Salt to taste

1	tsp	garam masala I (p 148)
2	tbsp	(30 g) oil
½	tsp	heeng (asafoetida)
2	tsp	jeera (cumin seeds)
5–6		sabut lal mirch (whole, dried red chilli)
1	tbsp	chopped (coriander leaves), for garnish

METHOD

1. To make pakories: Drain the water from the lentils and grind till fine, either in a blender or on a stone, using as little water as possible, preferably none (a wet grinding attachment of a food processor is better than a blender, and a grinding stone even better).

2. Whip the lentils till light (to test if done, a little bit of batter dropped into water should float).

3. In a frying pan, heat ½ cup oil (which should form about a 1 cm / ½ in layer in the pan). When hot, add teaspoonfuls of the batter (as many as possible). Reduce heat to medium, and let the pakories cook. When the base becomes golden and the top has little holes appearing on it, turn the pakories over and fry on the other side. Scoop out of the oil and set aside till needed. Put aside ⅓ cup of lentil mixture for gravy and make pakories with the rest.

4. Add to the remaining lentil mixture, turmeric, chilli powder, salt and garam masala. Add yogurt gradually to form a smooth paste. Then add the rest of the yogurt and 4 cups of water.

5. Heat the oil in a large, heavy-based pan. Add asafoetida, cumin seeds and the dried red chilli. When the cumin seeds begin to splutter, add the yogurt mixture and bring to a boil. Reduce heat and simmer till the gravy is a little thick (about 15 minutes).

6. Add the pakories to this mixture; simmer for about 10 minutes, and serve garnished with chopped coriander leaves.

BHARWAN KARELA I

*(Whole bitter gourd, stuffed with masala and sauted.
This is an excellent way to have bitter gourd!)*

INGREDIENTS

6–8 (500 g) **karelas (bitter gourd)**
1 tbsp salt

Mix together for masala:
Salt to taste
½ tsp haldi (turmeric)
½ tsp sonth (ginger powder)
1 tbsp dhania (coriander powder)
½ tsp chilli powder
1 tsp roasted jeera (cumin seeds)
⅛ tsp heeng (asafoetida)
1 tsp saunf (fennel seeds)   } roasted and
½ tsp methi dana (fenugreek seeds) } pounded coarsely
2 tbsp (30 g) sarson ka tel (mustard oil)

METHOD

1. Scrape off the rough surface of the bitter gourd; slit length-wise on one side, rub all over with 1 tablespoon salt and keep aside for about 30 minutes (this reduces bitterness).

2. Squeeze the bitter gourd to remove the bitter juice and scoop out the hard seeds, if any.

3. Stuff the filling firmly into the bitter gourd. In a pan, heat 2 tablespoons of oil and add the bitter gourd. Turn over a few times on high flame. Reduce heat and cook them covered, till tender, stirring a few times so that they are cooked and browned all round.

Notes: 1. For crisp outers, add double the quantity of oil, and saute a little longer.

2. 1 cup sliced onions can be fried, crushed and mixed with the masala, if desired.

MENU SIX

◆ Besan ki kadhi
◆ Sookhe aloo
◆ Tahiri (p 105)

BESAN KI KADHI

(A curry with dumplings, made with yogurt and chickpea/gram flour. Made almost all over India, this dish has its distinctive regional flavours. Everyone feels kadhi is best in their own home!)

INGREDIENTS

3 cups (600 g) **dahi (yogurt)**
1 cup (120 g) **besan (chickpea/gram flour)**
1 tsp haldi (turmeric)
1 tsp chilli powder
Salt to taste
1 tsp garam masala I (p 148)
6 cups (approx 1.5 l) water
¼ cup (60 g) oil
½ tsp heeng (asafoetida)
2 tsp jeera (cumin seeds)
5–6 sabut lal mirch (whole, dried red chillies)
1 tbsp ghee   } for tempering
1 tsp chilli powder }

Pakories:
1 cup (120 g) **besan (chickpea/gram flour)**
1 tsp salt
½ cup (120 g) oil

METHOD

1. Mix the chickpea flour, turmeric, chilli powder, salt and garam masala. Add the yogurt gradually to this mixture to form a smooth paste, then add the water.

2. Heat the oil in a large, heavy-based pan; add the asafoetida, cumin seeds and the whole red chillies. When the cumin seeds begin to splutter, add the flour and yogurt mixture and bring to boil. Simmer over low heat till it thickens a bit (about 15 minutes).

3. For the pakories: Mix the ingredients listed above into a smooth batter with enough water to form a thick dropping consistency (blobs of batter should fall off without lingering between your fingers). Let the batter rest for at least 15 minutes.

4. In the frying pan, heat ½ cup oil (it should form about a 1 cm layer in the pan). Beat the pakorie mixture till light and fluffy and add teaspoonfuls of the mixture (as many as fit in easily without the blobs touching each other). Reduce heat to medium and fry the pakories. When the pakories fluff up and the base becomes golden-brown, turn them over and brown on the other side. Scoop out the pakories from the oil and drop them into the kadhi. Repeat with the rest of the mixture. Transfer the hot kadhi into a serving dish.

5. Heat the ghee, add the chilli powder and pour over the kadhi immediately to garnish.

SOOKHE ALOO

(A potato dish that goes well with lentils and kadhi, as well as to fill in samosas, etc. This combination is a must in my home for lunch on Saturdays. The potatoes can be made spicier according to taste.)

INGREDIENTS

½ kg **potatoes,** boiled and peeled
¼ cup (60 g) oil
1 tbsp finely sliced ginger
⅛ tsp heeng (asafoetida)
2–3 sabut lal mirch (whole, dried red chilli)
2 tsp jeera (cumin seeds)
1 tbsp dhania (coriander seeds) — roasted
Seeds of 1 badi elaichi (black cardamom) — and
4 laung (cloves) — powdered
1 tsp saunf (fennel seeds)
Salt to taste
2 tsp amchoor (mango powder)
½ tsp chilli powder
½ tsp haldi (turmeric)
¼ cup chopped hara dhania (coriander leaves)

METHOD

1. Crush and break the potatoes between the palm of your hands and set aside.

2. Heat the oil; add the asafoetida, ginger and whole red chillies. When the chillies begin to darken, add the roasted and powdered ingredients and the potatoes, and mix well.

3. Add salt, mango powder, chilli powder, turmeric and 2 tablespoons of coriander leaves and saute over low heat for about 5 minutes. Garnish with the rest of the chopped coriander leaves and serve hot.

25

MENU SEVEN

- Aalan ka saag
- Chhunke hue sabut matar ki sabzi
- Sabut arbi

AALAN KA SAAG

(A unique combination made into a lentil-like preparation, this is a Mathur speciality. It can be eaten like soup when one is not particularly hungry.)

INGREDIENTS

5 cups water
½ cup (60 g) **besan (chickpea/gram flour)**
1 tbsp (15 g) ghee
2–3 sabut lal mirch (whole, dried red chilli) broken into large pieces
1 tsp jeera (cumin seeds)
¼ tsp heeng (asafoetida)
2 tbsp chhilke wali moong daal (split green gram), washed
½ tsp haldi (turmeric)
1 tsp chilli powder
Salt to taste
1 cup (30 g) palak (spinach) loosely packed, chopped
Chaat masala (p 149)
Lemon wedges

METHOD

1. Mix the chickpea flour with a little water to form a smooth paste. Add the rest of the water and set aside.
2. Heat the ghee and add the whole red chilli, cumin seeds and asafoetida. When they begin to darken, add the split green gram and saute for a few seconds.
3. Add to this, the water and chickpea flour mixture and bring to boil. Reduce heat and simmer. Add the turmeric,

chilli powder, salt and spinach. Continue simmering till the liquid looks smooth (about 15 minutes).

4. Fix the lemon wedges on the sides of the dish. Serve hot with chaat masala.

CHHUNKE HUE SABUT MATAR KI SABZI

(This is a dish made from fresh green peas. I learnt this unusual preparation from my friend Bina. It is a preparation very typical of her home—one that I like very much. It should be made only with tender green peas.)

INGREDIENTS

500 gms **sabut matar (fresh green peas, in their pods)**
2 tbsp oil
$\frac{1}{8}$ tsp heeng (asafoetida)
1 tsp jeera (cumin seeds)
2–3 sabut lal mirch (whole, dried red chillies)
Salt to taste
1 tsp chaat masala
1 tsp amchoor (mango powder)
2 tbsp chopped hara dhania (coriander leaves)

METHOD

1. Wash the peas (in their pods) and leave to drain the excess water.
2. Heat the oil in a kadahi and add the asafoetida, cumin seeds and whole red chillies.
3. When the seeds begin to splutter, add the peas and salt. Mix well, cover and simmer till the peas are cooked through. Takes 10–20 minutes, depending on how fresh the peas are.

4. Add the chaat masala and mango powder. Stir to mix and serve garnished with the chopped coriander leaves.

〰〰〰〰〰〰

SABUT ARBI

(Deep fried colacasia, cooked whole and sauted in a tangy masala. This can be served as a snack too.)

INGREDIENTS

500 g **arbi (colacasia)**
2 tsp   ajwain (thymol seeds)
2 tsp   amchoor (mango powder)
Salt to taste
½ tsp   chilli powder
¼ tsp   kali mirch (powdered black pepper)
2 tbsp chopped hara dhania (coriander leaves) ⎫
A few lemon wedges   ⎬ for garnish
Oil for deep-frying

METHOD

1. Wash the colacasia and boil till almost tender (about 5 minutes in a pressure cooker, depending on the size and thickness of the colacasia).

2. Peel the skin off when cool enough to handle, and press between palms to flatten.

3. Heat the oil and put in as many pieces as will fit without touching each other, and fry over high heat till golden brown and crisp.

4. When all the pieces are fried, heat a heavy-based pan over high flame and add the thymol seeds; stir for a few seconds. When they begin to pop, add the fried colacasia, mango powder, salt, chilli powder and black pepper. Stir well. Serve hot, garnished with chopped coriander leaves and lemon wedges.

〰〰〰〰〰〰

Dinner Menus Without Onions And Garlic

We now go on to *pakka khaana*, which has almost the same number of combinations and accompaniments as do the lunch menus. The main difference here is that the bread is usually fried and more often than not, no rice is served. Instead of the lentils, there is a gravied dish and raita instead of yogurt. Of course, combinations differ between homes. The more health conscious avoid paranthas and poories. Until recently, I served paranthas every time we had a vegetarian dinner! In many U.P. households, a gravied dish of potatoes was a must till recently.

The items common to all the menus are:

• Parantha/Poori (pp 93, 96)
• Dahi (Yogurt) (p 99)
• Chutney (Relishes) (p 133)
• Achaar (Pickles) (p 137)

MENU EIGHT

- Khatte ke bade
- Bharwan baingan
- Palak ki bhurji
- Missi parantha (p 94)

KHATTE KE BADE

(Taught to me by Pushpa Bhalla, an expert in the cooking of eastern U.P. dishes. This eastern U.P. delicacy of badas/bhallas in tamarind gravy is delicious if you like tangy and spicy things.)

INGREDIENTS

Bade:

1	cup	(180 g) **dhuli urad ki daal (split black gram),** soaked for 5–6 hours
¼	tsp	heeng (asafoetida)

A small bowl

A thin cloth to cover the bowl with

A large damp cloth to place the shaped bade on before frying

Oil for frying

(Save ¼ cup of the daal and fry bhallas as on p 102)

40	g	tamarind, soaked and strained
2	tsp	dhania (coriander powder)
½	tsp	chilli powder
½	tsp	haldi (turmeric)
½	tsp	garam masala II (p 148)
2	tsp	sugar

Salt to taste

¼	cup	ghee
1	tsp	jeera (cumin seeds)
¼	tsp	heeng (asafoetida)
2	tbsp	chopped hara dhania (coriander leaves)

METHOD

1. Add enough water to the tamarind juice to make up to 4 cups. Mix in the ground lentils, coriander powder, chilli powder, turmeric, garam masala, sugar and salt. Set aside.

2. Heat the ghee in a heavy-based pan and add the asafoetida and cumin seeds. When the seeds splutter, add the tamarind water and bring to a boil. Simmer over low heat for about 5 minutes.

3. Add the bade and continue simmering for 2–3 minutes. Serve hot, garnished with the fresh coriander leaves.

Note: Traditionally, fresh green tamarind is used; it is added to the water, boiled and then strained. Since it is seasonal and may be hard to find, dried tamarind is the closest substitute.

BHARWAN BAINGAN

(Small, whole brinjal, stuffed with masala. Thought by some to have no food value, brinjal certainly has one excellent quality—taste, especially when stuffed!)

INGREDIENTS

12–15 (½ kg) small round **baingans (brinjals)**

For filling, mix together:

1	tsp	roasted and powdered ajwain (thymol seeds)
¼	tsp	heeng (asafoetida)
2	tsp	ginger paste
1	tbsp	besan (chickpea/gram flour), roasted till slightly discoloured

Salt to taste

½	tsp	haldi (turmeric)

1 tbsp dhania (coriander powder)
½ tsp chilli powder
1 tsp saunf (fennel seeds) ⎫ roasted and
½ tsp methi dana (fenugreek seeds) ⎭ pounded coarsely
20 g (walnut-sized) ball of tamarind, soaked in water and strained
½ cup (120 g) sarson ka tel (mustard oil)
1 tbsp very finely sliced ginger for garnish

METHOD

1. Wash and wipe the brinjals and slit lengthwise from the base towards the stalk, just short of the stalk, dividing first into half. Then make another slit dividing each into quarters, thus making space to fill the masala.
2. Stuff the masala firmly into the brinjals.
3. Heat the oil in a pan till it gives off a strong aroma. Let it cool to get rid of the pungent smell.
4. Add the brinjals and turn around a few times on high heat. Reduce heat, cover and cook till tender, stirring a few times. Serve hot, garnished with sliced ginger.

PALAK KI BHURJI

*(Chopped spinach, very lightly spiced and sauted.
A quick and simple preparation. It is best to use
a stainless steel vessel for this as it helps retain
the green colour of the spinach.)*

INGREDIENTS

¾ kg **palak (spinach),** washed and chopped fine
2 tbsp ghee
2–3 sabut lal mirch (whole, dried red chillies)
1 tbsp thinly sliced ginger
1½ tsp salt

1 tsp sugar
1 tbsp malai (clotted cream)

METHOD

1. Heat the ghee in a heavy-based stainless steel broad pan and add the whole red chillies. When they begin to darken, add the ginger and saute till light brown.
2. Keeping the heat on high, add the chopped spinach, salt and sugar and mix well.
3. Continue to cook over high heat, till the spinach is tender and dry. This takes about 20 minutes, during which it needs to be stirred every few minutes. Spinach should be cooked on a high flame because it cooks quite fast and the high heat helps the water to evaporate quickly.
4. Serve hot, garnished with cream.

29

MENU NINE

*(A combination good with
poories and dahi ki pakori.
This is a useful party menu!)*

* Dahi ke aloo
* Khatta mitha kaddu
* Ghutti hui gobhi
* Dahi ki pakori
* Poori (p 96)

DAHI KE ALOO

*(A potato dish with gravy that goes well with poories.
Traditionally, tomatoes are not added to this dish.
But I found that tomatoes enhance the taste
so I did away with tradition!)*

INGREDIENTS

500 g		**potatoes,** boiled and peeled
¼	cup	ghee
$\frac{1}{8}$	tsp	heeng (asafoetida)
1	tsp	jeera (cumin seeds)
1	tbsp	finely shredded ginger
½	cup	(125 g) tomatoes grated (optional)
½	tsp	garam masala I (p 148)
2	tsp	dhania (coriander powder)

Salt to taste

½	tsp	chilli powder
½	tsp	haldi (turmeric)
½	cup	(100 g) dahi (yogurt)
3–4		coarsely chopped green chillies
1	tbsp	chopped hara dhania (coriander leaves)

METHOD

1. Break the potatoes, by holding each in the palm of your hand and closing the fist. Set these unevenly broken potatoes aside, till required.
2. Heat the ghee and add the cumin seeds and asafoetida. When the cumin seeds begin to splutter add the ginger and saute till slightly fried; then add the tomatoes and stir-fry till the fat separates.
3. Add the garam masala, coriander powder, salt, turmeric and chilli powder. Stir a few times till well mixed, and then add the potatoes and green chillies. Turn around over high heat, till they look slightly fried.
4. Add about 2 cups of water and bring mixture to boil. Reduce flame and simmer uncovered for about 15 minutes.
5. Beat the yogurt till smooth and add to the potatoes. Serve hot, garnished with the chopped coriander leaves.

KHATTA MITHA KADDU

*(Sweet and sour pumpkin—another must
with poories. This is a 'no regrets' recipe!)*

INGREDIENTS

750 g		**kaddu/sitaphal (pumpkin)** the orange or green variety
½	cup	(120 g) oil
$\frac{1}{8}$	tsp	heeng (asafoetida)
1	tsp	methi dana (fenugreek seeds) ⎫ roasted
1	tsp	saunf (fennel seeds) ⎬ and pounded
1	tsp	jeera (cumin seeds) ⎭ coarsely
1	tbsp	thinly shredded ginger
3–4		sabut lal mirch (whole, dried red chillies)

Salt to taste

½	tsp	haldi (turmeric)
1	tsp	chilli powder

1   tbsp   dhania (coriander powder)
1   tsp   garam masala II (p 148)
1   tbsp   sugar
Tamarind pulp made from 20 g tamarind
1   tbsp   chopped hara dhania (coriander leaves), for garnish

METHOD

1. Peel the pumpkin if using the red variety (not the green). Scoop out the fibres and seeds in the centre before cutting it into 2–3 cms cubes.

2. Heat the oil in a kadahi and add the asafoetida, the coarsely pounded fenugreek, fennel and cumin seeds. When they begin to splutter, add the ginger and the whole red chillies.

3. Saute till lightly coloured and add the pumpkin. Stir-fry on high heat till it looks glossy.

4. Add salt, tumeric, garam masala, coriander powder, chilli powder and sugar. Mix well.

5. Reduce heat, cover and simmer till cooked through. Stir 3–4 times (takes 20–30 minutes; the red variety takes longer to cook than does the green).

6. Add the tamarind, cook for 2–3 minutes, and serve hot, garnished with chopped coriander leaves.

GHUTTI HUI GOBHI

(This is Bachchan Singh's recipe for cauliflower, which is almost mashed by the time it is cooked through. It is made best in a haandi.)

INGREDIENTS

500 g   **phool gobhi (cauliflower)**
2   tbsp   (30 g) ghee

1   tsp   jeera (cumin seeds)
1/8 tsp   heeng (asafoetida)
1   tbsp   finely chopped ginger
2   tsp   dhania (coriander powder)
Salt to taste
½   tsp   haldi (turmeric)
¼   cup   (50 g) dahi (yogurt can be sour)   mixed together
¼   tsp   garam masala I (p 148)
2   green chillies, slit lengthwise, for garnish

METHOD

1. Wash the cauliflower and chop into very small pieces. The stalk which is not very tough, should be peeled and chopped fine.

2. In a heavy-based pan, heat the ghee and add the cumin seeds and asafoetida. When the seeds splutter, add the ginger and saute till light brown.

3. Add the cauliflower and saute over high heat till it looks glossy; then lower the heat and add the coriander powder, salt and turmeric.

4. Cover and cook till the cauliflower is soft (you should be able to press it with the back of a spoon without much pressure). You might have to sprinkle some water to prevent it from scorching. Takes about 15 minutes.

5. Add the yogurt, mix well and saute till the fat separates.

6. Serve hot, garnished with the green chillies.

DAHI KI PAKORI

(Lentil fritters in a chilled, yogurt sauce. My mother-in-law's cook was an expert at making these, and they featured regularly in all the family dinners we had at her house!)

INGREDIENTS (MAKES ABOUT 25)

Pakories:

1 cup   (180 g) **dhuli moong (husked green gram)** soaked in water for 4–6 hours

2 tbsp   **dhuli urad (husked black gram)** soaked in water for 4–6 hours

Oil for deep-frying

A large saucepan containing 6–8 cups of water with 1 tbsp of salt

Dahi:

2½ cups   (500 g) **dahi (yogurt),** beaten smooth

Salt to taste

2   tsp   roasted and powdered jeera (cumin seeds)

½   tsp   chilli powder

1   tsp   kala namak (black rock salt)

1   tbsp   chopped hara dhania (coriander leaves)

¼   tsp   kali mirch (powdered black pepper)

METHOD

1. Drain the water from the lentils and grind them very fine, either in a blender or on a stone, using as little water as possible, preferably none (a wet grinding attachment of a food processor is better than a blender, and a grinding stone even better).

2. Whip the lentils till light (a little bit of the batter dropped in water should float over it).

3. Heat the oil. To test if it is at the right temperature, drop a little batter in. If it comes up immediately, it is ready. Drop tablespoonfuls of batter into the oil. Lower the heat to medium, and let the pakories fry till golden on all sides. This takes about 3–4 minutes.

4. Lift the pakories out of the oil with a slotted spoon, and drop them in salted water. Continue till all the batter is used up.

5. Add salt, black pepper, 1 teaspoon powdered cumin seeds and ½ teaspoon black rock salt to the yogurt and mix well. Squeeze out the pakories, dip them in the yogurt mixture, and arrange on a serving dish. Pour the remaining yogurt sauce over them.

6. Garnish with the rest of the powdered cumin seeds, black rock salt, chilli powder and coriander leaves. Serve chilled.

MENU TEN

- Mangauri matar
- Bhuni hui kamal kakri
- Lobhia ki phali

MANGAURI MATAR

(Mangauris are green gram badis which make a good combination with green peas. This dish can be made with an onion and garlic masala too, if so desired.)

INGREDIENTS

2	cups	shelled **matar (peas)** (about 1 kg unshelled)
½	cup	(50 g) **mangauris** (p 151)
2	tbsp	oil
1	tsp	jeera (cumin seeds)
¹/₈	tsp	heeng (asafoetida)
1	tsp	finely chopped ginger
½	cup	(125 g) grated tomato
2	tsp	dhania (coriander powder)

Salt to taste

1	tsp	chilli powder
¼	tsp	garam masala I (p 148)
½	tsp	haldi (turmeric)

2 green chillies, slit a little
2 cups water

METHOD

1. Heat the oil in a heavy-based saucepan. Add the cumin seeds and asafoetida.
2. When the seeds splutter, add the ginger and saute over high heat till brown.
3. Add the grated tomatoes, coriander powder, salt, garam masala and turmeric. Stir-fry till the fat separates.
4. Add the mangauris, peas and green chillies. Stir a few times till the peas look a bit glossy and the mangauris darken a little.
5. Add the water and bring to boil. Cover the pan and simmer for about 10 minutes.
6. Serve hot. If you want the preparation to be dry, do not add water, reduce the quantity of salt, cover and simmer, till the mangauris and peas are cooked through (approx 10 minutes), stirring a few times to avoid scorching.

Note: If the mangauris are hard, it is better to cook them separately in water before adding them to the peas. This depends on the quality of the mangauris.

BHOONI HUI KAMAL KAKRI/BHEIN

(Sauted lotus stems, made into a dry preparation. Simple to make and quite delicious!)

INGREDIENTS

250 g		**kamal kakri (lotus stems)**
1	tbsp	chopped ginger
1	tsp	jeera (cumin seeds)
2	tsp	sabut dhania (coriander seeds)

ground together

Salt to taste

½	tsp	chilli powder
½	tsp	garam masala II (p 148)
2	tbsp	(30 g) oil
1	tsp	jeera (cumin seeds)
¼	tsp	heeng (asafoetida)
½	cup	(100 g) dahi (yogurt)
1	tbsp	chopped hara dhania (coriander leaves), for garnish

33

METHOD

1. Peel thin outer layer of the lotus stems and wash well. Wash carefully as they are often caked with dry mud. Slice the stems into ¼ cm thick pieces.
2. Boil 4 cups of water and add the sliced lotus stems. Simmer till tender. Takes 30–45 minutes. Should press with a slight pressure. Drain and cool.
3. Add the ground ingredients, and mix well.
4. In a heavy-based pan, heat the oil. Add the cumin seeds and asafoetida. When the seeds splutter, add the vegetable mixture and stir well.
5. Add the yogurt and cook over high heat till the liquid evaporates. Serve hot, garnished with chopped coriander leaves.

LOBHIA KI PHALI

*(Greens of black-eyed beans.
The greens and beans are both popular.)*

INGREDIENTS

500	g	**lobhia ki phali (greens of the black-eyed beans)**
2	tbsp	ghee
1	tsp	jeera (cumin seeds)
$\frac{1}{8}$	tsp	heeng (asafoetida)
1	tbsp	finely chopped ginger
¼	cup	(50 g) dahi (yogurt)
2	tsp	dhania (coriander powder)
½	tsp	haldi (turmeric)
¼	tsp	garam masala I (p 148)
Salt to taste		
½	tsp	chilli powder
2	tbsp	chopped hara dhania (coriander leaves), for garnish

METHOD

1. Chop the beans about ½ cm thick (or according to preference).
2. Heat the ghee and add the cumin seeds and asafoetida. When the seeds splutter, add the ginger and saute till a light brown.
3. Add the yogurt a little at a time, stirring vigorously till blended. After all the yogurt has been added, stir-fry till the fat separates; add the coriander powder, turmeric, garam masala, salt and chilli powder.
4. Mix well and add the greens. Stir-fry over high heat till a little glossy. Lower the heat, cover and cook till tender, stirring a few times to avoid scorching. Takes about 15 minutes. Serve hot, garnished with chopped coriander leaves.

Note: Sometimes I add potatoes to this. To do that, peel and cube the potatoes small. Add them with the chopped beans.

MENU ELEVEN

* Ghiya ke kofte
* Sookhi moong ki daal
* Frans bean aloo

GHIYA KE KOFTE

*(Deep fried balls of grated bottle gourd, with gravy.
Koftas ought to make a good snack!)*

INGREDIENTS (MAKES ABOUT 15)

Koftas:

500 g		(approx 4 cups) **(bottle gourd)** peeled and grated
½	tsp	ginger paste
½	tsp	chopped green chillies
1	tbsp	hara dhania (coriander leaves)

Salt to taste

$^1/_8$	tsp	kali mirch (powdered black pepper)
$^1/_8$	tsp	heeng (asafoetida)
¼	cup	(30 g) besan (chickpea/gram flour)

Oil for deep-frying

Gravy:

2	tbsp	(30 g) ghee
1	tsp	jeera (cumin seeds)
¼	tsp	heeng (asafoetida)
1	tsp	ginger, chopped fine
¼	cup	(50 g) dahi (yogurt)
¼	cup	khus khus (poppy seeds) soaked in milk for ½ an hour and ground to a paste
1½	tsp	dhania (coriander powder)

Salt to taste

½	tsp	chilli powder
¼	tsp	garam masala I (p 148)
¼	tsp	haldi (turmeric)

2	tbsp	malai (clotted cream)
1	tbsp	chopped hara dhania (coriander leaves)

} for garnish

METHOD

1. Mix together the grated bottle gourd, salt, ginger, green chillies, coriander leaves, black pepper, asafoetida and chickpea flour.

2. Heat the oil in a kadahi and drop about 1 tablespoonful of the mixture into it. Continue to drop tablespoonfuls of mixture into the hot oil. Put in as many as the kadahi will hold comfortably. Lower heat and fry till golden brown and set aside till required.

3. Heat the ghee in a pan. Add the cumin seeds and asafoetida. When the seeds splutter, add the ginger and saute till light brown. Add 1 tablespoon yogurt and stir vigorously till the water is absorbed and the fat separates. Then add the rest of the yogurt in 3 more instalments and follow the same procedure. Stir so that mixture does not curdle.

4. Add the poppy seed paste, coriander powder, salt, chilli powder, garam masala and turmeric; saute at medium heat till it is well fried and the fat separates.

5. Add about 3 cups water and bring to boil. Simmer for about 10 minutes. Add the koftas and simmer for another 2 minutes. Serve hot, garnished with clotted cream and coriander leaves.

Note: If the dish is being prepared well before it is to be served, keep the koftas separate and add them only before serving. They may disintegrate if left too long in the gravy.

35

SOOKHI MOONG KI DAAL

(Husked green gram lightly fried and cooked till tender; it retains its shape.)

INGREDIENTS

1	cup	(180 g) **dhuli moong ki daal (husked green gram)**, soaked for 5–6 hrs
¼	cup	(60 g) ghee
1	tsp	jeera (cumin seeds)
1/8	tsp	heeng (asafoetida)
1½	tsp	sliced ginger
1	tsp	dhania (coriander powder)

Salt to taste

½	tsp	chilli powder
¼	tsp	haldi (turmeric)
½	tsp	amchoor (mango powder)
1	tbsp	chopped coriander leaves
1	tsp	chopped green chillies

for garnish

Lemon wedges

METHOD

1. Wash the lentils well. Drain the water and leave in a colander for a few minutes. Heat the ghee in a heavy-based pan and add the cumin seeds and asafoetida.

2. When the seeds splutter add the ginger and saute till slightly coloured. Add the lentils, coriander, salt, chilli powder, turmeric and mango powder. Mix well.

3. Add 1¼ cups water and bring to boil. Cover and simmer, for 15–20 minutes or till cooked through (the water should be absorbed—as with rice; when done, no moisture remains and the grains are separate).

4. Serve hot, garnished with coriander leaves, green chillies and lemon wedges.

Notes: Chopped onions can be sauted with the ginger if desired.

Most lentils can be cooked this way, though the time taken to cook may differ.

Crisply fried onions are a popular garnish for this.

FRANS BEAN ALOO

(Frans bean/green beans, sauted with potatoes. I always find this name interesting. It is an example of how some words become part of the vocabulary of another country—French Beans to Frans Bean in India! This reminds me of the time I was asked what the Indian word for chutney was!)

INGREDIENTS

500 g		**French (green/string) beans**
250 g		**potatoes,** peeled
¼	cup	(60 g) ghee
1	tsp	jeera (cumin seeds)
¼	tsp	heeng (asafoetida)
1	tsp	finely chopped ginger
2 medium-sized (125 g) tomatoes, grated		
2	tsp	dhania (coriander powder)

Salt to taste

½	tsp	haldi (turmeric)
½	tsp	chilli powder
¼	tsp	garam masala I (p 148)

METHOD

1. Wash and string the beans. Cut them into small, horizontal pieces (about ½ cm/¼ in).

2. Heat the ghee in a heavy-based pan. Add the cumin seeds and asafoetida. When the seeds splutter, add the ginger and saute till slightly brown.

3. Add the tomatoes and stir-fry till the fat separates. Add the coriander powder, salt, turmeric, chilli powder and garam masala.

4. Add the beans and potatoes and saute over high heat till they look glossy.

5. Lower heat, cover and cook till tender, stirring occasionally to ensure that it does not scorch. Takes about 20–30 minutes. Serve hot.

Menu Twelve

* Aloo rasedaar
* Sookhe matar
* Saankhein
* Methi ka parantha (p 94)

ALOO RASEDAAR

(A popular vegetable, here are potatoes cooked the Varanasi way with gravy. This was taught to me by a friend. Especially popular when cooked with a minimum of fat.)

Ingredients

500	g	**potatoes,** boiled and peeled
1	tbsp	finely chopped ginger
$1/8$	tsp	heeng (asafoetida)
1	tsp	saunf (fennel seeds) } roasted and
1	tsp	methi dana (fenugreek seeds) } coarsely pounded
2	tsp	dhania (coriander powder)
½	tsp	haldi (turmeric)
½	tsp	chilli powder
Salt to taste		
1	tsp	amchoor (mango powder)
2	tbsp	ghee
2	tbsp	chopped hara dhania (coriander leaves), for garnish

Method

1. Break the potatoes by holding each in your palm and closing your fist. Set aside these unevenly broken potatoes.

2. Heat the ghee, add the asafoetida, fennel seeds, fenugreek seeds and the potatoes soon after (taking care not to let the spices burn).

3. Saute the potatoes well, making sure they are get coated with the ghee. Add the coriander powder, tumeric, chilli

powder and salt and mix well. Add enough water to cover the potatoes, add the mango powder and bring to boil. Simmer for 5–10 minutes. Serve hot, garnished with chopped coriander leaves.

ᛜᛜᛜᛜᛜᛜᛜ

SOOKHE MATAR

(This dish is enjoyed most in winter when peas are very tender and sweet, and cook very fast.)

INGREDIENTS

1	kg	**matar (peas)**, shelled
¼	cup	(60 g) ghee
2	tsp	jeera (cumin seeds)
$\frac{1}{8}$	tsp	heeng (asafoetida)
1	tbsp	finely sliced ginger
2	tsp	dhania (coriander powder)
1	tsp	amchoor (mango powder)
¼	tsp	garam masala I (p 148)
Salt to taste		
1	tbsp	chopped hara dhania (coriander leaves)

METHOD

1. Heat the ghee in a heavy-based pan. Add the cumin seeds and asafoetida. When the seeds begin to splutter, add the ginger and saute to a light brown.

2. Add the peas, coriander powder, mango powder, garam masala and salt. Saute over high heat till they look glossy. Lower heat and simmer till the peas are cooked. (Should take about 10 minutes, depending on the quality of the peas. Sometimes a little water may be required to cook them).

3. Serve hot, mixed with chopped coriander leaves.

SAANKHEIN

(Four kinds of lentils, with husked Bengal gram being the most predominant. A Kayasth recipe taught to me by Bina, which I find compliments this menu. Served mainly during the festival of Holi.)

INGREDIENTS

1	cup	**channa daal (Bengal gram)**
$\frac{1}{3}$	cup	**dhuli moong (husked green gram)**
$\frac{1}{3}$	cup	**dhuli urad (husked black gram)**
$\frac{1}{3}$	cup	**arhar (yellow lentils)**

soaked for 4–5 hours

Salt to taste		
½	tsp	heeng (asafoetida)
1	tsp	chilli powder
½	tsp	baking soda
2	tsp	ajwain (thymol seeds)
Oil for deep-frying		

METHOD

1. Grind the soaked lentils to a dough-like consistency without using water. The texture should be a little grainy.

2. Mix in the rest of the dry ingredients and shape the dough into slightly flat rounds 6 cm/2–3 inches in diameter. Heat the oil over high flame, put in as many balls as fit in without their touching each other. Turn after about 10 seconds and lower heat. Cook till firm on both sides, but not brown.

3. When cool, slice into 6 cm / ½ in thick slices. Before serving, deep-fry the slices, first over high heat, then lowering the heat till slices are crisp. Serve with a green chutney.

ᛜᛜᛜᛜᛜᛜᛜ

MENU THIRTEEN

- Jimikand ki sabzi
- Paneer pasanda
- Parwal aloo

JIMIKAND KI SABZI

(One of Snehji's recipes, this item is made for Diwali dinner in some homes.)

INGREDIENTS

1½ cups (250 g) **jimikand (yam)**, peeled and cut into about ¼ in cubes
2–3 green chillies, slit
1 tbsp chopped ginger
1 tsp roasted jeera (cumin seeds)
2 tsp roasted dhania (coriander seeds) } grind together
2 tsp roasted khus khus (poppy seeds)
Salt to taste
1 tsp chilli powder
1 tsp haldi (turmeric)
½ tsp garam masala II (p 148)
2 tbsp (30 g) ghee
1 tsp jeera (cumin seeds)
¼ tsp heeng (asafoetida)
2 large (250 g) tomatoes, grated
½ cup (100 g) dahi (yogurt)
1 tbsp chopped hara dhania (coriander leaves), for garnish

METHOD

1. Boil enough water to take in the yam when it is added. Add the cubed pieces into the boiling water, cover and simmer for about 20 minutes or until cooked through. Drain and set aside.

2. In a heavy-based pan, heat the ghee, add the cumin seeds and asafoetida. When the seeds splutter, add the tomatoes and stir-fry till fat separates.

3. Add the ground spices and mix well before adding the cubed yam. Stir-fry for about 5 minutes, add salt, chilli powder and garam masala.

4. Add 3–4 cups of water, depending on how much gravy you want. Bring to boil and simmer for about 5 minutes.

5. Beat the yogurt slightly to make it smooth and add to the gravy. Garnish with chopped coriander leaves and serve.

PANEER PASANDA

(Cottage cheese with gravy.)

INGREDIENTS

½ kg **paneer (cottage cheese)** (p 150), cut into broad slices about ¼ in (½ cm) thick
2 tbsp besan (chickpea flour)
¼ cup (60 g) ghee or butter
1 tsp jeera (cumin seeds)
1 tbsp finely chopped ginger
1 cup hung curd (200 g after water has drained)
¼ tsp haldi (turmeric)
2 tsp dhania (coriander powder)
Salt to taste
½ tsp chilli powder
¼ tsp garam masala I (p 148)
2–3 green chillies, slit
1½ cup water
1 tbsp chopped hara dhania (coriander leaves), for garnish
2 tbsp malai (clotted cream)

METHOD

1. Heat the ghee or butter in a pan and fry the pieces of cottage cheese. Lift them out and set aside. In the same ghee, add the cumin seeds, saute a little and add the ginger.
2. When the ginger turns a light brown, add the chickpea flour. Saute and add yogurt, turmeric, coriander powder, salt, chilli powder, and garam masala. Saute over medium heat till the fat separates.
3. Add the green chillies, saute a little, then add the water and bring to boil. Simmer for 3–4 minutes.
4. Add the fried pieces of cheese, simmer for about 2 minutes and serve hot, garnished with chopped coriander leaves and cream.

PARWAL ALOO

(One of the many ways of making this seasonal vegetable – readily available in U.P., but perhaps not in other parts of India – is to combine it with potatoes. Gherkins are also made into a sweetmeat, filled with khoya.)

INGREDIENTS

10–12 (500 g)		**parwals,** preferably of a uniform size
125	g	**potatoes**
½	cup (120 g)	oil
1	tsp	roasted and powdered jeera (cumin seeds)
½	tsp	chilli powder
¼	tsp	haldi (turmeric)
2	tsp	dhania (coriander powder)
Salt to taste		
¼	tsp	garam masala I (p 148)
1	tsp	amchoor (mango powder)
¼	tsp	heeng (asafoetida)
1	tbsp	hara dhania (coriander leaves), for garnish

METHOD

1. Cut the gherkins lengthwise into halves. Remove any fibres and seeds that are yellow and hard, as these remain tough even when cooked.
2. Peel the potatoes and cut them lengthwise to match the gherkins.
3. Heat the oil in a kadahi, and over high heat, add the potatoes. Stir-fry the potatoes till they are a creamish colour. Remove them with a slotted spoon and add the gherkins into the same oil. Fry to a light brown and till the edges fold towards each other.
4. Add the rest of the ingredients, except the coriander leaves. Lower heat, cover and cook till potatoes and gherkins are tender. Serve hot, garnished with coriander leaves.

MENU FOURTEEN

- Aloo dum
- Tali hui karari bhindi
- Gajar matar

ALOO DUM

(Medium-sized whole, fried potatoes in a gravy. This is a rich dish.)

INGREDIENTS

500 g   even-sized **potatoes**
Oil for deep-frying the potatoes

Gravy:

2	tbsp (30 g) ghee	
2	tej patta (bay leaves)	
1½	tsp jeera (cumin seeds)	
3–4	chhoti elaichi (green cardamoms)	
½	tsp methi dana (fenugreek seeds)	roasted and
3–4	laung (cloves)	pounded coarsely
1	tsp saunf (fennel seeds)	
1	tbsp finely chopped ginger	

½ cup (125 g) tomatoes, skinned, de-seeded and chopped
½ cup (100 g) (dahi) yogurt
Salt to taste
¼ tsp   haldi (turmeric)
1 tbsp   dhania (coriander powder)
½ tsp   chilli powder
2–3 green chillies, slit a little
1 tbsp   chopped hara dhania (coriander leaves) ⎫ for garnish
2 tbsp   cream ⎭

METHOD

1. Peel, wash and pat the potatoes dry. Prick with a fork, in 2–3 places. Deep-fry over high heat till light brown. Set aside on absorbent paper.
2. Heat the ghee in a heavy-based saucepan and add the bay leaves. When they darken a bit, add the roasted and pound spices. Stir a little, then add the ginger.
3. Stir-fry till colour changes slightly. Add tomatoes and continue stir-frying till the fat separates.
4. Add the yogurt and continue to stir till the fat separates again. Now add the salt, turmeric, coriander powder and chilli powder.
5. Mix well and add the fried potatoes and green chillies. Stir till the vegetables are coated with the masala, and begin to stick slightly to the pan.
6. Add enough water to cover the potatoes (approx 3 cups) and bring to boil. Simmer at low heat till the potatoes are cooked through and the gravy is well blended.
7. Serve hot, garnished with cream and chopped coriander leaves.

TALI HUI KARARI BHINDI

(Spicey ladies' fingers fried to a crisp.)

INGREDIENTS

500 g   **bhindi (ladies' fingers)**, washed and wiped dry
A large pinch of heeng (asafoetida)
1 tsp   jeera (cumin seeds)
Salt to taste
1 tsp   amchoor (mango powder)
½ tsp   chilli powder
Oil for deep-frying

41

METHOD

1. Top and tail the ladies' fingers—slice off the stalk end and the tail. Slice them into ½ cm/¼ in thick rounds.
2. Heat the oil until a piece of the vegetable dropped in, comes up at once. Add as many pieces as fit in comfortably. Fry over high heat for about 2 minutes. Then lower the heat and fry till crisp.
3. Lift the pieces out with a slotted spoon and leave to drain. Repeat till the whole lot is fried, increasing the heat before a fresh lot is put in. Set aside.
4. Heat about 1 tablespoon oil. Add the asafoetida and cumin seeds. When the seeds splutter add the fried ladies' fingers, salt, mango powder and chilli powder. Saute to mix well and serve.

GAJAR MATAR

(A colourful combination of carrots and peas, especially popular in the winter months.)

INGREDIENTS

2	cups	(1 kg unshelled) shelled **matar (peas)**
½	kg	**gajar (carrots),** cubed to match the peas
2	tbsp	ghee
¼	tsp	heeng (asafoetida)
½	tsp	methi dana (fenugreek seeds) ⎫ roasted and
1	tsp	saunf (fennel seeds) ⎭ coarsely ground
2	tsp	dhania (coriander powder)
½	tsp	chilli powder
¼	tsp	garam masala II (p 148)

Salt to taste

1	tbsp	lemon juice
2	tbsp	chopped hara dhania (coriander leaves), for garnish

METHOD

1. Heat the ghee in a heavy-based pan. Add the asafoetida and ground spices.
2. When the spices darken a bit, add the vegetables and stir till they look a little glossy.
3. Add the coriander powder, chilli powder, garam masala and salt. Mix well. Lower heat and cook uncovered till tender (approx 20 minutes).
4. Mix in the lemon juice and serve garnished with chopped coriander leaves.

Menu Fifteen

- Moong daal ki potli ki sabzi
- Bhindi sookhi
- Matar ki chaat

MOONG DAAL KI POTLI KI SABZI

(The name is derived from the fact that the lentils are tied up in a cloth. An innovation with green gram, which is generally made into a gravied dish, but can be eaten as a snack too. It was the name that first attracted my attention! This too, was taught to me by Bina.)

INGREDIENTS

Potli:

1 cup (180 grams) **moong daal chhilke wali (split green gram),** soaked for 4–5 hours
1 tbsp chopped hara dhania (coriander leaves)
1 tsp finely chopped green chillies
1 tsp jeera (cumin seeds)
Salt to taste
¼ tsp baking soda
Oil to deep-fry

Gravy:

2 tbsp (30 g) oil
1 tsp jeera (cumin seeds)
¼ tsp heeng (asafoetida)
1 cup (250 g) grated tomato
½ tsp haldi (turmeric)
1 tbsp dhania (coriander powder)
¼ tsp garam masala I (p 148)
½ tsp chilli powder
Salt to taste
2–3 green chillies, slit
Chopped hara dhania (coriander leaves), for garnish

METHOD

1. Grind the green gram coarsely (grainy texture), with the ginger. Add the coriander leaves, green chillies, salt and soda. Mix well.
2. Tie this mixture up in a cloth and boil in water for about 20 minutes, or till firm. Cool, and remove from cloth. Cut into square pieces of the size desired, and fry over high heat, till crisp and golden. Set aside.

Gravy:

1. Heat the oil, add the cumin seeds and asafoetida. When the seeds splutter, add the tomatoes and saute till the fat separates. Add turmeric, coriander powder, garam masala, chilli powder, salt and green chillies. Mix well.
2. Add 3–4 cups water and bring to boil. Simmer for about 5 minutes. Add the pieces of fried lentils and simmer for a few minutes more. Serve hot, garnished with the coriander leaves.

Note: If desired, you can add an onion and garlic and ginger paste after adding the asafoetida. Stir-fry till fat separates and then proceed.

BHINDI SOOKHI

(One of the various preparations of ladies' fingers, cut and sauted with spices. Most people like this vegetable, so it is a safe option.)

INGREDIENTS

500 g **bhindi ladies' fingers)**
1 tsp jeera (cumin seeds)
¼ tsp heeng (asafoetida)
½ tsp garam masala I (p 148)

2 tsp dhania (coriander powder)
½ tsp chilli powder
½ tsp haldi (turmeric)
2 tsp amchoor (mango powder)
Salt to taste
¼ cup (60 g) oil
3–4 green chillies, cut into 2–3 pieces each

METHOD

1. Wash and wipe the ladies' fingers dry. Slice them into 1cm (½ in) pieces.
2. Heat the oil in a kadahi. Add the cumin seeds and asafoetida. When the seeds begin to splutter, add the ladies' fingers and green chillies. Stir-fry at high heat till the vegetables are lightly coated with oil.
3. Add the garam masala, coriander powder, chilli powder, turmeric, salt and mango powder. Stir-fry enough to mix well. Lower heat.
4. Cook uncovered at low heat, stirring a few times, till soft. Some people like them absolutely tender while others like them less so. Cook depending on individual taste. Nevertheless, a well-cooked dish is one in which the ladies' fingers keep their shape, and are not cooked till they disintegrate. They should remain 'bite-like'.

Note: To cook with onions, thinly slice one large onion. Add after the cumin seeds splutter. Stir-fry till the moisture of the onions dries up and then add the ladies' fingers, and proceed.

MATAR KI CHAAT

(A spicy dish made with peas which look like chickpeas but are smoother and round. Although this is a snack served traditionally by roadside vendors, it makes an interesting addition to a dinner/lunch menu.)

INGREDIENTS

2 cups (360 g) **matar/vatana (yellow peas)** | soaked together
¾ tsp baking soda (adjustable) | for 4–6 hours
Salt to taste
2 tbsp finely shredded ginger
Ghee to fry the peas
½ cup sonth ki chutney (ginger powder chutney) (p 134)
¼ cup hari chutney (coriander chutney p 134)
1 cup (200 g) dahi (yogurt) beaten smooth
Chaat ka masala
Chilli powder | for garnish
Chopped hara dhania (coriander leaves)

METHOD

1. Discard the water in which the peas have been soaked. Cook in fresh water with salt and ginger, till tender. Takes about 15 minutes in a pressure cooker. (Takes 1 hour 15 minutes and more water in an ordinary pan.)
2. Cook at low heat till peas look quite mashed. If they are not soft enough, add some more water and cook, but only enough so it is absorbed. Once cooked, there should be no water left. The peas should take on a thick paste-like consistency, which, when cool, looks like soft dough.
3. When the mixture is cold, form into flat round cutlets (or tikkis).
4. Heat some ghee in a frying pan (enough to coat the base), and add as many cutlets to it as fit comfortably in

the pan without touching each other. Fry at medium heat till brown and crisp, first on one side and then the other. Fry all the pieces.

5. To serve, place the crisp, hot cutlets in the frying pan over high heat, and break up each into a few pieces with a spoon. Place them in a serving dish, pour some ginger powder chutney over them, followed by the green chutney and then the yogurt. Sprinkle some chaat masala and chilli powder over the yogurt, according to taste, and garnish with chopped coriander leaves.

MENU SIXTEEN

- Makhmali kofte
- Gajar methi
- Ghiya malaiwala

MAKHMALI KOFTE

(Koftas in a rich gravy. Smooth and soft, these are made with solidified milk and so are quite rich!)

INGREDIENTS (MAKES ABOUT 20)

Koftas:

½ cup (100 g) firmly packed Khoya (solidified milk) (p 150)
6 tbsp (45 g) maida (flour)
⅛ tsp baking soda
Ghee for deep-frying

Gravy:

¼ cup (60 g) ghee
1 tsp jeera (cumin seeds)
1 tbsp finely chopped ginger
2 tbsp khus khus (poppy seeds)
¼ cup dessicated coconut (soaked in water for 1 hour and ground to a paste)
1 tbsp dhania (coriander powder)
Salt to taste
1 tsp garam masala I (p 148)
¼ tsp kali mirch (powdered black pepper)
2 tbsp cornflour dissolved in ½ of cup milk
2 tbsp chopped hara dhania (coriander leaves), for garnish

METHOD

1. With the heel of your palm or the base of a small bowl, mash the solidified milk till smooth, so that no grains

remain. Mix in the flour and baking soda and knead into a firm dough. A food processor can be used for this. The dough should be firm, and pliable, but should not feel dry. If it does, wet your hands and work the dough again.

2. Shape the dough into marble-sized balls, that are smooth and creaseless.

3. Heat the ghee in a kadahi. To check if the oil is hot enough, drop a piece of dough into it. It should come up at once. Lower the heat and fry a cube of bread till light brown (this lowers the temperature of the oil slightly).

4. Lift out the cube of bread and add as many balls as will fit comfortably into the pan. Keeping the heat low, fry these till golden brown all over, turning if necessary. It is easier to stir the ghee slowly. This helps turn the balls over, without breaking them.

5. Lift balls out of the ghee and drain. Increase heat for a few seconds, then lower it before adding the next lot. Keep koftas aside while making the gravy.

Gravy:

1. Heat the ghee in a heavy-based pan and add the cumin seeds. When the seeds splutter, add the ginger and saute till light brown.

2. Add the ground paste, coriander powder, salt, garam masala and black pepper. Saute till fat separates. Add 3 cups water, bring to boil and simmer for about 5 minutes.

3. Add the cornflour solution, simmer for a couple of minutes and add koftas. Simmer again for 2–3 minutes and serve garnished with cream and coriander leaves.

GAJAR METHI

(The sweetness of carrots and the bitter taste of fenugreek leaves combine well to make a delicious dish.)

INGREDIENTS

½ kg **gajar (carrots)**
250 g **methi (fenugreek) leaves**
1 tsp methi dana (fenugreek seeds)
2 tsp dhania (coriander powder)
Salt to taste
½ tsp chilli powder
3–4 sabut lal mirch (whole, dried red chillies)
½ cup (120 g) sarson ka tel (mustard oil)

METHOD

1. Peel and dice the carrots into 1 cm (½ in) cubes. Clean the fenugreek leaves, wash well, changing the water a few times. Chop fine, discarding the tough stalks.

2. Heat the oil in a kadahi. Add fenugreek seeds and whole red chillies. Stir-fry and add the carrots and fenugreek leaves.

3. Stir-fry till leaves look slightly glossy, then add salt, chilli powder and coriander powder. Cook uncovered till the leaves are done (they will look a little shrivelled up and fried), and the carrots are soft. Serve hot.

GHIYA MALAIWALA

*(Bottle gourd with clotted cream.
Taught to me by our old cook, Devi Ram.
After all these years I still manage to
surprise people who generally do not eat
this vegetable, into enjoying this dish!)*

INGREDIENTS

2	cups	(500 g) **ghiya/lauki (bottle gourd),** peeled and cut into small pieces, 1½ cms ¾ in thick
2	tbsp	ghee
2	tsp	jeera (cumin seeds)
Salt to taste		
¼	cup	(60 g) malai (clotted cream)

2	tbsp	chopped hara dhania (coriander leaves) } for garnish
1	tbsp	finely chopped green chillies

METHOD

1. Heat the ghee in a heavy-based pan and add the cumin seeds. When they begin to splutter, add the bottle gourd and salt. Stir a few times over high heat, till the pieces look glossy.

2. Lower heat, cover and cook till tender. Takes 20–25 minutes depending on the freshness of the vegetable. It is done when it is easily pressed.

3. Add the clotted cream, mix well and serve hot, garnished with coriander leaves and green chillies.

Non-vegetarian Menus

People who are predominantly non-vegetarian, often pay little attention to vegetables. I have made combinations of the recipes by keeping taste and nutritional balance in mind. Some combinations are traditional. The accompaniments can be chosen from the vegetarian menus.

DUM PUKHT: A pan or haandi with a close-fitting lid is essential for cooking dum. Dum is food cooked in its own steam. Put the ingredients to be cooked into the pan and grease the edges of the mouth of the pan. Make a thick string of kneaded dough and line the greased edge with it. Place the lid on the pan and press to seal. Now cook at low heat or place on a griddle, also at low heat. Before serving, prize open the lid with the help of a sharp instrument. It is important that it is opened only just before serving.

MENU SEVENTEEN

- Murgh-e-kalmi
- Mutton stoo
- Tali hui karari bhindi (p 41)
- Roomali roti (p 92)

MURGH-E-KALMI

(A delectable dish of chicken in a yogurt marinate, spiced and grilled/barbecued.)

Oven temp: 450°F/220°C

INGREDIENTS

1 kg **chicken** (broiler), skinned and cut into 8–10 pieces
1 tsp ginger paste
1 tsp garlic paste
Salt to taste
1 cup (200 g) dahi (yogurt), placed in a colander to drain out excess water
2 laungs (cloves)
½ tsp dalchini (cinnamon), broken ⎫
½ tsp kala jeera (black cumin) ⎬ roasted and powdered
A large pinch of kesar (saffron) ⎭
2 tbsp nimbu (sour lime) juice
¼ cup (30 g) maida (refined flour)
1 egg slightly beaten
1 large onion sliced into rings ⎫
1 tbsp chopped pudina (mint) leaves ⎬ for garnish
1 lemon cut into wedges ⎭

METHOD

1. Wash the chicken and wipe dry. Prick in 2–3 places. Mix all the ingredients, except those for garnishing. Marinate the chicken for 2–3 hours in the mixture.

2. Before serving, place the marinated chicken on a drip-tray and grill till light brown, or bake in a hot oven for 15–20 minutes. It is best cooked in a tandoor. A drip-tray is essential, because the drippings need to escape. Chicken cooked in drippings becomes soggy.

3. Serve hot, garnished with onion rings, chopped mint leaves and lemon wedges.

MUTTON STOO

*(Similar to Korma-e-Vakil (p 50),
except that in this recipe whole spices
are added and cooked together.)*

INGREDIENTS

1	kg	**mutton/lamb,** cut into pieces
10		chhoti elaichi (green cardamoms)
10		laung (cloves)
1	tsp	seeds of badi elaichi (black cardamom)
3–4		sabut lal mirch (whole, dried red chillies)
3	tbsp	dhania (coriander seeds)
1	tsp	haldi (turmeric)
2	tsp	finely cut ginger
1	tbsp	garlic pods

Salt to taste

1	cup	(200 g) dahi (yogurt)
2	cups	(250 g) onions, sliced thin
½	cup	(120 g) ghee
2	tbsp	chopped hara dhania (coriander leaves), for garnish

METHOD

1. Mix all the ingredients together, except the ghee and coriander leaves.

2. Heat the ghee in a heavy-based pan, and add the meat mixed with other ingredients. Stir a few times over high heat, till pieces look opaque. Lower heat, cover and simmer for half an hour.

3. Uncover and simmer further till the meat is tender, and the fat separates. If required, sprinkle a little water to avoid scorching.

4. Add water and simmer for about 5 minutes if you want a gravy, (amount of water added depends on how thin you want the gravy) and serve garnished with the coriander leaves.

Menu Eighteen

KORMA-E-VAKIL

(Mutton korma less rich than the Shahi Korma, but rich in fat nevertheless! The kind of dish that can be enjoyed only if it has its characteristic fat floating over it! As the name suggests, this is as made by Vakil Mohammed, who never cooks less than one whole animal at a time!)

INGREDIENTS

1 kg **mutton/lamb,** cut into pieces
1 cup (240 g) ghee
2 cups (250 g) onions, sliced thin

Mix together:

10 chhoti elaichi (green cardamoms)
10 laung (cloves)
1 tsp seeds of badi elaichi (black cardamom), powdered
1 tbsp chilli powder
3 tbsp dhania (coriander powder)
1 tsp haldi (turmeric)
1 tsp ginger paste
1 tsp garlic paste
1 cup (200 g) dahi (yogurt)
Salt to taste
2 tbsp chopped hara dhania (coriander leaves), for garnish

METHOD

1. Heat the ghee in a heavy-based pan and fry the onions till brown and crisp. With a slotted spoon, scoop them out and grind to a paste with a little water. Set aside.

2. Add the mixed spices to the meat and put it into the hot ghee over high heat.

3. Stir to mix well; when the meat pieces begin to look opaque, lower heat, cover and simmer for about an hour or till the meat is tender. Stir a few times to make sure it does not scorch. Time taken for meat to cook through depends on quality of meat and width of vessel. If it cooks through before the water dries up and fat separates, remove pieces of meat, cook the masala till fat separates, and then put meat back into pan. If it does not cook through, add a little water and cook till tender.

4. Add the onion paste and cook some more till well blended, and serve garnished with coriander leaves. If you want some gravy, add water according to taste and simmer for another five minutes before serving.

Dum Pukht: If you want to cook it dum style (p 48), add the fried, ground onions to the meat; after the meat pieces begin to look opaque (step 3) transfer the meat mixture to a haandi and dum for ½ an hour and serve.

FISH FRIE

(Another recipe from Vakil Mohammed who believes in cooking in large quantities. He told us he once cooked 200 kg of fish!)

INGREDIENTS

1 kg **singhara** (or any other large fish with a single bone) cut into 2½ cm (1 in) thick slices, without bones and with the skin on (wt 1 kg after cleaning and de-boning)

1 tbsp pissi peeli mirch (dried yellow peppers, powdered)
1 tbsp chilli powder
2 tsp ajwain (thymol seeds, powdered)
2 tbsp besan (chickpea/gram flour)
Salt to taste
2 tsp garlic paste
Sarson ka tel (mustard oil) to deep-fry the fish
Chaat masala and lemon wedges, for garnish

METHOD

1. Mix all the ingredients except the oil and apply to the fish. Marinate for about ½ an hour.
2. Heat the oil in a kadahi; when hot (a piece of fish put in should come up at once), add as many pieces as fit in comfortably. Fry over high heat till lightly coloured, and the masala forms a coat over it.
3. Remove fish from oil, and set aside over a colander (to drain excess oil). Heat oil again, before frying the remaining pieces.
4. Before serving, heat the oil and add the pieces of fish to it; press them down a little and fry till cooked through and crisp on top. (When cooked through they are opaque when cut.)
5. Drain on absorbent paper and serve hot, sprinkled with chaat masala and lemon wedges on the side.

MENU NINETEEN

- Nargisi kofta
- Daal gosht
- Methi aloo

NARGISI KOFTA

(Egg wrapped in a coating of minced meat , fried and served in gravy. Rather like an Indian equivalent of Scotch Eggs, these can also be served without gravy.)

INGREDIENTS (MAKES 6 KOFTAS)

Mix together:

2 cups (500 g) **keema (minced mutton/lamb)**
½ tsp garlic paste
½ tsp ginger paste
Salt to taste
¼ tsp kali mirch (powdered black pepper)
¼ tsp garam masala III (p 149)
5–6 hard boiled eggs, cooled and shelled
A little flour (maida) to roll the eggs in

Gravy:

1 tbsp chopped ginger
1 tbsp chopped garlic
1½ cups (250 g) roughly chopped onions, boiled in very little water
1 cup (240 g) oil
2 tej patta (bay leaves)
2 tsp kala jeera (black cumin seeds)
6–7 chhoti elaichi (green cardamoms) ⎫
6–7 laung (cloves)   ⎬ lightly roasted and powdered
1 tsp broken cinnamon (dalchini)   ⎪
1 blade mace (javitri)   ⎭
Salt to taste

½ tsp   haldi (turmeric)
2 tbsp   dhania (coriander powder)
½ tsp   chilli powder
1 cup   (250 g) finely chopped tomatoes
A large pinch of kesar (saffron)
½ tsp   kewra (vetiver) or
          ½ tsp almond essence   } dissolved together
2 tbsp   warm milk
¼ cup   chopped hara dhania (coriander leaves)
2 tbsp   cream

METHOD

Koftas:

1. Divide the meat into 5 or 6 portions, and shape each into a round pattie. Roll the eggs in the flour, dust off the excess flour, and place in the centre of each pattie. Bring the meat up around the egg, to form an even coating around it. Smooth the surface so that no creases remain. Refrigerate for at least an hour.

2. In a kadahi, heat some of the oil listed with the ingredients for the gravy. Fry the koftas in it, first over high heat; then lower the heat, so that they are cooked through. When they are evenly brown, remove from oil and set aside. Fry as many koftas as fit comfortably in the kadahi. Be careful not to break them.

Gravy:

1. Grind the ginger, garlic and boiled onions to a fine paste and set aside.

2. Heat the rest of the oil in a saucepan and add the bay leaves and powdered spices. When the spices darken a little, add the onion mixture. Stir-fry till brown and fat separates.

3. Add the tomatoes, salt, turmeric, coriander powder and chilli powder, and stir-fry again till fat separates.

4. Add about 2 cups water. Bring to boil and simmer for about 10 minutes. Add half the chopped coriander leaves and the milk into which saffron etc. have been mixed.

Serve:

1. Cut the koftas lengthwise. Arrange on a serving dish and pour the hot gravy over them.

2. Serve, garnished with the cream and the rest of the chopped coriander leaves.

Note: Some like to serve koftas whole. To do this, when the gravy is ready, add the koftas, simmer for a couple of minutes, garnish and serve.

DAAL GOSHT

(A combination of meat and urad ki daal.)

1. Cook ½ kg mutton as in Korma-e-Vakil (p 50).

2. Soak ½ cup husked black gram, for about an hour. Add the soaked lentils to the meat. Add ½ teaspoon chilli powder, ¼ teaspoon turmeric and salt to taste.

3. Simmer for about 10 minutes or until the lentils are cooked through, but not soft enough to disintegrate. Serve garnished with coriander leaves.

Menu Twenty

- Pasande
- Murgh rasedaar
- Mooli ki bhurji
- Roomali roti (p 92)

PASANDE

(In a pasande preparation, the meat is flattened, making it tender and ensuring that it simply melts in the mouth! Today, cooking this dish is easier as one can get the meat prepared by a butcher.)

INGREDIENTS

Mix together and marinate for 4–5 hours

1 kg	(wt after de-boning) **mutton,** cut into 3½ cms (1¼ in) cubes and beaten flat (pasandas),
Salt to taste	
1 tbsp	ginger paste
1 tbsp	garlic paste
2 tsp	chilli powder
2 tbsp	dhania (coriander powder)
2 tbsp	khus khus (poppy seeds), soaked, roasted and ground
1 tsp	kalonji (onion seeds)
2½ cups (500 g) dahi (yogurt)	

½ cup (120 g) oil
6–7 chhoti elaichi (green cardamoms)
6–7 laung (cloves)
2 pieces dalchini (cinnamon)
1 cup (125 g) onions, chopped fine
1 cup (250 g) tomatoes cut fine
½ cup tomato puree

10–12 blanched and slivered almonds ⎫
¼ cup cream   ⎬ for garnish
2 tbsp chopped hara dhania (coriander leaves) ⎭

METHOD

1. Heat the oil in a large saucepan; add the cardamoms, clove and cinnamon. When these darken, add the onions and fry to a dark brown.

2. Add the flattened meat along with the marinate and cook uncovered, over low or high heat (depending on how often you stir it), till the water has evaporated and the fat separates. By this time the meat should be cooked too. If not yet tender, add some water and cook till tender.

3. Add the tomatoes and puree, and saute till fat separates again, taking care not to break the meat pieces. Add half the almonds. Dish can be served dry. To make a gravy, add a little water and cook for a few minutes longer.

4. Garnish with cream, the rest of the almonds and the coriander leaves, and serve.

MURGH RASEDAAR

(A chicken curry which can be a base for many innovative preparations.)

INGREDIENTS

1 kg	**chicken** (broiler), skinned and cut into pieces
¼ cup	(60 g) oil
1 tbsp	jeera (cumin seeds)
2–3 tej patta (bay leaves)	
1 tsp	ginger paste
1 tsp	garlic paste
2 cups	(approx 500 g) grated onions
½ cup	(125 g) grated tomatoes
½ cup	(100 g) dahi (yogurt)
2 tsp	garam masala II (p 148)

Salt to taste
½ tsp haldi (turmeric)
2 tbsp dhania (coriander powder)
1 tsp chilli powder
2 tbsp chopped hara dhania (coriander leaves), for garnish

METHOD

1. Heat the oil in a heavy-based saucepan. Add cumin seeds and bay leaves. When the seeds begin to splutter, add the onions, garlic and ginger. Saute over high heat till brown.

2. Add the tomatoes and stir-fry till the fat separates, then add the yogurt, stir-frying vigorously so that it blends well and does not curdle.

3. Cook till fat separates, then add the garam masala, salt, turmeric, coriander powder and chilli powder. Mix well.

4. Keeping the heat high, add the chicken pieces and stir till they look a little opaque. Add 1½ cups water and bring to boil; lower heat, uncover and simmer till chicken is cooked through. Takes about 15 minutes. The amount of water added depends on the thickness of the gravy you want.

5. Serve hot, garnished with chopped coriander leaves.

MOOLI KI BHURJI

(A tangy radish preparation, which also includes the leaves of the radish.)

INGREDIENTS

2 large (1 kg) **mooli (radish)**, including the leaves
2 tbsp sarson ka tel (mustard oil)
⅛ tsp heeng (asafoetida)

1 tsp jeera (cumin seeds)
Salt to taste
1 tsp sugar
½ tsp chilli powder

METHOD

1. Wash the radish leaves well and chop fine. Scrape the radish, wash and chop fine.

2. Heat the oil and add the asafoetida and cumin seeds. When they begin to splutter, add the chopped vegetables, salt, sugar and chilli powder. Stir-fry till the leaves are slightly limp but still crunchy, and serve.

Menu Twenty-one

- Murgh mussallam
- Keema matar
- Kathal ki sabzi

MURGH MUSSALLAM

(A chicken cooked whole with a thick paste of masala, as I learnt from Hasina Siddique.)

Ingredients

1 (1 kg approx) **desi murghi (country chicken)**
¼ cup (25 g) chopped kaccha papita (raw papaya) ground with a tsp of salt
¼ cup (60 g) ghee
1 (125 g) large onion grated

Grind together:

5–6 sabut lal mirch (whole, dried red chilli)
1 tsp khus khus (poppy seeds), roasted } dry grind
1 tsp jeera (cumin seeds)
Salt to taste
1 (125 g) large onion
1 tbsp chopped ginger
1 tbsp chopped garlic
¼ cup thick strained yogurt
2 tsp garam masala II (p 148)
2 tbsp nariyal ka burada (dessicated coconut)
A large pinch of kesar (saffron)
½ tsp kewra (vetiver) or } dissolved together
      ½ tsp almond essence
2 tbsp warm milk
1 tbsp blanched and shredded almonds
2 hard boiled eggs cut into halves, lengthwise
2 tbsp chopped hara dhania (coriander leaves)

Method

1. Clean inside of the chicken and remove innards. Smear chicken with the papaya paste, outside and inside. Leave on for 5 minutes, wash off and wipe dry.
2. Heat the ghee in a heavy-based pan and stir-fry the chicken over high heat till brown. Remove the chicken and fry the onions in the same ghee till brown and crisp.
3. Meanwhile, apply the ground ingredients to the chicken both inside and outside.
4. When the onions are a dark brown, increase heat and add the chicken. Fry, turning on all sides, so that the whole chicken is fried; lower heat and cook, turning every 5–7 minutes (to avoid scorching), till the chicken is tender. Takes 30–40 minutes.
5. Add the garam masala, coconut and saffron mixture, and simmer till the fat separates.
6. Transfer on to a serving dish and cover with the masala in the pan. Arrange the boiled eggs around it, garnish with the coriander leaves and almonds and serve.

Note: If you do not wish to serve the chicken whole, cut it up, arrange on a serving dish and proceed. (I find this to be a more convenient way to serve it, even though it is traditionally served whole.)

KEEMA MATAR

(Minced mutton or lamb, cooked with green peas. This can be made as a side dish with a meal or can be used as a filling for samosas.)

Ingredients

½ kg (wt after de-boning) **keema (minced mutton/lamb)**
1 cup shelled (1 kg) **matar (green peas)**

½ cup (120 g) ghee
2 tsp jeera (cumin seeds)
4 laung (cloves)
A small piece of dalchini (cinnamon) the length of a clove
4 sabut kali mirch (peppercorns)
Seeds of 1 badi elaichi (black cardamom)
2 tej patta (bay leaves)
1 cup (250 g) grated onions
1 tsp ginger paste
1 tsp garlic paste
2 cups (250 g) chopped tomatoes
Salt to taste
1 tbsp dhania (coriander powder)
½ tsp haldi (turmeric)
½ tsp chilli powder
1 tbsp chopped hara dhania (coriander leaves)

METHOD

1. Heat the ghee in a heavy-based pan and add the cumin seeds, cloves, cinnamon, peppercorn, cardamom and bay leaves.
2. When the seeds start to splutter, add the garlic, ginger and onions, and stir-fry till fat separates.
3. Add the tomatoes, salt, coriander powder, turmeric and chilli powder. Continue to stir-fry till fat separates.
4. Increase heat to high and add the mince and peas. Stir a few times till the mince looks fried, then lower heat and saute till cooked through and fat separates once again.
5. Serve hot, garnished with chopped coriander leaves.

Note: In case you are using cooked peas, add them after the mince is done.

KATHAL KI SABZI

(A dry preparation of jackfruit. Because of its texture this vegetable looks a little like meat.)

INGREDIENTS

500 g **kathal (jackfruit)** and some oil to grease your hands
½ cup (120 g) oil
1 tsp jeera (cumin seeds)
1 cup (250 g) grated onions
1 tsp finely chopped ginger
1 tsp finely chopped garlic
1 cup (250 g) grated tomatoes
2 tsp dhania (coriander powder)
2 tsp salt
1 tsp chilli powder
½ tsp haldi (turmeric)
¼ tsp garam masala I (p 148)
2–3 green chillies, slit
1 tbsp hara dhania (coriander leaves), for garnish

METHOD

1. Oil your hands well. Keep some oil handy while cutting the jackfruit as you will need to smear your palms with oil from time to time. Oil prevents hands from getting sticky and itchy.
2. Peel the jackfruit and slice into rounds of desired thickness. Slice rounds into halves, and remove any thick stem in the centre, before cutting slices into smaller pieces. Do not wash. Scrape any dirt off. (Water makes it slimey, sticky and impossible to handle.)
3. Heat the oil and fry the pieces over high heat, till light brown. Drain and set aside.
4. Add cumin seeds to the same oil. When the seeds begin to splutter, add the onions, garlic and ginger. Stir-fry till

brown, add the tomatoes, and fry till fat separates. Add coriander powder, salt, chilli powder, tumeric, and garam masala. Stir to mix well.

5. Add the green chillies and jackfruit, stir a few times before adding about ½ cup water. Bring to boil and simmer till the vegetable is cooked through. (You should be able to cut it with a spoon or spatula, without much effort.)

6. Serve hot, garnished with coriander leaves.

MENU TWENTY-TWO

*   Malai kofta dum
*   Simple fish frie
*   Badi aloo matar
*   Naan (p 91)

MALAI KOFTA DUM

(Meat balls baked in a cream sauce. The cream gives this dish a very rich and distinctive flavour.)

Oven temp: 325°F/160°C

INGREDIENTS (MAKES ABOUT 15 KOFTAS)

Meat balls:

2	cups	(500 g) **keema (minced mutton/lamb)**
½	tsp	garlic paste
½	tsp	ginger paste
Salt to taste		
¼	tsp	kali mirch (powdered black pepper)
¼	tsp	garam masala I (p 148)
Oil for deep-frying		

Cream sauce:

1	cup	(240 g) malai (thick clotted cream)
1	cup	(250 g) grated onions
½	tsp	garam masala I (p 148)
2	tsp	dhania (coriander powder)
Salt to taste		
½	tsp	chilli powder
2	tbsp	chopped hara dhania (coriander leaves)
1	tsp	finely chopped green chillies

Mix together

2   tbsp   chopped hara dhania (coriander leaves), for garnish
An oven proof serving dish with a lid, large enough for the koftas to fit comfortably

METHOD

1. Shape the meat ball mixture into walnut-sized rounds, and refrigerate for at least an hour.

2. Heat the oil and put as many meat balls as fit in comfortably; lower heat to complete cooking. Fry all the meat balls in this way. They will shrink a little and turn a darkish brown.

3. In the oven proof dish, put in a layer of the meat balls and cover with a layer of the cream mixture. Repeat till all the meat balls are in the dish.

4. Bake in a pre-heated oven for about half an hour. Garnish with the coriander leaves and serve.

Alternatively: Cook dum (p 48)

SIMPLE FISH FRIE

*(Called so because it is hardly spiced,
requires no preparation and is easy to make.
A favourite in Mrs Iqbal's home!)*

INGREDIENTS

1	kg	**fish,** filleted and cut into 1 cm/½ in thick slices
1	tsp	salt
2	tsp	lemon juice

Sarson ka tel (mustard oil) to deep-fry
½   tsp   salt
Garam masala I (p 148)/chaat masala (p 149) to garnish

METHOD

1. Marinate the fish in the salt and lemon juice for 15 minutes and then wash off and wipe dry.

2. Heat the oil, and when a piece of fish tossed in comes up at once, add ½ teaspoon salt and fry the fish — put

in as many pieces as fit in comfortably without the pieces touching each other. Turn pieces over and lower heat. Cook till pieces are an even brown.

3. Remove from oil, drain on an absorbent paper and serve hot, garnished with the garam masala/chaat masala.

BADI ALOO MATAR

(Black gram nuggets, cooked with potatoes and peas, in a gravy. In some parts of the state mangauris made from green gram are preferred.)

INGREDIENTS

250	g	**potatoes**, boiled in their jackets and peeled
5–6		**badis** (p 151), or more if small
2	cups	shelled (1 kg) **green peas**
¼	cup	(60 g) ghee
1	tsp	jeera (cumin seeds)
1	tbsp	finely chopped ginger
½	cup	(125 g) grated tomatoes

Salt to taste
½   tsp   haldi (turmeric)
¼   cup   dahi (yogurt), beaten smooth
Approx 2½ cups water
1   tbsp   chopped hara dhania (coriander leaves), for garnish

METHOD

1. Break the potatoes in the palm of your hand and set aside. Heat the ghee and add the nuggets in very quickly. Stir till they get slightly darker. Remove from ghee.

2. In the same ghee, add cumin seeds and ginger. Saute till ginger is light brown, then add the tomatoes.

3. Stir-fry till fat separates. Add the potatoes and peas. Cook over high heat till lightly fried. Add salt, turmeric, and the nuggets. Add enough water to cover the mixture and bring to boil.

4. Simmer till peas are cooked and nuggets are soft, but retain their shape (about 15 minutes). If nuggets take very long to cook, it is advisable to cook them in some water after frying them. Then add nuggets with water to potato mixture.

5. Mix in the yogurt and serve garnished with coriander leaves.

MENU TWENTY-THREE

- Chicken frie
- Keema dum
- Baingan ki lonje
- Moti roti (p 89)

CHICKEN FRIE

(A tangy, fried chicken dish, which is spicey and dry. Easy and quick to make, it is also good as a snack.)

INGREDIENTS

1 kg **chicken** (broiler), cut into 8 pieces

Mix together for marinate:

½ tsp ginger paste
½ tsp garlic paste
Salt to taste
2 tsp chilli powder
2 tbsp (30 g) vinegar
2 tbsp (15 g) besan (chickpea/gram flour)
2 tsp ajwain (thymol seeds)
4–5 laung (cloves)
1 tsp methi dana (fenugreek seeds) — roasted and powdered
4–5 sabut kali mirch (peppercorns)
Seeds of 2 badi elaichi (black cardamoms)
2 tsp jeera (cumin seeds)

½ cup (120 g) sarson ka tel (mustard oil)
Lemon twists and hara dhania (coriander leaves), for garnish

METHOD

1. Prick the chicken in 2–3 places, marinate in the mixture and keep for 3–4 hours.

2. Heat the oil in a heavy-based pan and put the chicken pieces into it.

3. Deep fry over a medium flame, till the chicken is tender. Takes 15–20 minutes.

4. Serve garnished with lemon twists and coriander leaves.

KEEMA DUM

(Minced mutton/lamb cooked with spices on low heat, without stirring very much. This was taught to me by Pushpa Bhalla, who grew up on this dish, in Varanasi.)

INGREDIENTS

½ kg **keema (minced mutton/lamb)**
2 cups (250 g) onions, sliced thinly
¼ cup (60 g) ghee
1 tsp ginger paste
1 tsp garlic paste
¼ cup (25 g) chopped kaccha papita (raw papaya), unpeeled
1 tbsp sabut dhania (coriander seeds)
6 laung (cloves)
6 chhoti elaichi (green cardamoms)
1 tsp jeera (cumin seeds)
½ tsp pieces of dalchini (cinnamon)
Seeds of 1 badi elaichi (black cardamom)
½ tsp pieces of javitri (mace)
$\frac{1}{8}$ tsp grated jaiphal (nutmeg)
4 sabut kali mirch (peppercorns)
2 tbsp (30 g) sarson ka tel (mustard oil)

} roasted and powdered together

Salt to taste
1 tsp chilli powder
1 piece of coal
½ tsp ghee

} for smoking

2 laung (cloves), powdered
2 tbsp chopped hara dhania (coriander leaves)

METHOD

1. Heat ¼ cup ghee. Fry the onions till brown and crisp; remove and grind to a paste with some water.

2. Mix the mince meat with the ginger and garlic paste and chopped papaya. Add the roasted and powdered ingredients and the onion paste. Marinate for at least 2 hours.

3. Heat the oil in a heavy-based saucepan with a tight-fitting lid (or seal the lid with wheat flour dough). Add the mince meat, salt and chilli powder, mix well, cover and cook thoroughly over low heat. (Takes about 20 minutes). Do not stir while cooking. The fat will separate when cooked.

4. Before serving, set alight a piece of charcoal. Place it in a small bowl or in aluminium foil shaped like a cup. Place this in the centre of the cooked mince meat, pour the ½ teaspoon ghee and the powdered clove over it and cover immediately. Leave thus for about 5 minutes, remove the coal and bowl/foil; serve mince garnished with chopped coriander leaves.

BAINGAN KI LONJE

(Brinjal, the long variety, stuffed with a mixture of spices and cooked.)

INGREDIENTS

10–12 (½ kg) long **baingans (brinjals)**
½ cup (60 g) ghee
1 cup (125 g) onions, thinly sliced
½ tsp ginger paste
Salt to taste

2   sabut lal mirch (whole, dried red chillies)
5   laung (cloves)
1 tsp   pieces of dalchini (cinnamon)   } powder together
Seeds of 1 badi elaichi (black cardamom)
½ tsp   sabut kali mirch (peppercorns)
5   laung (cloves)
2 tbsp   (30 g) sugar
2 tbsp   nimbu (sour lime) juice
2 tbsp   chopped hara dhania (coriander leaves), for garnish

METHOD

1. Slit the brinjals lengthwise down to the base of the stalk.

2. Heat the ghee in a kadahi and saute the onions till brown and crisp. Remove onions from ghee and set ghee aside till ready to use again.

3. Grind together the onions, ginger, salt and half the powdered ingredients. Apply a layer of this mixture into the slits made in the brinjals.

4. Heat ghee again and add the cloves. When they begin to darken a little, add the brinjals and any leftover masala and saute over high heat till they look glossy.

5. Lower heat, cover and cook till tender, stirring a few times to avoid scorching.

6. Mix in the sugar, lime juice and the rest of the powdered masala. Garnish with the coriander leaves and serve.

MENU TWENTY-FOUR

* Murgh shahi korma
* Boti kabab
* Boot/Hare channe ki sabzi
* Varki parantha (p 90)

MURGH SHAHI KORMA

*(Chicken in a rich or shahi gravy. A good party dish,
it can also be made with just a salad to complement it.)*

INGREDIENTS

1   (1 kg) **chicken** (broiler), skinned and cut into 8 pieces
½ cup   (120 g) ghee
2 tsp   jeera (cumin seeds)
1 cup   (250 g) grated onions
2 tbsp   khus khus (poppy seeds) roast and dry grind separately
8–10   kaju (cashew nuts)
¼ cup   milk   } soaked for half an hour and ground to a paste
2 tbsp   nariyal ka burada (dessicated coconut)
½ tsp   haldi (turmeric)
½ tsp   chilli powder
½ tsp   garam masala I (p 148)
1 tbsp   dhania (coriander powder)
Salt to taste
2–3 green chillies, slit
¼ cup   (60 g) khoya (solidified milk) (p 150), mashed into a paste with water
¼ cup   (60 g) thick cream   } for garnish
2 tbsp   chopped hara dhania (coriander leaves)

METHOD

1. Heat the ghee in a heavy-based pan and add the cumin seeds.

2. When the seeds splutter, add onions and saute till light brown. Add the ground paste and saute again till fat separates.

3. Increase heat, add the chicken pieces, and stir-fry until coated with the masala. Add the turmeric, chilli powder, garam masala, coriander powder, salt and the green chillies. Stir-fry to mix well.

4. Add 2 cups water and the milk paste, bring to boil and simmer uncovered for 15–20 minutes or till chicken is tender.

5. Serve hot, garnished with the cream and coriander leaves.

BOTI KABAB

(Cubes of mutton or lamb marinated in light spices and grilled or barbecued.)

Oven temp: 450°F/220°C and 300°F/150°C

INGREDIENTS

1 kg (de-boned) **mutton/lamb,** cut into 2½ cms/1 in square cubes,
¼ cup (20 g) raw papaya, chopped
1 tbsp peeled garlic
1 tbsp roughly chopped ginger — ground to a paste
1 cup (200 g) dahi (yogurt)
Salt to taste
¼ cup bhuna channa (roasted gram), powdered
Onion slices and lemon wedges, for garnish

METHOD

1. Pierce the pieces of meat with a fork or skewer. Mix in all the ingredients except the roasted gram and marinate for 6 hours or even better, overnight.

2. Mix in the powdered gram and skewer the meat pieces. Bake in a pre-heated oven over a drip-tray, for 15–20 minutes. Then lower the temperature and bake for another 10 minutes or till tender. Alternatively, the pieces can be grilled on a barbecue. This gives it a better flavour.

3. Serve garnished with the onions and the lemon wedges. A green chutney is a good accompaniment.

BOOT KI SABZI/HARE CHANNE KI SABZI

(Hara channa is enjoyed not only with gravy, but also just sauted in light spices or freshly shelled. Sometimes the channas are roasted directly over a flame in their pods, then shelled and eaten, especially during the festival of Holi.)

INGREDIENTS

250 g shelled **hara channa**
¼ cup (60 g) ghee
⅛ tsp heeng (asafoetida)
1 tsp jeera (cumin seeds)
1 tbsp finely shredded ginger
½ cup (125 g) tomatoes grated (optional)
½ tsp garam masala I (p 148)
2 tsp dhania (coriander powder)
Salt to taste
½ tsp chilli powder
½ tsp haldi (turmeric)
½ cup (100 gms) dahi (yogurt)
1 tbsp chopped hara dhania (coriander leaves)

METHOD

1. Heat the ghee, add the cumin seeds and asafoetida. When the cumin seeds begin to splutter add the ginger

and saute till lightly fried. Then add the tomatoes and stir-fry till fat separates.

2. Add the garam masala, coriander powder, salt, tumeric and chilli powder. Stir a few times till well mixed. Add the channas and stir-fry over high heat, till they look slightly fried.

3. Add about 2 cups water, and bring the mixture to boil. Simmer uncovered for about 15 minutes.

4. Beat the yogurt till smooth and add to the channas. Serve hot, garnished with chopped coriander leaves.

Note: If you do not want gravy, do not add water.

MENU TWENTY-FIVE

- Murgh do piaza
- Bhuni kaleji
- Frans bean gajar

MURGH DO PIAZA

(A chicken prepartion with onions added in two stages.)

INGREDIENTS

1	kg	**chicken** (broiler) skinned and cut into 8 pieces
¼	cup	(60 g) ghee
1	tbsp	jeera (cumin seeds)
1		tej patta (bay leaf)
4		sabut kali mirch (peppercorns)
4		laung (cloves)
½	tsp	methi dana (fenugreek seeds)
1	tsp	saunf (fennel seeds)

roasted and powdered

1	tsp	ginger paste
1	tsp	garlic paste
1	cup	(250 g) grated onions
½	cup	(100 g) dahi (yogurt)
1	tsp	garam masala I (p 148)

Salt to taste

½	tsp	haldi (turmeric)
1	tbsp	dhania (coriander powder)
1	tsp	chilli powder

2–3 green chillies, slit

2	cups	(500 g) onions, sliced a little thick
2	tbsp	chopped hara dhania (coriander leaves), for garnish

METHOD

1. Heat the ghee in a heavy-based saucepan, and add the cumin seeds, bay leaf, peppercorns, cloves, powdered

fenugreek and fennel seeds. When the seeds begin to splutter, add the garlic and ginger paste and the onions. Saute over high heat till brown.

2. Add the yogurt, stir-frying vigorously so that it blends well and does not curdle.

3. Cook till fat separates. Add the garam masala, salt, tumeric, coriander and chilli powder.

4. Keeping the heat high, add the chicken pieces and stir till they look a little opaque and are coated with the masala. Lower heat, uncover and simmer for about 10 minutes. Add the green chillies and sliced onions. Continue cooking over low heat, till chicken is cooked through and fat separates. Takes 10–15 minutes. The onions should be crunchy.

5. Serve hot, garnished with chopped coriander leaves.

Note: You can make 'mutton do piaza' similarly, although, of course, it takes longer to cook.

BHUNI KALEJI

*(Liver sauted and spiced, this
can be served as a snack too.)*

INGREDIENTS

500	g	**liver** (mutton) washed and wiped dry
½	tsp	ginger paste
½	tsp	garlic paste
½	tsp	chilli powder
¼	cup	(50 g) dahi (yogurt)
¼	tsp	garam masala III (p 149)
Salt to taste		
2	tbsp	(30 g) ghee
½	cup	(125 g) grated onions

2 tbsp hara dhania (coriander leaves) and lemon wedges, for garnish

METHOD

1. Chop the liver into small pieces and mix in the ginger, garlic, chilli powder, yogurt, garam masala and salt.

2. Heat the ghee, add the onions and saute till golden brown. Add the liver mixture and saute till fat separates. Add ½ cup of water and pressure cook for 5 minutes. Stir-fry to dry the water completely, and separate the fat.

3. Serve garnished with coriander leaves and lemon wedges.

FRANS BEAN GAJAR

(Green/String Beans, sauted with carrots.)

INGREDIENTS

500	g	**frans (green/string) beans** (4 cups after cutting)
250	g	**carrots**, peeled (1½ cups, diced)
¼	cup	(60 g) ghee
1	tsp	jeera (cumin seeds)
¼	tsp	heeng (asafoetida)
1	tsp	finely chopped ginger
1	cup	(250 g) onions, grated
1	cup	(250 g) tomatoes, grated
2	tsp	dhania (coriander powder)
Salt to taste		
½	tsp	haldi (turmeric)
½	tsp	chilli powder
½	tsp	garam masala I (p 148)

METHOD

1. Wash and string the beans. Cut into small, horizontal pieces of about ½ cm/¼ in.

2. Cut the carrots into cubes of 1 cm/½ in.

3. Heat the ghee in a heavy-based pan; then add the cumin seeds and asafoetida. When the seeds splutter, add the ginger and onions. Saute till light brown.

4. Add the tomatoes and stir-fry till fat separates. Add the coriander powder, salt, turmeric, chilli powder and the garam masala.

5. Add the beans and carrots and saute over high heat till they look glossy.

6. Lower heat and cook covered, till tender, stirring off and on to ensure that it does not scorch. Takes about 20–30 minutes. Serve hot.

MENU TWENTY-SIX

- Magaz masala
- Bhindi gosht
- Dhuli moong ki daal
- Roomali roti (p 92)

MAGAZ MASALA

*(Brain, cooked in a gravy of spices
that complements it very well.)*

INGREDIENTS

2	pcs	(approx 225 g) **goat/lamb brain,** * smeared with ½ tsp haldi (turmeric) and 2 tsp salt for about 15 minutes, then washed well
2	tbsp	(30 g) ghee
4		laung (cloves)
4		sabut kali mirch (peppercorns)
½	tsp	pieces of dalchini (cinnamon)
1	tsp	jeera (cumin seeds)
1	tsp	methi dana (fenugreek seeds)

roasted and coarsely pounded

2		(250 g) medium-sized onion
2	tsp	chopped ginger
2	tsp	chopped garlic

ground together

2		(250 g) medium-sized tomatoes, grated
2	tsp	dhania (coriander powder)
½	tsp	haldi (turmeric)
Salt to taste		
1	tsp	chilli powder
2	tbsp	strained dahi (yogurt)
2		green chillies chopped coarsely
¼	cup	chopped hara dhania (coriander leaves)

* You must ask the butcher to clean it, so that it's ready to be cooked.

METHOD

1. Chop brain into 2 cm/1 in cubes and set aside till ready to use.
2. Heat the ghee and add the roasted, coarsely pounded spices to it. When they darken a little, add the ground onion paste. Stir-fry till fat separates and mixture is brown.
3. Add the tomatoes and fry till fat separates again. Add the coriander powder, turmeric, salt and chilli powder. Mix well and add the yogurt, stirring vigorously to dissolve any lumps.
4. When the yogurt is well blended, add the green chillies and the chopped pieces of brain. Stir-fry till well mixed. Add about half a cup of water and bring to boil. Put in half the coriander leaves and simmer for about 5 minutes or till the water dries (brain cooks very fast).
5. Serve garnished with the remaining chopped coriander leaves.

BHINDI GOSHT

*(A combination of meat and ladies' fingers. It is quite
a common practice to add some vegetable to the meat.
This serves to balance the diet. In many homes, vegetables
are not relished by themselves, so this is a nice way
to ensure that they are consumed!)*

1. Cook ½ kg mutton as in Korma-e-Vakil (p 50).
2. Take ½ kg ladies' finger either whole or cut into large chunks.
3. Heat 2 tablespoons of oil. Fry the ladies' fingers so that they do not become sticky. Now add them to the meat gravy. Simmer for about 10 minutes or until the vegetable is cooked through.

4. Serve garnished with coriander leaves. You can add vegetables of your choice, viz., potatoes, turnips, cauliflower, beetroot, etc.

DHULI MOONG KI DAAL

*(Husked green gram is considered light and easy
to digest and so is called Bimaron ki daal
(lentils for the sick) in many homes.)*

INGREDIENTS

1 cup (180 g) **dhuli moong (husked green gram)**
Salt to taste
½ tsp haldi (turmeric)
2 tbsp (30 g) ghee
1 tsp jeera (cumin seeds)
⅛ tsp heeng (asafoetida)
1 tbsp ginger finely chopped
½ cup (125 g) finely chopped onions
½ cup (125 g) finely chopped tomatoes
1 tsp dhania (coriander powder)
½ tsp chilli powder
½ tsp garam masala I (p 148)
2 tbsp chopped hara dhania (coriander leaves), for garnish

METHOD

1. Pick, clean and wash the lentils till the water comes out clean. Place them in a heavy-based pan with 3 cups of water, turmeric, ginger and salt. Partially cover pan and place over high heat.
2. Bring to boil and then simmer till cooked (25–30 minutes).
3. Heat the ghee in a heavy-based pan and add the asafoetida and cumin seeds. When they begin to splutter, add the onions.

4. Saute onions till brown, add the tomatoes and stir-fry till fat separates. Add coriander powder, chilli powder and garam masala. Mix well and add the cooked lentils. Bring to boil and simmer for about 1 minute.

5. Garnish with coriander leaves and serve hot.

Note: In case you do not want to add onions and tomatoes you can omit them and proceed as above.

MENU TWENTY-SEVEN

◆ Galauti kabab
◆ Reshmi biryani
◆ Cachoomber raita (p 101)

GALAUTI KABAB

(Called so because they are so soft, that they literally melt in the mouth. Lucknow is home to some special recipes for this, but they are kept secret. I have tried to get as close to the original as possible!)

INGREDIENTS

½ kg   **keema (minced mutton)**

Grind together:

75–100 g chopped kaccha papita (raw papaya)
Salt to taste
1 tbsp chopped ginger
1 tbsp chopped garlic
8 laung (cloves)
Seeds of 2 badi elaichi (black cardamom)
2 tsp   khus khus (poppy seeds), roasted and dry ground
4 sabut kali mirch (peppercorns)
½ tsp   pieces of dalchini (cinnamon)
2 tbsp nariyal ka burada (dessicated coconut), lightly roasted
2 blades javitri (mace)
5 chhoti elaichis (green cardamoms)
1 tsp   chilli powder
¼ tsp   grated jaiphal (nutmeg)
1 cup   (125 g) sliced onions, fried brown and crisp in ½ cup (120 g) ghee
¼ cup   finely chopped hara dhania (coriander leaves)
1 tbsp (or to taste) finely chopped green chillies
3 tbsp roasted besan (chickpea/gram flour)

1 egg
Ghee to pan fry the kababs
Lemon juice to sprinkle over the kababs

METHOD

1. Marinate the minced meat in the ground ingredients for 4–5 hours.

2. Mix together the coriander leaves, green chillies, chickpea flour and egg. Add to the meat and work at it for some time, almost kneading it like dough.

3. Shape mixture into round patties of desired size, and refrigerate for half an hour or so.

4. Heat the ghee in a heavy-based frying pan or griddle (enough to coat base). Fry the kababs, browning first one side and then the other, over medium heat.

5. Arrange them on a serving dish, sprinkle lemon juice and serve.

RESHMI BIRYANI

(A chicken biryani in which the rice and chicken are cooked together.)

INGREDIENTS

1	kg	**chicken** (broiler), cut into 8 pieces
1	kg	onions, sliced uniformly
		Oil for frying the onions
1	cup	finely chopped hara dhania (coriander leaves)
½	tsp	garlic paste
½	tsp	ginger paste
1	tbsp	dhania (coriander powder)
½	tsp	haldi (turmeric)
2	tsp	chilli powder
½	tsp	garam masala II (p 148)
1	cup	(200 g) dahi (yogurt)
		Salt to taste

Rice:

2	cups	(360 g) **basmati rice***
		Salt to taste
		Water
		Some dough to seal the pan

* Some people use sela (parboiled) rice for all biryanis, which takes a little longer to cook. It is really a matter of choice.

METHOD

1. Marinate the chicken in the garlic and ginger paste, coriander powder, turmeric, chilli powder, garam masala, yogurt and salt, for at least 3–4 hours.

2. Heat enough oil in a heavy-based broad pan or kadahi to take in the onions comfortably (the onions should be covered with the oil). Fry onions till brown and crisp.

3. Strain out onions and set aside.

4. Fill a pan with 2½ times the amount of water as you have rice. Bring water to boil. Add the rice and salt and cook till rice is almost done (takes about 8 minutes). Drain the rice and set aside.

5. Take a large heavy-based pan with a lid. Grease the edges.

6. Heat half cup of the oil remaining in the pan and add the chicken to it, spreading it to form a layer.

7. Over the chicken, make a layer of half the rice, onions and coriander leaves.

8. Repeat the same layers a second time and cover the pan with the lid, sealing it with some dough (the grease on the edges will ensure that the dough comes off easily later).

9. Cook on high heat for 10 minutes, then place on a griddle and leave on low heat to cook for about an hour. Alternatively, you could cook it in a moderately hot oven for an hour.

10. Break the seal and serve either in the same pan or transfer on to a serving dish.

Menu Twenty-eight

- Shahi biryani
- Sookhe kofte
- Maash ki daal
- Cachoomber (p 133)
- Dahi (p 99)

SHAHI BIRYANI

(A mutton biryani which makes a delicious meal with just yogurt and cachoomber.)

INGREDIENTS

½ kg	**mutton/lamb,** cut into small pieces	
1 cup	(125 g) onions finely sliced	
Ghee for frying the onions		
1 cup	(250 g) onions grated	
1 tsp	garlic paste	
1 tsp	ginger paste	mix together and
1 tsp	haldi (turmeric)	marinate the meat
1 tsp	kala jeera (black cumin seeds)	in it for about
Salt to taste		4 hours
1 cup	(200 g) dahi (yogurt)	
1 tsp	garam masala II (p 148)	
1 tsp	jeera (cumin seeds)	
1	tej patta (bay leaf)	
¼ cup	(60 g) malai (clotted cream)	
2 tbsp	chopped hara dhania (coriander leaves)	

Rice:

2 cups (360 g) **basmati rice** cleaned and soaked in water*
2 chhoti elaichi (green cardamoms)
2 laung (cloves)
½ tsp kala jeera (black cumin seeds)
A piece of dalchini (cinnamon), about the size of a clove, broken up

Salt to taste

½ tsp   kesar (saffron), soaked in ¼ cup of warm milk

2 tbsp   ghee

* Some people use sela (parboiled) rice for all biryanis, which takes a little longer to cook. It is really a matter of choice.

METHOD

1. Heat enough ghee in a broad heavy-based pan or kadahi as will take in the onions comfortably (the onions should be covered with the melted ghee). Fry the onions till brown and crisp.

2. Strain onions from ghee and transfer on to an absorbent paper and set aside.

3. In ½ cup of the ghee that is left in the pan, add the cumin seeds and bay leaf, stir a few times till they change colour a little, and keeping the heat high, add in the meat mixture.

4. Stir-fry meat over high heat till the pieces look opaque. Lower heat, partially cover and simmer, stirring a few times till meat is tender.

5. Saute till water dries up and fat separates. Add water and cook further, in case meat has not cooked through (takes approx 45 minutes). If meat cooks through before water dries up, uncover pan, and let water evaporate over high heat.

6. Remove pan from stove and add the fried onions, cream and coriander leaves and mix well.

7. While meat is cooking (step 5), drain the rice and set aside. Heat 2 tablespoons of ghee and add the black cumin seeds, cardamom, clove and cinnamon. Stir a few times, and add the rice and salt.

8. Now add 2½ cups of water, and bring to boil. Lower heat, cover and let the rice cook for 8 minutes.

9. Shut off heat, leaving pan on stove. The rice should be almost done.

10. Half an hour before serving, divide the rice and meat into halves each. Take half the meat out of the pan, leaving one layer at the bottom. Spread this layer well, in the pan. Now cover this with a layer of half the rice, sprinkle half the saffron flavoured milk over it, then add the second layer of meat and finally the other half of the rice.

11. Sprinkle the rest of the milk and saffron mixture over rice. Seal pan with wheat flour and place on a griddle over low heat for half an hour.

12. Alternatively, arrange in an oven proof dish and place in a pre-heated oven (300°F/140°C), for about half an hour.

13. Serve in the same dish or mix gently and transfer on to a serving dish.

SOOKHE KOFTE

(Delicious meat balls which can be served as a snack and can also be cooked in a gravy. A speciality of Manju Bhatnagar of Kanpur.)

INGREDIENTS

500 g   **keema (minced mutton),** (wt after mincing)

2 tbsp   strained yogurt

1 tsp   ghee

Grind to a smooth paste:

10–12 almonds

1 tbsp   chopped ginger

3–4 green chillies

1 tbsp   khus khus (poppy seeds) roast and dry grind

5–6 pudina (mint leaves)
½ cup   bhuna channa (roasted gram)
2 tsp   roasted jeera (cumin seeds)
½ tsp   garam masala II (p 148)
Salt to taste
2 tbsp   (30 g) ghee
1 tbsp   finely shredded ginger
1 tsp   chilli powder
2 tbsp   finely chopped hara dhania   } for garnish
         (coriander leaves)

METHOD

1. Mix the ground ingredients and meat together. Grind to a slightly grainy consistency, a little finer than the finely minced meat.

2. Mix in the yogurt and the 1 teaspoon of ghee and shape into balls of desired size.

3. Heat the ghee in a heavy-based frying pan or kadahi and add the meat balls to it. Cover and cook for about 3 minutes.

4. Uncover, and turn the meat balls, which should be brown on the underside by now. Sprinkle the shredded ginger over them, and cook till brown all around.

5. Transfer the meat balls to serving dish, sprinkle the chilli powder and coriander leaves and serve.

MAASH KI DAAL

(Husked black gram, very lightly spiced, garnished with fried onions. This is one of the main daals cooked in the home of Nafees Ifraeem.)

INGREDIENTS

1 cup   (180 g) **dhuli urad ki daal (husked black gram),** soaked for 5–6 hrs
1 tbsp   finely chopped ginger
1 tsp   (or to taste) finely chopped green chillies
Salt to taste
½ cup   (60 g) ghee
1 cup   (125 g) uniformly sliced onions

METHOD

1. Drain the water. Add to the lentils, ginger, green chillies and salt in 1¼ cups water.

2. Bring to boil, cover and simmer for 30–40 minutes or till cooked through. The water should be absorbed, but the lentils must remain moist and soft.

3. Heat the ghee and saute the onions till brown and crisp.

4. Transfer the cooked lentils on to a serving dish and serve garnished with the fried onions.

Menu Twenty-nine

- Lassooni kabab
- Palak gosht
- Sabut masoor ki khichdee (p 105)

LASSOONI KABAB

(Strong on garlic as the name suggests,
these are very tender chicken kababs.
One can make a meal of these with a Roomali
Roti wrapped around, accompanied
with some onions and green chutney.)

Oven temp: 450°F

Ingredients

500	g	boneless **chicken breasts**
2	tsp	garlic paste
1	cup	(200 g) dahi (yogurt), strained for an hour
¼	cup	chopped hara lahsan (green garlic)
1	tbsp	salt
¼	tsp	kali mirch (powdered black pepper)
¼	cup	malai (clotted cream)

Melted ghee to brush the kababs
Lemon wedges and onion rings, for garnish

Method

1. Beat the chicken pieces as flat as possible and marinate in the garlic paste, yogurt, green garlic, salt, black pepper and cream for 2–3 hours.
2. Skewer the pieces and grill or bake in a pre-heated oven over a drip-tray for 10 minutes. Brush with the melted ghee and bake for a further 5–10 minutes, till tender.

3. Serve hot, garnished with lemon wedges and onion rings.

Note: These would taste even better cooked in a tandoor.

PALAK GOSHT

(A combination of mutton/lamb and spinach.
A one dish meal, if had with a roti of your choice.)

1. Cook Korma-e-Vakil as on p 50, making sure that not much liquid remains.
2. Add to this, 2 cups (½ kg) finely chopped spinach.
3. Simmer for about 5 minutes and serve.

Note: The quantity of spinach can vary according to taste. Pureed spinach can be effectively used too.

Menu Thirty

- Murgh korma
- Seekh kabab
- Kale channe ki sabzi

MURGH KORMA

(Chicken with a little gravy. The best thing about this is that you can put everything in together and sit back until it cooks!)

INGREDIENTS

1	kg	**chicken** (broiler) cut into 8 pieces
2	cups	(250 g) onions, sliced thin

Ghee to fry the onions and chicken

10		chhoti elaichi (green cardamoms)
10		laung (cloves)
1	tsp	seeds of badi elaichi (black cardamom), powdered
1	tbsp	chilli powder
3	tbsp	dhania (coriander powder)
1	tsp	haldi (turmeric)
1	tsp	ginger paste
1	tsp	garlic paste
½	cup	(100 g) dahi (yogurt)

mix together

Salt to taste

2 tbsp chopped hara dhania (coriander leaves), for garnish

METHOD

1. Heat enough ghee in a heavy-based broad pan as will comfortably take in the onions (should be covered with the melted ghee). Fry them till brown and crisp.

2. Remove fried onions from ghee and transfer to an absorbent paper and set aside. Mix the chicken pieces into the spice mixture.

3. Heat ¼ cup of the remaining ghee; add the chicken to it over high heat.

4. Stir to mix well; when chicken pieces are coated with spices, lower heat, uncover and simmer till tender. If you feel the chicken may cook before the water dries up, increase the heat, because the water must evaporate by the time the chicken is cooked through. Stir a few times to prevent scorching.

5. If chicken cooks through before water evaporates and fat separates, remove the chicken pieces, cook the masala till the fat separates, and then put chicken pieces back into pan.

6. While the chicken is cooking, grind the fried onions to a paste with a little water and set aside.

7. When the chicken is cooked and the fat separates, add the onion paste, simmer for about 5 minutes and serve garnished with coriander leaves.

SEEKH KABAB

(Skewered mutton kababs cooked over a grill. These are ideally cooked over a charcoal grill.)

Oven temp: 375°F/205°C

INGREDIENTS (MAKES 8 KABABS, ABOUT 15 CMS/6 IN LONG)

Mix together:

2	cups	(500 g) **keema (minced mutton/lamb)**
1	tbsp	vinegar
2	tbsp	chopped methi (fenugreek) leaves or 2 tsp dried methi
½	tsp	garlic paste
½	tsp	ginger paste

Salt to taste

Non-vegetarian

73

¼ tsp   kali mirch (powdered black pepper)
¼ tsp   garam masala II (p 148)
2 tbsp   chopped hara dhania (coriander leaves)
1 tsp   finely chopped green chillies

Seekh (skewers) greased, to make the kababs
Oil for brushing
Some chaat masala, onion rings and lemon wedges, for garnish

METHOD

1. Mix all the ingredients, cover and refrigerate to marinate for at least 5 hours.

2. About 25 minutes before serving, shape the meat mixture* into long tubes around the skewers and place on a grill over a drip-tray, or into a pre-heated oven (also on a drip-tray). If cooking them over a charcoal grill, you must rotate them so that they brown and cook evenly. Takes 20–25 minutes to cook.

3. Brush the kababs with oil and cook for another 2 minutes.

4. Using oven mittens or a cloth, carefully push the kabab off from one end, on to a serving dish. Garnish with chaat masala, onions and lemon. Serve with a green chutney.

* It helps to wet your hands while shaping the meat on to the skewer.

KALE CHANNE KI SABZI

(Whole Bengal gram with gravy. Boiled and spiced with salt, pepper and onions, this gram also makes a very good and healthy snack.)

INGREDIENTS

2 cups   (360 g) **kala channa (whole Bengal gram)**

3 cups   roughly chopped (500 g) onions
1 tbsp   chopped ginger
8 cloves garlic peeled
2 tsp   garam masala I (p 148)   } ground to paste
1 tej patta (bay leaf)
1 tbsp   jeera (cumin seeds), roasted
2 cups   finely chopped (500 g) tomatoes
Salt to taste
½ tsp   haldi (turmeric)
2 tbsp   dhania (coriander powder)
1 tsp   chilli powder
2–3 green chillies
½ cup   (120 g) ghee
2 tbsp   chopped hara dhania (coriander leaves), for garnish

METHOD

1. Pick and wash the lentils and soak in water for 4–6 hours, or overnight.

2. Drain the water and cook till tender.

3. When cooked, strain and keep the liquid and lentils separate.

4. Heat the ghee in a heavy-based saucepan and add the onion paste. Stir-fry onions well until the fat begins to separate.

5. Add the chopped tomatoes and stir-fry well, till fat separates. Add the salt, turmeric, coriander powder and chilli powder and stir till well mixed.

6. Add the lentils and green chillies and stir a few times over high heat.

7. Measure 4 cups of the liquid, adding water if necessary. Add this to the lentil mixture and bring to boil; then simmer till gravy is well blended and not watery (approx 10 minutes).

8. Serve hot, garnished with the coriander leaves.

MENU THIRTY-ONE

- Methi murgh
- Kakori kabab
- Tamatar ka bharta

METHI MURGH

(The quantity of fenugreek leaves can vary and if fresh leaves are not available dried ones can be used. Although they are less visible, the flavour predominates.)

INGREDIENTS

1	kg	**chicken** (broiler), skinned and cut into 8 pieces
¼	cup	(60 gm) oil
1	tbsp	jeera (cumin seeds)
2		tej patta (bay leaves)
5		chhoti elaichi (green cardamom)
½	tsp	pieces of dalchini (cinnamon)
4		laung (cloves)
½	tsp	ginger paste
½	tsp	garlic paste
2	cups	(500 g) grated onions
½	cup	(125 g) grated tomatoes
½	cup	(100 g) dahi (yogurt)
Salt to taste		
½	tsp	haldi (turmeric)
2	tbsp	dhania (coriander powder)
1	tsp	chilli powder
1	cup	(100 g) finely chopped methi leaves (fenugreek leaves)
2	tbsp	malai (clotted cream), for garnish

METHOD

1. Heat the oil in a heavy-based saucepan and add the cumin seeds, bay leaves, green cardamoms, cinnamon and cloves. When the seeds begin to splutter, add the ginger, garlic and onions and saute over high heat till brown.
2. Add the tomatoes and stir-fry till fat separates, then add the yogurt, stir-frying vigorously so that it blends well and does not curdle.
3. Cook till fat separates and then add the salt, turmeric, coriander powder and chilli powder and mix well.
4. Keeping heat high, add the chicken pieces and stir till coated with the spices. Lower heat and cook, stirring occasionally, till chicken is cooked through. Takes about 15 minutes, by which time the fat should separate. If it does not, stir-fry over high heat till it does.
5. Add the fenugreek leaves and stir-fry till the fat separates again. Serve garnished with the cream.

KAKORI KABAB

(Also called Reshmi kabab in some homes, this is a smoother, melt-in-the-mouth version of the Seekh Kabab, a speciality of Lucknow. It is believed by some to have been invented for an old begum who had lost all her teeth.)

INGREDIENTS (MAKES 10–12 KABABS, ABOUT 15 CMS/6 IN LONG)

2	cups	(500 g) **keema** (minced mutton/lamb)

Mix together and marinate:

½	tsp	garlic paste
½	tsp	ginger paste
Salt to taste		
¼	tsp	kali mirch (powdered black pepper)
2	tbsp	chopped hara dhania (coriander leaves)
1	tsp	finely chopped green chillies

Non-vegetarian

75

2   tbsp   (25 g) chopped kaccha papita (raw papaya)
4   laung (cloves)
Seeds of 1 badi elaichi (black cardamom)
½   tsp   pieces of dalchini (cinnamon)
1   tsp   jeera (cumin seeds)
1   blade mace (javitri) — about ½ a petal
½   tsp   grated jaiphal (nutmeg)
2   cups   (250 g) onions, sliced thin and fried crisp and brown
½   cup   (120 g) ghee
¼   cup   bhuna channa (roasted gram), powdered
1   egg
Skewers for the kababs
Ghee to brush over kababs
Some chaat masala, onion rings and lemon wedges, for garnish

METHOD

1. Marinate the mixed ingredients for about 4 hours. Grind the mixture to form a smooth, thick paste. Ensure it is not grainy.

2. Knead this mixture well and mix in the egg and roasted gram.

3. Cover and refrigerate for another hour.

4. About 25 minutes before serving, shape the meat mixture* into long tubes around the skewers and place the kababs on to a grill over a drip-tray, or into the pre-heated oven (also on a drip-tray). If cooking the kababs over a charcoal grill, rotate them frequently so that they brown and cook evenly. Takes 15–20 minutes to cook.

5. Brush them with ghee and cook for another 2 minutes.

6. Using oven mittens or a cloth, carefully push the kabab off from one end, on to a serving dish. Garnish with chaat masala, onions and lemon. Serve with a green chutney.

* It helps to wet your hands while shaping the meat on to the skewer.

TAMATAR KA BHARTA

(Mashed tomatoes stuffed with potatoes and garnished with chutney. A popular dish sold by roadside vendors in Varanasi, according to Alka.)

INGREDIENTS

8–9 (1 kg) firm, ripe **tomatoes** of uniform size
1   cup   (240 g) oil
7–8 (1 kg) potatoes, boiled and mashed
Salt to taste
2   tsp   dhania (coriander powder)
¼   tsp   kali mirch (powdered black pepper)
1   tsp   chilli powder
2   tsp   roasted and powdered jeera (cumin seeds)
¼   tsp   heeng (asafoetida)
2   tsp   amchoor (mango powder)
2   tbsp   finely chopped hara dhania (coriander leaves)
2   tsp   finely chopped green chillies (or to taste)

Mix together for filling

1   cup   (100 g) dahi (yogurt) beaten smooth
1   cup   (approx), sonth ki chutney (ginger powder chutney) (p 134)
½   cup   (approx), hara dhania chutney (p 134) (coriander chutney)
Chopped hara dhania (coriander leaves) and chaat masala, for garnish

METHOD

1. Wash the tomatoes. Cut thin slices off the top and scoop out the seeds and loose pulp, so that you have empty tomato shells.

2. Stuff the tomato shells tight with the potato filling.

3. Heat half the oil in a kadahi, and fry the tomatoes one at a time over high heat, turning them around, so that all sides get coated with oil. Place all in the kadahi again, cover, and cook over low heat till skin of tomatoes begins to shrink a little. Takes about 10 minutes.

4. These are best served individually.

   To serve: Heat about a tablespoon of oil in a frying pan. When hot, place a tomato in it, and break it up into small pieces at random (bharta), with a spatula.

5. Continue to stir-fry this mixture over high heat for about a minute, till it looks well fried. Transfer to a serving plate, pour some yogurt over it, followed by the ginger powder chutney and green chutney. Garnish with chaat masala and coriander leaves and serve hot.

MENU THIRTY-TWO

- Machchli ka khalia
- Shaami kabab
- Mangauri chawal (p 106)

MACHCHLI KA KHALIA

*(Fish with gravy, simple to make, and delicious.
This tastes good not only with rice, but with paranthas too.)*

INGREDIENTS

½	kg	**fish** (Sole, Singhara or Pomfret), filleted and cut into chunks of 5 cms/2 in
1	tsp	salt mixed with 1 tbsp lemon juice
1	cup	(200 g) dahi (yogurt)
2	tsp	dhania (coriander powder)
1	tsp	chilli powder
½	tsp	ginger paste
½	tsp	garlic paste
1	tsp	haldi (turmeric)

Salt to taste

1	tsp	methi dana (fenugreek seeds)

2–3 green chillies, slit

¼	cup	(60 g) sarson ka tel (mustard oil)
2	tbsp	chopped hara dhania (coriander leaves), for garnish

METHOD

1. Marinate the fish in the salt and lemon juice mixture for 15 minutes. Wash off and leave to drain.

2. Mix together the yogurt, coriander powder, chilli powder, garlic and ginger paste, tumeric and salt.

3. Marinate the fish in this mixture for a couple of hours.

4. Heat the oil in a kadahi and when it begins to give off a strong aroma, add the fenugreek seeds. As soon as the

seeds darken a little (don't let them become a dark brown; if they do, they will make the dish bitter), add the fish, the marinate mixture and the green chillies.

5. Stir-fry over high heat till the mixture is a little fried. Add 2 cups water and bring to boil; simmer uncovered over low heat. Stir once or twice, or shake the pan, while the fish is cooking, taking care not to break the pieces of fish.

6. Simmer till fish is cooked through. Takes 15–20 minutes. Serve hot, garnished with the coriander leaves.

Note: I make this dish with a fish that can be filleted, but it can be made with any fish of your choice.

SHAAMI KABAB

(A combination of mutton/lamb and lentils made into cutlets and pan-fried.)

INGREDIENTS (MAKES 18–20 OR MEDIUM-COCKTAIL SIZED KABABS)

½ cup	(90 g) **channa daal (split and husked Bengal gram)***	
2 cups	(500 g) **keema (minced mutton/lamb)** (wt after de-boning)	
2 tsp	chopped garlic	
1 tbsp	chopped ginger	
4	sabut kali mirch (peppercorns)	
4	laung (cloves)	
2	chhoti elaichi (green cardamoms)	
½ tsp	crushed dalchini (cinnamon)	
Salt to taste		
½ cup	chopped onions	
1 tsp	finely chopped green chillies	
2 tbsp	finely chopped pudina (mint leaves)	mix together
½ tsp	salt	
1 tsp	lemon juice	

Oil for pan-frying
Onion rings and lemon wedges, for garnish

* If you want the kababs more firm, you can increase the daal to ¾ cup.

METHOD

1. Cook the minced meat with the garlic, ginger, peppercorn, cloves, green cardamom, cinnamon, salt and lentils in about 2 cups of water. Cook on low flame for 1½ hours. If using a pressure cooker add approximately ¼ cup of water and cook for 15 minutes. Very little water should be used so that the mixture does not have any extra moisture, once it is cooked.

2. After the mixture cools a bit, grind to a thick, dough-like paste. Refrigerate for at least an hour.

3. Take about a tablespoon of the mixture at a time, pat it into a round, flat shape. Place about a teaspoon of the onion mixture in the centre, close by bringing the edges together, and gently press it flat again, without tearing, making sure that the filling does not spill out.

4. Heat enough oil in a heavy-based pan to form a thin layer. When hot, place as many kababs in the pan as will fit in comfortably. Fry to a dark brown, first on one side, then the other. Serve garnished with the lemon wedges, onion rings and green chutney (p 134).

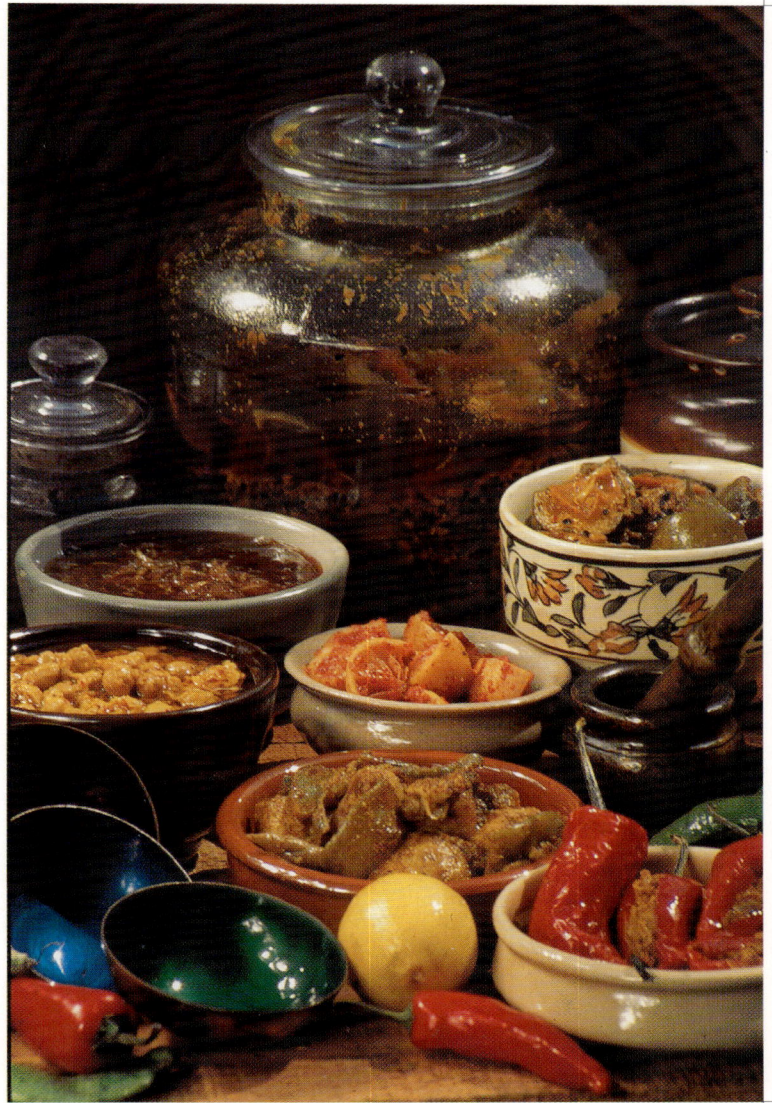

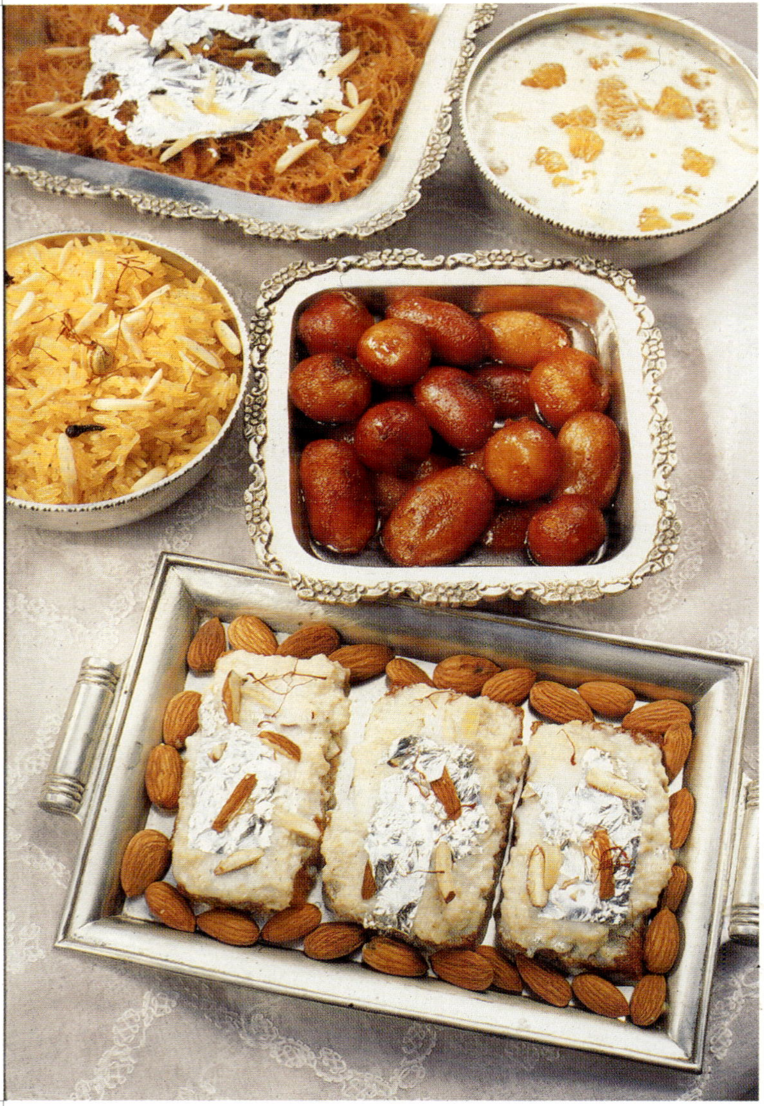

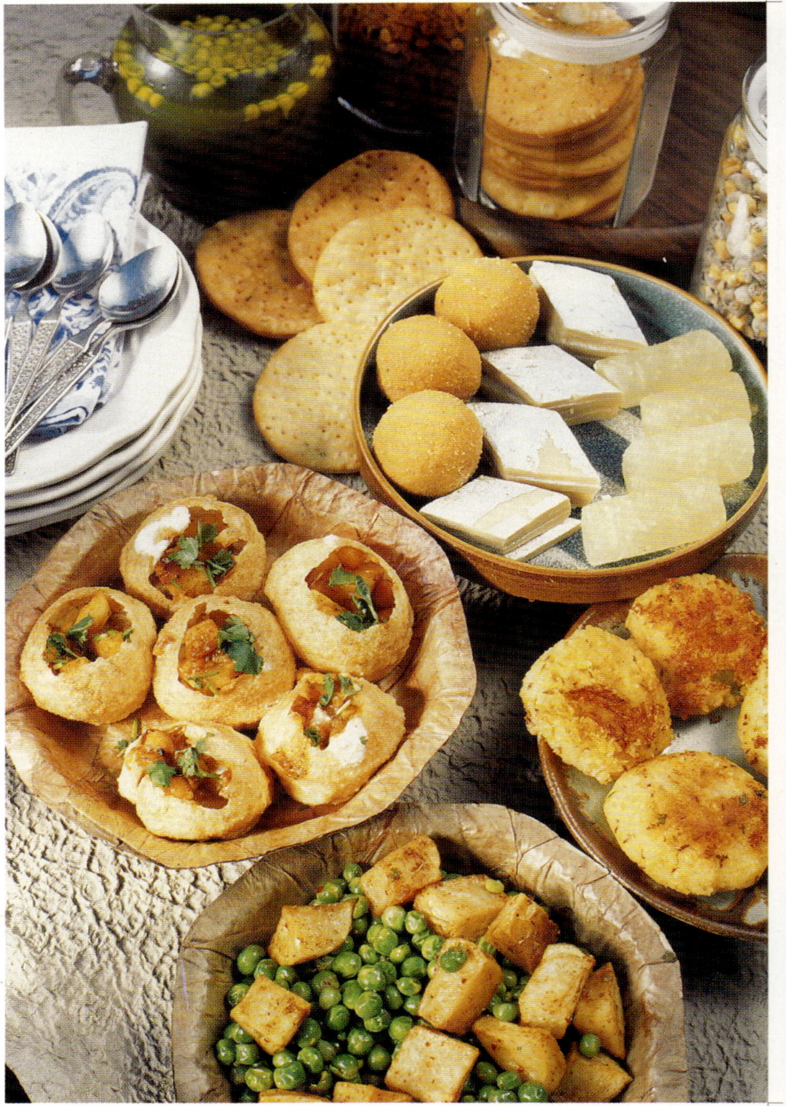

Menu Thirty-three

- Murgh saagwala
- Gola kabab
- Lobhia ki daal

MURGH SAAGWALA

*(A combination of chicken and spinach,
this is a very wholesome dish.)*

Cook Murgh Rasedaar as on p 53. Make sure that there is not much gravy in it. Add to this, 2 cups (½ kg) of finely chopped spinach. Simmer for about 5 minutes and serve.

Note: The quantity of the spinach can vary according to taste. You can also use pureed spinach.

GOLA KABAB

*(A dry preparation of minced mutton
and spices bound together
with wheat flour aata.)*

INGREDIENTS

½	kg	**keema (minced mutton/lamb)**
1½	tsp	finely chopped garlic
1½	tsp	finely chopped ginger
½	cup	(125 g) finely chopped onions
Salt to taste		
2	tsp	finely chopped green chillies
2	tbsp	finely chopped hara dhania (coriander leaves)
¼	cup	aata (whole wheat flour)
Oil to deep-fry		

METHOD

1. Mix together all the ingredients except the oil, and form into walnut shaped kababs. Refrigerate for about an hour.
2. Heat the oil in a kadahi and add as many kababs as fit in comfortably. Lower heat and fry till brown and cooked through.
3. Serve hot, with a green chutney (p 134).

LOBHIA KI DAAL

(Black-eyed beans cooked in a gravy.)

INGREDIENTS

2	cups	(360 gms) **lobhia (black-eyed beans)**	
Salt to taste			
3	cups	(500 g) coarsely chopped onions	
1	tbsp	chopped ginger	
1	tbsp	chopped garlic	
2	tsp	garam masala I (p 148)	ground to a paste
1		tej patta (bay leaf)	
1	tbsp	roasted jeera (cumin seeds)	
2	cups	(500 gms) finely chopped tomatoes	
½	tsp	haldi (turmeric)	
2	tbsp	dhania (coriander powder)	
1	tsp	chilli powder	
2–3 green chillies			
½	cup	(120 g) oil	
2	tbsp	chopped hara dhania (coriander leaves), for garnish	

METHOD

1. Pick, clean and wash the beans. Put them in 3 cups of water and add the salt. Cook till soft (takes approx 1 hour).

If using a pressure cooker put only 2 cups of water and cook for 12 minutes. Drain the beans and set the water aside till ready to use.

2. Heat the oil in a heavy-based saucepan and add the onion paste. Stir-fry till golden and fat begins to separate.

3. Add the chopped tomatoes and fry till fat separates again. Add turmeric, coriander powder and chilli powder, stir a few times till well mixed.

4. Add the beans and the green chillies and fry lightly over high heat.

5. Add the water drained from the beans (and more according to the consistency you desire) and bring to boil; simmer till gravy is well blended and not watery (approx 10 minutes).

6. Serve hot, garnished with chopped coriander leaves.

MENU THIRTY-FOUR

- Raan mussallam
- Machchli kabab
- Ghiya channe ki daal

RAAN MUSSALLAM

(Sarlaji, who told me about this recipe, said it was Bhopali and so not strictly U.P. cuisine. However, it complements U.P. food very well and hence my decision to include it in this book.)

INGREDIENTS

1   leg of **mutton** (about 1 kg)*
1   cup   (200 g) dahi (yogurt)
1   tbsp   ginger paste
1   tbsp   garlic paste
Salt to taste
¼   cup   chopped kaccha papita (raw papaya)
1   tsp   chilli powder
2 medium-sized (200 g) onions, finely sliced
Ghee to fry the onions
4   chhoti elaichi (green cardamoms)
10   laung (cloves)
Seeds of 2 badi elaichi (black cardamoms)
½   tsp   broken pieces of dalchini (cinnamon)
¼   tsp   grated jaiphal (nutmeg)
2   blades javitri (mace)
1   tsp   kala jeera (black cumin seeds)
2   tsp   khus khus (poppy seeds), roast and dry grind
1   tsp   kewra water (vetiver) (optional)
Dough to seal the saucepan
2   tbsp   malai (clotted cream)   ⎫
2   tbsp   blanched, chopped almonds ⎬ for garnish

* Ask the butcher to remove all the fat and bend it at the knee.

METHOD

1. Make deep cuts into the leg of mutton on both sides, in the shape of a cross (for marinate to seep through).

2. Mix the yogurt, ginger, garlic, papaya, salt and pepper together. Smear this mixture all over the leg of mutton and leave to marinate overnight or for at least 6 hours.

3. Heat ghee in a broad-based pan (should be broad enough to cook the leg of mutton). Add the green cardamom and when it changes colour add the onions to it (the onions should be covered with the melted ghee). Fry till brown and crisp. Take out half the fried onions and grind them to a paste with the cloves, black cardamom seeds, cinnamon, nutmeg, mace, black cumin seeds, and then add the ground poppy seeds.

4. Into the onions that are left in the pan, add the mutton leg; over high heat, turn the leg over in the ghee to seal the juices. Cover and lower heat. Cook till meat is tender, turning it once every half an hour.

5. If the meat becomes tender before the liquid dries up, increase the heat, adjusting it such that the meat cooks through and the fat separates at about the same time.

6. When tender, add the ground onion paste and the vetiver.

7. Grease the edges of the pan and lid with oil. Seal the lid with kneaded dough and place over a griddle at low heat for about half an hour. Alternatively, cook in a moderate oven for half an hour.

8. Serve garnished with cream and almonds.

MACHCHLI KABAB

(Fried fish balls which can either be part of a main course or served as a snack. Spice it up more if you prefer it so!)

INGREDIENTS

1	kg	**fish** (Singhara, Sole or Surmai) filleted and skinned
1	tsp	salt
1	tbsp	lemon juice
1	tsp	ginger paste
1	tsp	garlic paste
Salt to taste		
¼	cup	finely chopped onion
¼	tsp	kali mirch (powdered black pepper)
1	tbsp	finely chopped green chillies
2	tbsp	chopped hara dhania (coriander leaves)
1	egg, with yolk and white separated	
Oil for deep-frying		

METHOD

1. Marinate the fish in the salt and lemon juice for about 15 minutes and wash off.

2. Pat the fish dry and finely mince in food processor or with knife.

3. Mix in the ginger and garlic, salt, onion, black pepper, green chillies, coriander leaves and egg yolk. Form into walnut-sized balls.

4. Refrigerate for about an hour.

5. Heat the oil in a kadahi. Meanwhile, beat the egg white slightly to break up the fibres. Dip each kabab into it and fry in the hot oil, lowering the heat once you have put in as many kababas as the kadahi will hold comfortably.

6. Fry at medium heat till brown and cooked through (the insides should be opaque when cut open).

7. If serving later, fry over high heat for 2–3 minutes only, and not as instructed in step 6. Fry again just before serving.

GHIYA CHANNE KI DAAL

(Bengal gram, cooked with ghiya.
This makes a good neutraliser
on any menu!)

INGREDIENTS

180 g **channe ki daal (Bengal gram)**
Salt to taste
1   tsp   haldi (turmeric)
1   tbsp finely chopped ginger
2   tbsp (30 g) ghee
1   tsp   jeera (cumin seeds)
2   tej patta (bay leaves)
¼   cup   (60 g) grated tomatoes
2–3 green chillies, slit
½   tsp   garam masala II (p 148)
2   tsp   dhania (coriander powder)
1   tsp   chilli powder
2   cups (500 g) **ghiya/lauki (bottle gourd)** peeled and cut
            into small pieces, 1½ cms / ¾ in thick
1   tbsp chopped hara dhania (coriander leaves), for garnish

METHOD

1. Pick, clean and wash the lentils. Add the salt, turmeric and ginger. Cook in 5 cups of water, till soft (takes approx 1 hour). If using a pressure cooker add only 3 cups of water and cook for 12 minutes.

2. Heat the ghee in a pan, add the cumin seeds and bay leaves. When the seeds splutter, add the tomatoes and stir-fry till fat separates.

3. Add the green chillies, garam masala, coriander powder, chilli powder and pieces of bottle gourd. Mix well. Add the lentils to this mixture and bring to boil; simmer for about 10 minutes and serve hot, garnished with chopped coriander leaves.

Menu Thirty-five

- ◆ Makhmali murgh
- ◆ Machchli masala
- ◆ Gobhi dum

MAKHMALI MURGH

*(Chicken cooked in a velvety sauce. Your
curiosity should make you try this one!)*

INGREDIENTS

1	kg	**chicken** (broiler), cut into 8 pieces
¼	cup	(60 g) ghee
1	tsp	jeera (cumin seeds)
½	tsp	sabut kali mirch (peppercorns)
1	cup	(250 g) grated onions
1	tsp	garlic paste
1	tsp	ginger paste
1	tbsp	dhania (coriander powder)
1	tbsp	tomato puree

Salt to taste

2		green chillies, finely chopped
4		cherry tomatoes
1	tsp	vinegar
1	tsp	sugar
4	tbsp	hara dhania (coriander leaves), finely chopped
2	tbsp	cornflour dissolved in ½ cup water
½	cup	(120 g) milk

METHOD

1. Place the chicken in a saucepan with 2 cups of water. Bring to boil and then simmer till cooked through (about 20 minutes).

2. When cool, drain the chicken pieces. Mix the milk and the stock together; it should add up to 2 cups (add more water if required).

3. Heat the ghee in a heavy-based pan and add the cumin seeds and peppercorns. When they splutter, add the onions, ginger and garlic, and saute till the onions are transparent.

4. Add the coriander powder, tomato puree, salt and green chillies. Stir well to mix. Add the chicken, stock and milk mixture to this masala and bring to boil. Add the cornflour mixture, and bring to boil again. Simmer for 2 minutes.

5. Add the tomatoes, vinegar, sugar and half the coriander leaves. Mix and serve hot garnished with the rest of the coriander leaves.

MACHCHLI MASALA

*(Fish fried whole with a combination of spices.
The crisp crust of the fish tastes very good.)*

INGREDIENTS

1	kg	**fish** (Pomfret, or part of a larger fish) in one piece, scaled and cleaned with skin kept intact
1	tsp	salt and 2 tsp lemon juice, mixed together
1	tbsp	ajwain (thymol seeds), roasted
1	tbsp	chopped ginger
1	tbsp	chopped garlic
½	tsp	haldi (turmeric)
1	tsp	chilli powder

Grind to a paste

Salt to taste

2–3		green chillies
¼	cup	(60 g) sarson ka tel (mustard oil)

Lemon juice and chaat masala, for garnish

METHOD

1. Make slits along the length (along the bone) of the fish, on one side, going deep into the fish, but not cutting through to the other side, thus creating a pocket. Repeat on the other side of the bone, and you will have two such pockets on either side of the bone of the fish. (Most often the fishmonger will do it for you.)

2. Apply the salt and the lemon juice to the fish inside and outside. Leave for about 15 minutes and wash off. Drain and wipe dry.

3. Apply the ground paste all over the fish, and on the inside too. Heat the oil and add the fish to it, browning over high heat, first on one side, then the other.

4. Lower heat, cover and cook, till crisp and brown on both sides. (Takes about 10–15 minutes, depending on the thickness of the fish.)

5. Transfer on to a serving dish, garnish with lemon juice and chaat masala and serve.

GOBHI DUM

*(Whole cauliflower, fried and cooked
with a thick masala paste.)*

INGREDIENTS

1	medium (½ kg)	**phool gobhi (cauliflower)**
¼	cup (60 g)	oil
1	tsp	jeera (cumin seeds)
1		tej patta (bay leaf)
1	cup (250 g)	grated onions
½	tsp	garlic paste
½	tsp	ginger paste
1	cup (250 g)	grated tomatoes

1	tbsp	kasoori methi (dried fenugreek leaves)
Salt to taste		
1	tbsp	dhania (coriander powder)
1	tsp	chilli powder
½	tsp	garam masala II (p 148)
½	tsp	haldi (turmeric)
2–3		green chillies, slit
Dough to seal the pan		
1	tbsp	malai (clotted cream)
2	tbsp	hara dhania (coriander leaves)

for garnish

METHOD

1. Chop off the leaves and hard base of the cauliflower and wash well. Drain the water and wipe cauliflower dry to make it easier to fry.

2. Heat the oil in a deep pan (since the fat will splash at first). When heated, add the cauliflower and cook over high heat stirring till it is a light brown all over.

3. Remove from the ghee, and set aside. In the same ghee, add the cumin seeds and bay leaf. When the seeds splutter, add the onions, garlic and ginger. Saute till light brown.

4. Add the tomatoes, dried fenugreek leaves, salt, coriander, chilli powder, garam masala and turmeric. Saute till fat separates. Add the green chillies and saute till they look glossy.

5. Add ¾ cup water and bring to boil; simmer for 2–3 minutes.

6. Place cauliflower in a pan with a lid, pour the masala over it, covering it well. Brush the lid (especially the edges) with oil and seal it with the dough. Place on griddle over high heat for 5 minutes; lower heat and cook for about half an hour. Alternatively, cook in a pre-heated oven (320°F/160°C) for half an hour.

7. Just before serving, break dough seal and transfer cauliflower on to serving dish. Garnish with cream and coriander leaves and serve.

Note: If you wish to avoid the extra calories, you can steam the cauliflower instead of frying it.

MENU THIRTY-SIX

- Surkh murgh
- Andaa karee
- Moong daal ki khichdee

SURKH MURGH

(A dry preparation of chicken, called surkh because it is red. Nafees, who taught me this, said it was a great favourite in her home and once you have tasted it you will know why!)

INGREDIENTS

1 whole **chicken** (broiler)*
1 jaiphal (nutmeg), powdered
Salt to taste
2 tsp chilli powder
2 medium-sized potatoes cut into 2 pieces each
¼ cup (60 g) ghee
2–3 sabut lal mirch (whole, dried red chillies) ⎫ for garnish
2 tbsp chopped hara dhania (coriander leaves) ⎭

* To get the real flavour, use country chicken, although this will require cooking it for longer.

METHOD

1. Apply the nutmeg on to the chicken, inside and out, and leave for an hour.
2. Wash the chicken and drain. Wipe dry and refrigerate uncovered for about half an hour.
3. Mix the salt with the chilli powder and apply it all over the chicken.
4. Heat the ghee in a deep kadahi or pan and stir-fry the potatoes and the whole red chilli. Scoop out and set aside.

85

Add the chicken to the same ghee; then, keeping the heat on high, stir it so that it is seared all over.

5. Lower heat, add the potatoes and cover. Cook till chicken and potatoes are tender, stirring every 10 minutes. Takes about 30 minutes. Alternatively, after searing you can cook it covered, in an oven (320°F/160°C) for the same length of time.

6. Serve garnished with the fried red chillies and coriander leaves.

ANDAA KAREE

(This is made from boiled eggs that are fried, and though you could avoid frying them, they are tastier fried!)

INGREDIENTS

6 **eggs**, hard boiled and peeled
½ cup (120 g) oil

Gravy:

4 laung (cloves)
4 sabut kali mirch (peppercorns)
½ tsp pieces of dalchini (cinnamon) } roasted and coarsely pounded
1 tsp jeera (cumin seeds)
1 tsp methi dana (fenugreek seeds)
2 medium (250 g) onion
2 tsp chopped ginger } ground together
2 tsp chopped garlic
2 cups (500 g) tomatoes grated
2 tsp dhania (coriander powder)
½ tsp haldi (turmeric)
Salt to taste
1 tsp chilli powder
2 green chillies chopped coarsely
¼ cup chopped hara dhania (coriander leaves)

86

METHOD

1. Heat the ghee and fry the eggs till slightly coloured and set aside.

2. To the same ghee, add the coarsely ground spices and when they darken a little, add the ground onion paste and stir-fry till brown.

3. Add the tomatoes, coriander powder, turmeric, salt and chilli powder. Stir-fry till fat separates.

4. Add the green chillies and fry till they look a little glossy. Now add about 1½ cups water, bring to boil and then simmer for about 5 minutes.

5. Add half the coriander leaves and the eggs and serve, garnished with the rest of the chopped coriander leaves.

Note: This dish can also be served by putting the gravy in the serving dish, cutting the eggs in half, lengthwise, and placing them in the gravy before garnishing with the rest of the chopped coriander leaves.

MOONG DAAL KI KHICHDEE

(A combination of rice and lentils, which with yogurt and pickle, makes a good light meal.)

INGREDIENTS

1 cup (180 g) **basmati rice**
½ cup (90 g) **moong daal chhilke wali (split green gram)**
2 tbsp ghee
1 tsp jeera (cumin seeds)
A pinch of heeng (asafoetida)
1 tbsp dhania (coriander powder)
Salt to taste

Method

1. Pick and wash the rice and lentils, and soak together in water for at least half an hour.
2. Put the rice and lentil mixture in a colander to drain the water. Heat the ghee in a heavy-based saucepan and add the cumin seeds and asafoetida. When the seeds splutter, add the rice and lentil mixture. Saute over high heat, till well mixed and excess water evaporates. Add the coriander powder and salt and mix well.

3. Add 2¼ cups water, cover and bring to boil. Lower heat and simmer for 10 minutes by which time the khichdee should be cooked, and ready to serve.

Note: You can make this spicier, by adding some more ground spices like garam masala and chilli powder. The lentils used could be changed according to taste.

There is a large variety of breads, for example, rotis, paranthas and poories. Here, I have provided the recipes of only a few. Some breads are inconvenient and impractical to make at home. But today, there are professionals in the bigger towns who make them to order. With time and practice you will find that none of them is very difficult to make!

PHULKA/CHAPATI

(A detailed recipe for the beginner.)

INGREDIENTS (MAKES ABOUT 12, 13 CM/5 IN ROUND CHAPATIS)

2 cups   (300 g) **aata (whole wheat flour)**
1 cup   (240 g) water, approximately
Some dry flour to help with rolling

METHOD

1. Place the flour in a bowl or paraat. Make a depression in the centre, and pour half the water into it. Mix the flour and water, starting from the centre and continue to add water, a little at a time, until you can gather up all the flour into a slightly sticky ball (the wet portions when rolled around the dish, help pick up the dry tidbits). Knead this into a smooth and soft dough—fold the dough towards you, then push down and away with the heel of your palm. When smooth and soft (enough to press a finger into it without much pressure), flatten it out and make depressions with your finger tips and sprinkle some water. Rest thus for at least 30 minutes.

2. Knead it a little once more, and form into a long roll. Break off walnut-sized pieces.

3. Dust your palms and fingers with dry flour. Roll the pieces of dough between your palms; into smooth balls, and then flatten them and set aside.

4. On a surface well dusted with flour, roll the flat disks into thinner disks of about 13 cm/5 in diameter. Rolling these evenly takes some practice. When rolling do not press the rolling pin too hard over the dough. Hold it lightly over the dough and let it roll to and fro in your hands. Holding your left hand steady, push the disk (with the help of the rolling pin) with the right hand, so that it keeps turning clockwise, thus helping to give it a round shape. Roll thinly and as evenly as possible, without tearing, dusting it with flour when needed. (As mentioned above, it takes practice to get them even and perfectly round, so do not despair if you take time! When you have mastered the technique, you will be able to roll one while the other is on the griddle, so that you don't have to roll ahead of time!) Repeat with the rest of the dough pieces, till all are rolled out. Keep them covered till ready to roast.

5. Place the griddle over high heat. Wait till hot enough—its ready when a drop of water thrown on it, evaporates immediately with a sizzle.

6. Place a rolled chapati over the hot griddle and as soon as the edges start rising and you notice a few bubbles beginning to form on the surface, lift it with a pair of tongs (the experts use their fingers!), and place it over a direct flame, with the uncooked side down. It should

start puffing up immediately. When fully puffed, or a spotty brown on the under-side, flip it over to cook the other side a little more.

7. Take it off the flame and serve hot, with a brushing of ghee, if so desired.

Note: If not serving immediately, keep piling them on top of each other, in a closed container. Keep covered so that the chapatis do not dry out. You will have to press them down. Chapatis also freeze well.

ROTE/MOTI ROTI I

(This roti was taught to me by Sharda Bhabhi; it tastes good with Urad Daal, Kadhi, etc.)

INGREDIENTS (MAKES 4)

2	cups (300 g)	**aata (whole wheat flour)**
¼	cup (30 g)	**besan (chickpea/gram flour)**

Salt to taste
1 tsp ajwain (thymol seeds)
$^1/_8$ tsp heeng (asafoetida)
½ tsp chilli powder
2 tbsp (30 g) ghee
Water to mix the dough
Ghee or butter to smear the roti with

METHOD

1. Mix all the ingredients (except the ghee for smearing) and knead into a firm dough.
2. Break the dough and shape into balls of about 5 cms/2 in diameter. Roll into rounds ½ cms/¼ in thick.
3. Place a griddle on high heat. After it is hot, put the roti on it, and cook a little on both sides, till it is very slightly cooked—it just about forms a firm upper crust.

4. Remove from heat and pinch the surface on one side, in a pattern, deep, but not reaching the bottom. (This is usually done in a spiral pattern, but close enough so that two-third of the surface is pinched). This helps cook the roti through and prevents it from puffing up.
5. Now cook over direct flame, over a wire rack, turning constantly till both sides have brown specks all over and the roti is cooked through. (This takes almost 10 minutes.)
6. Smear the cooked roti with ghee or butter and serve.
7. If they are to be stored, keep them in a closed container till ready to eat.

Note: These keep well for 4–5 days and taste good even without a meat or vegetable dish. Good for picnics and to take on journeys.

MOTI ROTI II

(A roti made for everyday meals in many Muslim households. Although they are thick, they stay soft for many hours.)

INGREDIENTS

The ingredients for this roti are the same as those for chapatis (p 88). When kneaded, the dough is so soft that it does not hold a shape. Such rotis are not rolled out, but are flattened by slapping the dough between the palms with the help of dry flour.

METHOD

1. Make the dough as for Chapati (p 88) and leave to rest for at least half an hour.
2. Take a shallow griddle and clean thoroughly on both sides, making sure the underside is smooth and clean. Place it upside down, over the flame, and heat.

3. Take a portion of the dough depending on the size of the roti you want to make. Roll the piece of dough in flour and make into a round ball. Pat it between the palms to make it larger. Do not try to roll it as it will be difficult to lift up. Press until each is about ½ cms/¼ in thick.

4. Check to see that the griddle is hot.

5. Place roti over the inverted griddle. When bubbles start appearing on the surface, flip the roti over and cook till the other side is also done. Store in a covered container till ready to eat.

Note: The experts make these as thin as Roomali Rotis, which have a little maida in them and become leathery when cold. These rotis, however, stay soft.

VARKI PARANTHA

(A parantha made with a combination of semolina and whole wheat flour.)

INGREDIENTS (MAKES ABOUT 12, 13 CM/5 IN ROUND PARANTHAS)

1½ cups (225 g) **aata (whole wheat flour)**
1½ cups (180 g) **soojee (semolina)**
Salt to taste
1 cup (240 g) water, approximately
Some dry flour to help with rolling
Ghee as required

METHOD

1. Soak the semolina in water till it loses its grainy texture.

2. Mix with a little water, the flour, semolina and salt; make into a dough and roll out paranthas (like Chapatis; see p 88).

3. Place a parantha over the hot griddle and as soon as the edges start rising and you notice a few bubbles beginning to form on the surface, smear it with a generous helping of ghee, letting it flow around and under the parantha. Cook till the underside is brown, flip over and cook on the other side till brown.

4. Take off the griddle and serve hot.

Note: If not being served immediately, keep in a closed container.

MISSI ROTI I

(Missi means mixed. This is a chapati made from the flour of a combination of three cereals. It is, therefore, very healthy and high in fibre content.)

INGREDIENTS

1 kg **kaala channa (horse gram),** with the skin on
1 kg **jau (barley)**
1 kg **genhu (wheat)**
Grind the three cereals together and use the mixed flour to make Chapatis (p 88) or Paranthas (p 93)

MISSI ROTI II

(An instant version of missi roti, since one generally has chickpea/gram flour at home.)

Mix equal quantities of chickpea/gram flour and whole wheat flour, and make Rotis/Chapatis as above.

Note: Missi aata can make a very healthy meal, if you add salt and some spices to taste—salt, asafoetida and a little chilli powder. In many homes chopped onions, coriander leaves and green chillies are also added. These rotis or paranthas can be eaten with yogurt and pickle, and no other dishes need be made!

BIRAIEE ROTI

(A roti stuffed with husked Bengal gram.)

INGREDIENTS (MAKES ABOUT 12, 13 CM/5 IN ROUND ROTIS)

2 cups (300 g) **aata (whole wheat flour)**
1 cup water
Some dry flour to help in rolling

Filling:

1 cup (180 g) **channa daal (husked Bengal gram)**
½ tsp haldi (turmeric)
Salt to taste
4 laung (cloves)
4 sabut kali mirch (peppercorns)
Seeds of 1 badi elaichi (black cardamom)
1 tsp jeera (cumin seeds)

METHOD

1. Knead the dough as you would chapati dough, and leave to rest.

2. Boil the lentils with ingredients for the filling, using just enough water to cook the lentils and be absorbed into them. No extra water should remain visible.

3. When cool enough to handle, grind the lentil mixture.

4. Make round balls of the dough and flatten into round patties between your palms. Press flat with your fingers, to make them about 6 cm/2½ in.

5. Pinch the edges about one-third way towards the centre so that they are thinner than the centre, and form a sort of cup. Take some of the lentil mixture and place it in the centre of the cup, then pinch the edges to seal.

6. Roll out this stuffed ball as thinly as you can, without tearing. Use dry flour to dust while rolling.

7. Clean a griddle on both sides. Place inverted on high heat. Cook the rolled out roti over it, first on one side, then the other and serve hot. The rotis can also be kept in a covered container until ready to serve.

NAAN

(This is leavened bread made from refined flour, in a tandoor, but which can be baked or grilled too.)

Temp: 425°F/220°C

INGREDIENTS (MAKES 6–8)

4 cups (480 g) **maida (refined flour)**
1¼ cups (250 g approx) **dahi (yogurt)**
1 tsp baking soda
Salt to taste
Kalonji (onion seeds), for garnish

METHOD

1. Mix together the flour, salt and baking powder. Knead into a soft, smooth dough using as much yogurt as required (a finger should press into it with very little pressure).

2. Cover with a damp cloth and leave to rise in a warm, draught-free place, till double in volume. If in a hurry, place the container in a larger container of hot water. The time taken for the dough to rise varies according to

the weather—about 3 hours in summer and 7 hours in winter.

3. Punch the dough and leave to rise again. This time it will take much less time.

4. Break the dough into pieces of desired size and smooth into rounds. Cover with a damp cloth and keep for at least 15 minutes.

5. Roll the balls into flat ovals or rounds. You can also flatten them, by slapping them between your palm—as experts do, stretching and pulling with your hands when required.

6. Smear the surface with water and sprinkle with onion seeds. Grease a baking tray and bake the naans in a pre-heated oven for about 5 minutes. Better still is to grill them, if your grill has elements both above and below. If you have a tandoor, wet one side of the naan with water and stick it to the walls of the tandoor. You can also stick it to a hot griddle and turn the griddle upside down over the flame. The naan will fall off when cooked.

7. Brush the hot naan with butter or ghee and serve.

ᏚᎿᏒᏚᎿᏒᏚᎿᏒ

ROOMALI ROTI

(A large thin roti served folded like a handkerchief or roomal, from which it gets its name. Popular with rich meat dishes.)

INGREDIENTS

3 cups   (450 g) **aata (whole wheat flour)**
1 cup   (120 g) **maida (refined flour)**
2 cups   (approx) water, to knead dough
Dry flour to help with rolling

METHOD

1. Mix the wheat flour and refined flour together, and knead into a soft, sticky, dough (quite wet); cover and set aside for 2–3 hours.

2. Shape the dough into small walnut-sized rounds.

3. Place a shallow griddle upside down over the stove, and heat it. While waiting for the griddle to get hot, roll out the roti. This takes a lot of practice, because the roti should be almost translucent. The dough is so sticky and soft, that you must frequently dust it with flour.

4. When it is rolled out, keeping the heat on high, place the roti over the griddle, and leave for 10–12 seconds, or until small bubbles start appearing over the surface, and the underside is a light brown. Turn over at once, and cook till the other side is a speckled brown too. Remove from griddle, fold it into quarters, and serve.

ᏚᎿᏒᏚᎿᏒᏚᎿᏒ

FRIED PARANTHA

(This one is a meal in itself. It is quite big and often has to be shared. It is commonly eaten in the homes of the Muslims of U.P.)

INGREDIENTS

3 cups   (450 g) **aata (whole wheat flour)**
1 cup   (120 g) **maida (refined flour)**
2 tbsp   (30 g) ghee
2 cups   (approx) water, to knead the dough
Dry flour to help with rolling
Ghee for frying the paranthas
4 eggs
Salt to taste
½ cup   finely chopped onions

92

Chopped green chillies to taste
4 tbsp chopped hara dhania (coriander leaves)

Method

1. Mix the whole wheat flour, refined flour and the two tablespoons of ghee together. Knead into a soft, sticky, dough (quite wet), cover and set aside for 2–3 hours.
2. Divide the dough into 4 rounds, cover and leave to rest for about 15 minutes.
3. Heat a griddle over the stove. While it is getting hot, roll out one round to about $1/8$ in thick. The dough is sticky and soft, so you may need to dust it with flour frequently. Better still, pat it thin with your palms if you can (although this takes a lot of practice).
4. Keeping the heat on high, place the roti over the griddle, break an egg on to the centre of it, sprinkle with two tablespoons of onion, salt, green chillies and 1 tablespoon coriander leaves. Lower heat to medium.
5. To seal, fold over four ways towards the centre, so that the ends overlap, thus forming a square. Make a trail of ghee around it to fry the underside. When the underside is fried (speckled brown), smear the top with a generous helping of ghee and turn over to fry to a golden brown. Serve hot with a chutney or yogurt.

Note: Along with this filling you can also add cooked minced meat, shredded chicken or any other filling you think may taste good!

SAADA PARANTHA

(Saada parantha is eaten regularly in almost every vegetarian home at dinner time.)

Ingredients

2 cups (300 g) **aata (whole wheat flour)**
Water to knead the dough
½ cup (120 gms approx), ghee
Dry flour for dusting

Method

1. Knead the flour with water, into a soft and pliable dough, as for Roti/Chapati (p 88).
2. Cover dough and leave to rest for at least 30 minutes.
3. Break dough into 8 pieces, and shape each into a round, smooth ball, using a dusting of flour, if it sticks.
4. Take a ball, and using a rolling pin, roll it into a round of about ½ cm/¼ in thickness.
5. Smear the surface of the round with a little ghee, fold in half, smear the surface with ghee again, and make another fold from corner to corner, thus making a triangle.
6. Roll the triangle as thin as you can with a light hand.
7. Repeat with the rest of the pieces, keeping the rolled paranthas covered, while you work on the rest of the dough. With enough practice you will be able to work fast enough to roll one, and fry the other at the same time.
8. Heat the griddle till very hot. Place a parantha on it and lower the heat a bit. When the edges start lifting slightly, make a trail of ghee along the outer edge of the parantha, so that some ghee trickles under it.

9. When underside is golden brown, smear some ghee on uncooked surface, increase heat and turn parantha over. Lower heat and cook on the other side. Serve hot.

MISSI PARANTHA

Made like Saada Parantha (p 94), using the flour of Missi Roti I (p 90) or Missi Roti II (p 90).

METHI KA PARANTHA

(Made by mixing fenugreek leaves into the dough. Delicious to have with a potato gravy preparation and yogurt. A terrific winter menu!)

INGREDIENTS (MAKES 12–15)

3   cups (200 g) **methi (fenugreek leaves),** chopped fine
½   cup   (60 g) **besan (chickpea/gram flour)**
1   cup   (150 g) **aata (whole wheat flour)**
Salt to taste
¼ tsp   heeng (asafoetida)
½ tsp   chilli powder
2 tbsp   (30 g) ghee
1 tsp   finely chopped green chillies
1 tbsp   chopped hara dhania (coriander leaves)
½ cup   (approx 120 g) ghee for frying

METHOD

This is made by kneading all ingredients together, and then rolling and cooking like a Saada Parantha (p 93).

MATAR KA PARANTHA

(Parantha stuffed with green peas. I enjoy eating these with plain yogurt—a meal in itself.)

INGREDIENTS

The dough used is the same as that used for Phulka/Chapati. Follow the same method from points 1 to 3 (p 88)
½   cup   (approx 120 g) ghee
Filling:
1   cup   (160 g) shelled and boiled green peas (water should be drained well)
⅛ tsp   asafoetida, powdered
1½ tsp   roasted jeera (cumin seeds)
½ tsp   chilli powder

grind together

A small bowl of water to dip your fingers in while working

METHOD

1. After you have flattened the round balls between your palms, press flat a little more with your fingers, to make rounds of about 6 cm/2½ in.
2. Pinch the edges to about one-third way towards the centre, so that the edges are thinner than the centre, and form a sort of a cup.
3. Place a tablespoonful of the ingredients ground together in the centre of the cup.
4. Dip your fingers in the water so that any filling sticking to them is washed off, and wet the edges before bringing them together to enclose the filling. Pinch to seal.
5. Roll out to smoothen and then dip in dry flour to coat well before rolling, again.
6. On a surface dusted with dry flour, roll out the parantha as thinly as you can without tearing it, as you would roll a chapati. More care is needed with this, as the wet filling inside causes it to tear more easily.

7. Heat the griddle till very hot.

8. Lower the heat and place one parantha on the hot griddle. When the edges start lifting, make a trail of ghee along the outer edge of the parantha, so that some ghee trickles under it. Then smear some ghee on the surface.

9. When underside is a golden brown, increase heat and turn parantha over. Lower heat and cook on the other side. Take off when both sides are brown. Serve hot.

Note: These have to be cooked as they are rolled, since the filling is a little wet. This makes the parantha tear quite easily. Nevertheless, if a large number of paranthas have to be made, you can cook them a little on both sides, and keep them aside. Fry them again just before serving.

MOOLI KA PARANTHA

(My mother loved having these when in Delhi because she felt that the radish in Bombay was not tasty enough!)

INGREDIENTS

Mix together:

2 cups   grated **safed mooli (white radish)**
2 tbsp   chopped hara dhania (coriander leaves)
1 tsp   finely chopped ginger
1 tsp   finely chopped green chillies (or according to taste)
Salt to taste
1 tbsp   lemon juice

METHOD

Make like Matar ka Parantha (p 94), substituting the radish mixture for the green pea mixture.

ALOO KA PARANTHA

(It is only very rarely that someone does not like this—whatever the age group!)

INGREDIENTS

Mix together:

2 cups   (500 g) **potatoes,** boiled and mashed
2 tbsp   chopped hara dhania (coriander leaves)
1 tsp   finely chopped green chillies (or according to taste)
Salt to taste
1 tbsp   lemon juice

METHOD

Make like Matar ka Parantha (p 94), substituting the potato mixture for the green pea mixture.

KEEME KA PARANTHA

(A good way to use up leftover minced meat and make a special dish!)

Follow the recipe for Keema Dum on p 60, and make like Matar ka Parantha (p 94), substituting the minced meat mixture for the green pea mixture.

DAAL KA PARANTHA

(On the day I make urad daal badis, I keep some daal aside and make Daal ka Paranthas for lunch!)

Follow the recipe for the filling of Khasta Kachauri (p 126), and make like Matar ka Parantha (p 94), substituting the lentil mixture for the green pea mixture.

POORI

(Have these with sweet and sour pumpkin and gravied potatoes to really enjoy them. Of course, some would argue that poori and kheer (a sweet preparation with milk, powdered rice and sugar) is a better combination!)

INGREDIENTS (MAKES 10–12)

2 cups   (300 g) **aata (whole wheat flour)**
Water to knead
2 tsp   (20 g) ghee
Salt to taste
Oil for deep-frying
A poori press (p 11)

METHOD

1. Add the salt to the flour and rub the ghee into it. Adding water, knead the flour into a stiffish dough (a little pressure would be needed to press a finger into it).

2. Cover dough and leave to rest for at least 30 minutes.

3. Break dough into 10–12 pieces, and shape each into a round, smooth ball. Smear your palms with some oil if the dough sticks to them.

4. Roll each ball into a round of about ¼ cm/$\frac{1}{8}$ in thickness or use a poori press to roll.

5. Heat the oil in a kadahi, (check if the oil is hot enough by tossing a small piece of dough into it; if the piece comes up at once, it's hot enough). Slip the rolled poori into the oil. As soon as it comes up, press the centre gently with a slotted spoon, so that the poori puffs up. Keeping the heat on high, turn it over and fry till light brown on both sides.

6. Remove from oil with slotted spoon, drain and place on absorbent paper before transferring to a serving dish.

Note: If you need to make quite a few for a party, you can half fry the pooris earlier—put them into the oil and take them out as soon as they come up. Fry again over high heat just before serving. When fried partially and stored, they settle down but will puff up again when you refry them, as long as they don't tear (p 5 about frying).

BATHUE KI POORI: Mix boiled and ground pigweed into the dough before adding the water. Make the pooris as above.

PALAK KI POORI: Mix ground spinach into the dough before adding the water. Make the pooris as above.

BEDVIN (PITHEE WALI POORI OR KACHAURI)

(Pooris filled with a lentil mixture. This is quite a festive food with its typical combinations.)

INGREDIENTS (MAKES 10–12)

Filling:

½ cup   (90 g) **dhuli urad ki daal (husked black gram),** soaked in water for 3–4 hrs
$\frac{1}{8}$ tsp   heeng (asafoetida)

1½	tsp	jeera (cumin seeds)
½	tsp	garam masala I (p 148)
½	tsp	chilli powder
1½	tsp	dhania (coriander powder)
⅛	tsp	kali mirch (powdered black pepper)

Dough:

2	cups	(300 g) **aata (whole wheat flour)**
1	tbsp	oil or ghee

Salt to taste
Water to knead (approx ¾ cup)
Oil for deep-frying

METHOD

1. Mix the salt and oil or ghee into the flour. Knead into a soft and pliable dough with water. (Very little pressure is required to press a finger into it.) Cover the dough and rest for at least half an hour.

2. Grind the lentils coarsely, and add the rest of the ingredients for the filling. Shape into small rounds of about 2 cms/¾ in diameter. You will need to wet your palms off and on, to make sure the filling does not stick to them.

3. Make walnut-sized smooth balls with the dough and flatten between your palms.

4. Take one round, and pinch and wet the edges all around. Place a round of filling in the centre. Bring the edges together and pinch to seal. Flatten by pressing gently and roll into rounds about ⅛ in thick, or thinner if you can do it without tearing the dough. Grease the surface of the rolling-pin, if necessary.

5. Heat the oil till such time as a piece of dough tossed in, comes up immediately. Fry the Bedvins in it over high heat, till golden on both sides.

Note: You can half fry these beforehand, and refry over high heat before serving.

MATAR KI POORI

(When made with maida, this poorie is the Bengali Luchi.)

INGREDIENTS

Filling:

1	cup	(160 g) shelled matar (peas) boiled and drained
⅛	tsp	heeng (asafoetida)
1½	tsp	roasted jeera (cumin seeds)
½	tsp	chilli powder

} grind together

Dough:

2	cups	(300 g) **aata (whole wheat flour)**
1	tbsp	(30 g) oil or ghee
1½	tsp	salt

Water to knead (approx 3/4 cup)
Oil for deep-frying

METHOD

Follow the method for Bedvin p 96, substituting the peas filling for the lentil filling.

PARAT-WALA PARANTHA

(A parantha made by layering rounds of dough and rolling, so that the paranthas are more like flaky pastry. Years ago, there were experts at Fatehpur Sikri who made paranthas with 60 layers! My friends would telephone an expert in Agra and place their order, so that he had enough time to make the paranthas while they drove to Sikri. We will have to be satisfied with 5–6 layers, though, of course, if you are enterprising enough, you can go right ahead and try your hand at more!)

INGREDIENTS

4 cups (600 g) **aata (whole wheat flour)**
1 cup (480 g) ghee softened and mixed well with 1 tbsp aata
Ghee for frying the paranthas

METHOD

1. Knead the flour into a dough (Chapati dough; see p 88) and leave to rest for about 15 minutes.

2. Shape walnut-sized balls of the dough and roll them out into 1 cm/½ in thick rounds.

3. Take one round, smear it with the ghee mixture and place another round over it. Repeat till you have used up 6 rounds. Do not smear the last one with ghee.

4. Using dry flour to dust, roll out these layers together, with a light hand, so that the dough does not tear. Roll as thin as you can without tearing, turning it over every now and then and dusting with flour.

5. Heat a heavy-based griddle. Pour in ghee to form a layer. Place rolled out parantha over griddle carefully and lower heat to cook slowly.

6. Smear the top with ghee and turn over to cook other side. Dribble a trail of ghee around the parantha. Turn around 2–3 times and add ghee until parantha is cooked through. When done, the outer layers become brown and crisp. The parantha will be layered on the inside, rather like a flaky pastry.

CHOORIE KA PARANTHA

(Made with a combination of split green gram and wheat flour. Taught to me by Brijan Bhabhiji, who goes all nostalgic over it!)

INGREDIENTS

2 cups (300 g) **aata (whole wheat flour)**
½ cup (90 g) **dhuli moong ki daal (split green gram)**
1 tbsp ghee
Salt to taste
$\frac{1}{8}$ tsp heeng (asafoetida)
½ tsp chilli powder
Ghee for frying

METHOD

1. Powder the lentils coarsely in a grinder, or with a mortar and pestle, and soak for 2–3 hours in 2 cups of water.

2. Rub 1 tablespoon ghee into the wheat flour. Then, mix the soaked lentils and the rest of the ingredients (except the ghee for frying), into a roti-like dough (p 88) using more water if required. Leave to rest for about 15 minutes.

3. Proceed to make paranthas as Varki Parantha (p 90).

Yogurt Dishes

DAHI/YOGURT/CURDS

(We take the making of yogurt for granted until we have to do it! It is only then that we realise that it is quite an art in itself.)

INGREDIENTS

2½ cups (500 g) **milk**
1 tsp **dahi (yogurt),** as a starter

METHOD

1. Boil the milk and transfer it into the container in which the yogurt is to be set. A ceramic bowl is best.
2. Cool the milk to a luke warm temperature—a drop of it on your wrist, should feel neither hot nor cold. The temperature of the milk is important.
3. Beat the teaspoonful of yogurt till smooth, add 2 table-spoons of milk to it, and mix well. Add this to the rest of the milk and stir with a spoon to mix well.
4. Cover the container and keep in a draught-free place to set. Do not move the container while the yogurt is setting.
5. Once set, place the yogurt in the refrigerator to chill before serving.

Note: The time taken for the yogurt to set, varies depending on the room temperature: in warm weather, it takes 3–4 hours. As it gets cooler, you have to cover the container with layers of cloth or a cosy. The colder it gets, the longer it takes to set. It sets overnight when it is very cold. A quick way to set it, is: switch on your oven to maximum temperature, for 5 minutes switch it off, and place your covered container of milk in it. Takes 2–3 hours for the yogurt to set.

ALOO KA RAITA

(You can sometimes serve this with ginger powder chutney on the side, making it taste rather like chaat.)

INGREDIENTS

½ kg **potatoes,** boiled, peeled and diced
2 cups (400 g) **dahi (yogurt)**
Salt to taste
¼ tsp kali mirch (powdered black pepper)
2 tsp jeera roasted and powdered (cumin seeds)
¼ tsp chilli powder
2 tbsp hara dhania chopped (coriander leaves)

METHOD

1. Beat the yogurt smooth, adding a little water if required, to make into a thick pouring consistency.
2. Add the salt, black pepper, 1 teaspoon of the cumin seed powder and 1 tablespoon coriander leaves and mix well. Add the potatoes.
3. Transfer the raita to a serving bowl. Garnish with the rest of the cumin powder, chilli powder and coriander leaves, and serve chilled.

PUDINE KA RAITA

*(A cool raita made with mint,
it is very refreshing in summer.)*

INGREDIENTS

½ cup **pudina (mint)** leaves, chopped very fine
2 cups (400 g) **dahi (yogurt)**
Salt to taste
1 tsp sugar
¼ tsp kali mirch (powdered black pepper)
2 tsp jeera roasted and powdered (cumin seeds)
¼ tsp chilli powder

METHOD

1. Beat the yogurt till smooth; add a little water (if necessary) to make into a thick pouring consistency.
2. Mix in the salt, sugar, black pepper, 1 teaspoon of the cumin powder and mint leaves.
3. Transfer the yogurt mixture to a serving bowl and garnish with the rest of the cumin powder and chilli powder. Serve chilled.

GHIYE KA RAITA

*(Some may not relish the thought,
but this is really quite good!)*

INGREDIENTS

2 cups (250 g) **ghiya (bottle gourd,)** peeled and grated
1 tbsp (15 g) oil
1 tsp jeera (cumin seeds)
2½ cups (500 g) thick **dahi (yogurt)**

Salt to taste
½ tsp kali mirch (powdered black pepper)
2 tsp jeera roasted and powdered (cumin seeds)
1 tsp ginger finely chopped
2 tbsp hara dhania chopped (coriander leaves)

METHOD

1. Heat the oil and add the cumin seeds. When they splutter, add the grated bottle gourd and saute till well mixed.
2. Cover and cook over low heat till soft and transparent. Remove from heat and leave to cool.
3. Beat the yogurt till smooth; add a little water to make it into a thick pouring consistency.
4. Add the salt, black pepper, 1 teaspoon of the cumin powder, chopped ginger and 1 tablespoon of the coriander leaves to the yogurt and mix well. Add in the bottle gourd.
5. Transfer to a serving bowl, garnish with the rest of the cumin powder and chopped coriander leaves. Serve chilled.

BATHUE KA RAITA

*(Raita made with pigweed.
This is a seasonal (winter) green.)*

INGREDIENTS

2½ cups (500 g) **dahi (yogurt)**
1½ cups (500 g) **bathua (pigweed)**, blanched and ground
Salt to taste
½ tsp kali mirch (powdered black pepper)
2 tsp jeera (cumin seeds) roasted and powdered
1 tsp chilli powder

METHOD

1. Mix the blanched and ground pigweed, yogurt, salt, pepper powder, 1 teaspoon cumin powder and half teaspoon chilli powder.
2. Arrange the mixture into a serving bowl and garnish with the rest of the cumin powder and chilli powder. Serve chilled.

PALAK KA RAITA: Substitute spinach for pigweed.

KACHNAAR KA RAITA: Substitute bauhinia flowers for pigweed but blanch and keep whole.

CACHOOMBER RAITA

(An ideal combination with biryani or pulao.)

INGREDIENTS

2 cups (400 g) **dahi (yogurt)**
Salt to taste
¼ tsp kali mirch (powdered black pepper)
2 tsp roasted and powdered jeera (cumin seeds)
2 tbsp chopped hara dhania (coriander leaves)
2 tsp (or to taste) finely chopped green chillies
1 cup (200 g) onions, diced small
1 cup (200 g) tomatoes, de-seeded and diced small
¼ tsp chilli powder

METHOD

1. Beat the yogurt till smooth; add the salt, pepper powder, 1 teaspoon cumin powder, 1 tablespoon chopped coriander leaves, green chillies and mix well.
2. Add in the onions and tomatoes. Transfer to a serving bowl and garnish with the rest of the cumin powder, chilli powder and chopped coriander leaves. Serve chilled.

BOONDI KA RAITA

(Boondi can be a substitute for Dahi ki Pakori. Boondis are available packed, in the market, but you can also make them at home.)

INGREDIENTS

Boondi:
½ cup (60 g) **besan (chickpea/gram flour)**
¼ tsp baking soda
Salt to taste
Oil for deep-frying

Raita:
2 cups (400 g) **dahi (yogurt)**
Salt to taste
¼ tsp kali mirch (powdered black pepper)
2 tsp roasted and powdered jeera (cumin seeds)
1 tsp sugar
2 tbsp chopped hara dhania (coriander leaves)
¼ tsp chilli powder
A colander for the batter

METHOD

1. Mix the flour and salt and enough water to make a smooth paste of dropping consistency (approx ¼ cup). Beat the batter to make it light. Fold in the baking powder.
2. Heat the oil till a drop of batter thrown in comes up at once. Lower heat. Holding the colander over the hot oil, pour the batter into it; force it out into the oil with a spatula.

3. Fry till golden. Then with a draining spoon, lift the boondis formed and transfer them into a container of cold water. Repeat till all the batter is used up, increasing the heat for a few seconds before adding a fresh lot.

4. Beat the yogurt till it is of a thick pouring consistency, adding a little water if required.

5. Add the salt, black pepper, 1 teaspoon of the cumin powder, sugar and 1 tablespoon of the coriander leaves to the yogurt. Mix well.

6. Gently squeeze the water out of the boondis; add to the raita and mix well.

7. Transfer to a serving bowl. Garnish with the rest of the cumin powder, chilli powder and coriander leaves, Serve chilled.

Note: You can always make extra boondis, transfer them to an absorbent paper and store in an airtight jar. Before using, soak in hot water, squeeze and proceed, as with fresh boondi.

KHIRE KA RAITA

(Cucumber raita is quick and easy to make and is extremely refreshing.)

INGREDIENTS

2 cups grated (500 g) **khira (cucumber)**
2 cups (400 g) **dahi (yogurt)**
Salt to taste
¼ tsp kali mirch (powdered black pepper)
2 tsp roasted and powdered jeera (cumin seeds)
1 tsp sugar
2 tbsp chopped hara dhania (coriander leaves)
1 tsp finely chopped green chillies
¼ tsp chilli powder

METHOD

1. Peel and grate the cucumber.

2. Beat the yogurt till smooth; add the salt, black pepper, sugar, 1 teaspoon cumin powder, 1 tablespoon coriander leaves and green chillies. Mix well.

3. Add the grated cucumber to the yogurt mixture.

4. Transfer to a serving bowl and garnish with the rest of the cumin powder, chilli powder and coriander leaves. Serve chilled.

DAHI KI PAKORI

Refer to page 32.

DAHI BHALLA

(Made in a different shape, this is also called Dahi ki Gunjiya)

INGREDIENTS (MAKES 8–10)

The Bhallas:

1 cup (180 g) **dhuli urad ki daal (split black gram),** soaked 5–6 hours
¼ tsp heeng (asafoetida)
A small bowl
A thin cloth to cover the bowl
A larger damp cloth, to place the shaped bhallas on before frying
Oil for frying
A large container of salted water, to put the bhallas in as soon as they are fried

Dahi:

2½ cups (500 g) **dahi (yogurt),** beaten smooth
Salt to taste
2 tsp jeera (cumin seeds) roasted and powdered
2 tbsp chopped hara dhania (coriander leaves)
¼ tsp kali mirch (powdered black pepper)
½ tsp chilli powder
1 tsp kala namak (black rock salt)
Chaat masala

METHOD

1. Wash the lentils by rubbing them between your palms and rinsing 3–4 times till the skin is washed off. Drain out water and grind lentils to a smooth paste, without adding any water (this can be done in a wet grinder attachment of a food processor, but the ideal way to do it is on a grinding stone).

2. Cover and keep paste to rest for about half an hour. Add asafoetida and beat well to make it light and fluffy—a drop of it in a cup of water should float up at once.

3. To shape the bhallas: cover a small bowl with a thin, wet cloth, bunching it at the bottom. Make sure that the cloth goes around the bowl and is held taut over its rim. Wet your palms (so that they do not stick), and pat some batter into a flat thin round, about ¼ cm/ $^1/_8$ in thick, over the stretched cloth. Push the centre of the batter, to form a hole. Ease out by tilting the bowl a little to let the shaped round fall off on to your palm. Place it on the larger cloth. Repeat with the rest of the batter. When you have had enough practice you will be able to shape them fast enough to drop them straight into the hot oil.

4. Heat the oil in a kadahi or a frying pan. To check if the oil is hot enough drop some batter into the oil; if it comes up immediately, drop as many bhallas into it, as fit in comfortably without one touching the other. Lower heat to medium, and fry till golden on both sides. Takes about 3–4 minutes. Repeat with the rest of the batter.

5. Scoop out fried bhallas with slotted spoon and put into the salted water. Repeat with the rest of the batter.

6. Mix the salt, 1 teaspoon cumin powder, 1 tablespoon coriander leaves and black pepper into the yogurt.

7. Squeeze out the fried bhallas and arrange them on a serving dish.

8. Cover with the yogurt, garnish with the rest of the cumin powder, coriander leaves, chilli powder, black rock salt and the chaat masala. Chill and serve with Sonth ki Chutney (p 134).

Note: To make Dahi ki Gunjiya, sprinkle a mixture of sliced ginger, green chillies and coriander leaves on one half of the lentil mixture, spread out on the bowl. Fold to cover it with the other half (so that it is like a sandwich) and fry. Proceed as for bhallas.

Rice Dishes

There is a seemingly infinite variety of rice recipes, of which I have selected only a few. I hope you will enjoy them and will innovate on your own, for example, by using various vegetables instead of just peas or meat, or by using different spices, etc. Most pulaos need only yogurt and salad as accompaniments. For biryanis and pulaos basmati rice (long grain rice) is often used.

SAADE CHAWAL

(Plain boiled rice, which is cooked almost every day for lunch.)

INGREDIENTS

1 cup   (180 g) **basmati rice**
Water

METHOD

1. Pick the rice to clean it of any stones or grit and wash well till the water runs clear.
2. Soak the rice for at least an hour and then drain.
3. Fill a heavy-bottomed pan with 1½ cups of water. Place the rice in it and bring to boil.
4. Cover and simmer over low heat, till cooked through, and water is absorbed. Takes about 10 minutes.

Note: In case you do not have the time to soak the rice, place the washed rice to cook in 2 cups of water.

CHAWAL-E-JEERA

(Rice flavoured with cumin seeds. An accompaniment for many a gravied dish.)

INGREDIENTS

2   cups   (360 g) **basmati rice**
½   cup   (125 g) sliced onions
2   tsp   **jeera (cumin seeds)**
Salt to taste
A few drops of lemon
2   tbsp   (30 g) ghee
Water

METHOD

1. Clean and wash the rice till the water runs clear, and soak for at least an hour.
2. In a heavy-bottomed saucepan, heat the ghee and add the cumin seeds. After they splutter, add the onions. Saute till onions are golden brown.
3. Drain rice, add to the ghee and stir-fry a few times to mix well. Add 3 cups of water and salt.
4. Leave uncovered and bring to boil. Sprinkle a few drops of lemon juice, cover and cook over low heat for about 10 minutes. By this time the water will have been absorbed. Serve hot.

TAHIRI

(A rice pulao made with badis and green peas.)

INGREDIENTS

2	cups	(360 g) **basmati rice,** washed and soaked for at least an hour
2	tbsp	(30 g) ghee
1	tbsp	jeera (cumin seeds)
1	tbsp	shredded ginger
2	cups	shelled (1 kg unshelled) **matar (green peas)**
2	tbsp	coarsely powdered **Urad Daal Badis** (p151)
2	tbsp	dhania (coriander powder)
1	tsp	powdered garam masala I (p 148)

Salt to taste
1 tsp   haldi (turmeric)
Water

METHOD

1. In a heavy-based pan, heat the ghee and add the cumin seeds and ginger.
2. When the ginger browns a little, add the peas, powdered badis, garam masala, salt and turmeric. Stir-fry well.
3. Leave uncovered. Add 4 cups water and bring to boil. Lower heat and cover. The rice should be done in 10 minutes. Serve hot.

SABUT MASOOR KI KHICHDEE

(Rice and Egyptian lentils with yogurt make a good, light meal.)

INGREDIENTS

1	cup	(180 g) **basmati rice**
½	cup	(90 g) **sabut masoor ki daal (Egyptian lentils)**
2	tbsp	ghee
1	tsp	jeera (cumin seeds)
1	tbsp	chopped ginger
1	tsp	chopped garlic
1	cup	(250 g) onions finely sliced
2	tsp	dhania (coriander powder)

Salt to taste
¼ tsp   garam masala I (p 148)
½ tsp   chilli powder
2–3 chopped green chillies (or to taste)
2   tbsp   chopped hara dhania (coriander leaves), for garnish
Water

METHOD

1. Pick and wash the rice and lentils. Soak in water for at least an hour.
2. Heat the ghee in a heavy-based saucepan and add the cumin seeds. When the seeds splutter, add the ginger, garlic and onions. Saute till the onions are transparent. Add the coriander powder, salt, garam masala, chilli powder and stir a few times till well mixed.
3. Add the rice and lentils, and saute over high heat, till well mixed and excess water dries up. Add green chillies and 3 cups water and bring to boil. Lower heat, cover and simmer for 15 minutes, by which time the khichdee should be cooked.
4. Serve hot, garnished with the coriander leaves.

Note: The lentils used can vary according to taste.

GHUTTI HUI KHICHDEE

(A meal for a convalescent, but one which is quite welcome when one has been eating out too often!)

INGREDIENTS

1	cup	(180 g) **basmati rice**
½	cup	(90 g) **dhuli moong ki daal (husked green gram)**
2	tbsp	ghee
1	tsp	jeera (cumin seeds)
⅛	tsp	heeng (asafoetida)

Salt to taste
Water

METHOD

1. Pick and wash the rice and lentils clean. Fill a heavy-based saucepan or haandi with about 4 cups water and the salt. Place rice in the pan.
2. Bring to boil and then lower heat. Simmer till the rice and lentils are tender and soft, rather like gruel. Adjust the water according to the consistency you desire.
3. Heat the ghee and add the cumin seeds. When the seeds splutter, add the rice and lentils. Mix well.
4. Serve hot with pickle and yogurt.

MANGAURI CHAWAL

*(Rice pulao made with mangauris.
These are badis made of green gram.)*

INGREDIENTS

¼	cup	**mangauris** (p 9)
1	cup	(180 g) **basmati rice**

2	tbsp	(30 g) ghee	
1	tsp	jeera (cumin seeds)	roasted and powdered coarsely
1	tsp	saunf (fennel seeds)	
½	tsp	methi dana (fenugreek seeds)	

Salt to taste

½	tsp	garam masala II (p 148)
½	tsp	chilli powder
1	tsp	amchoor (mango powder)
2	cups	water
2	tbsp	chopped hara dhania (coriander leaves)

METHOD

1. Pick and wash the rice well. Soak in water for at least half an hour.
2. Heat the ghee in a pan. Add the mangauris to it. Turn them over immediately, lift out of the ghee and set aside. The mangauris should look just a little darker than they usually do.
3. In the same ghee add the cumin, fennel and fenugreek seeds. As soon as they darken a bit add the drained rice, stir a few times and add the salt, garam masala, chilli powder and mango powder. Stir-fry till well mixed.
4. Add the water and bring to boil. Lower heat, cover and simmer for about 10 minutes or until cooked through and water is absorbed.
5. Transfer to a serving dish, garnish with chopped coriander leaves and serve hot.

SHAHI BIRYANI

(A rich mutton biryani. Refer to p 69)

RESHMI BIRYANI

(Chicken biryani. Refer to p 68)

SHORBA-E-PULAO

(A mutton pulao cooked in a stock of meat and spices.)

INGREDIENTS

2   cups (360 g) **basmati rice**
250 g **mutton/lamb,** cut into pieces as for a curry
8   laung (cloves)
8   chhoti elaichi (green cardamoms)
½ tsp   broken pieces of dalchini (cinnamon)
Seeds of 1 badi elaichi (black cardamom)
8   sabut kali mirch (black peppercorns) ⎬ powdered together
1   tej patta (bay leaf)
Salt to taste
1   tsp   chopped garlic
1   tsp   chopped ginger
¼   cup   (60 g) ghee
1   cup   (125 g) sliced onions
Water

METHOD

1. Pick and clean the rice and soak in water for at least an hour.
2. Clean and wash the meat well. Put the meat, powdered spices, bay leaf, salt, garlic and ginger in a heavy-based pan, with 4 cups of water. Bring to boil. Cover and simmer till meat is tender. Alternatively, cook meat with 2 cups of water in a pressure-cooker for 15 minutes, with all the above ingredients.
3. Strain the meat, and keep the meat and the liquid (stock) separately.
4. Place a pan large enough to hold the meat and rice together, over high heat. Heat the ghee in the pan. Fry the onions in ghee till light brown. Add the cooked meat and rice and stir-fry over high heat, till it looks a bit fried.
5. Make the meat stock upto 4 cups by adding water if required. Add to the rice and meat mixture. Bring to boil, cover and simmer over low heat till all the water is absorbed. Serve hot.

BOOT WALE CHAWAL/ CHHOLIA CHAWAL

(A rice pulao made with hara channa/chholia/boot.)

INGREDIENTS

2   cups (360 g) **rice**
2   cups shelled **hara channa**
1   tbsp   jeera (cumin seeds)
¼   tsp   heeng (asafoetida)
1   tsp   chilli powder
2   tbsp   dhania (coriander powder)
1   tsp   powdered garam masala I (p 148)
Salt to taste
1   tsp   haldi (turmeric)
2   tbsp   (30 gms) ghee
Water

METHOD

1. Clean and wash the rice well. Soak in water for at least an hour. Drain and set aside.

2. In a heavy-based pan, heat the ghee and add the cumin seeds and asafoetida.

3. When the seeds splutter, add the channa and rice, and the dhania powder, garam masala, chilli powder, salt and turmeric powder and stir a few times till well mixed.

4. Leave uncovered. Add 4 cups water and bring to boil. Then lower heat, cover and simmer. The rice should be done in 10 minutes.

5. Serve hot with yogurt.

Desserts and Sweets

In urban areas sweets are rarely made at home as they are easily available in the shops. But there are some who still like to make them at home. An important part of making sweets is the syrup, the consistency of which determines what the sweet will finally be like. Desserts are usually made at home. Before going on to the recipes, here are some aspects of syrup-making.

SYRUPS

Use as little heat as possible to make a syrup. The best way is to pour cold water over sugar and allow it to dissolve by leaving it in water for a few hours. Keep in a covered vessel, stirring occasionally to help it dissolve. It is very important that the sugar be dissolved completely before the mixture is boiled. This is to prevent the sugar from crystallising later.

The different types of syrup are:

1. Thin syrup: a little taken up in a spoon pours out like oil. This is good to store for mixing into cold drinks, or for making rasgullas, etc.
2. One thread consistency: a drop cooled on the thumb, when pressed between the thumb and the forefinger and pulled apart, forms a thread. Good for gulab jamuns and other sweets that need soaking in syrup, without hardening.
3. A setting consistency: a thin layer appears on blowing on the syrup. Good for jams, chutneys, etc.
4. Soft ball consistency: A drop in a cup of cold water, sets at once into a soft mass. Good for barfis, etc.
5. Hard ball consistency: A drop in a cup of cold water, sets into a hard ball of crackling consistency. Good for chikkies (peanut brittles), candies, etc.

Syrups need quite a lot of practice before one really learns the art of making them. They are a little easier if a saccharometer (or candy thermometer) is used.

CHAWAL KI KHEER

(A popular dessert throughout the country, but the name of the dessert and its consistency differs from region to region. This kheer is made on Sharad Poornima, a full moon night in winter. It is covered with a piece of cloth, placed on the terrace or any open space, to 'soak in the moonlight', and is eaten the next day.)

INGREDIENTS

5 cups (1 kg) **full cream milk**
¼ cup (50 g) **rice,** picked and washed
2 chhwara (dried dates) de-seeded and cut into thin strips
½ cup (120 g) sugar
10–12 kishmish (raisins)
4 chhoti elaichi (green cardamoms)
10–12 almonds, blanched and shredded
2–3 vark (leaves of beaten silver), p 110, optional

METHOD

1. Take a heavy-based saucepan with a capacity of at least double the volume of the milk. Fill with milk and rice and bring to boil. Add the dates.

2. Lower heat and simmer, stirring off and on to avoid scorching or forming lumps, till the rice has cooked and the milk has thickened. Takes about 25 minutes. Thicken to preferred consistency. Once the rice has cooked, you can decide how thick you want the kheer to be.

3. When thick enough, add the sugar, raisins and green cardamom, and continue stirring till the sugar dissolves. Cooking for another 10–15 minutes.

4. Take off heat, transfer to a serving bowl, garnish first with the silver leaf (see below) and then almonds. Kheer can be served hot or chilled.

Leaves of beaten silver (Vark): are sold between small sheets of paper. To use, unfold the sheet on the palm of your hand, paper side down. The surface you wish to cover should be moist. Now take your palm (with the paper) as close to the surface as possible, and lightly and quickly turn the leaf on to that surface. Remove the paper, leaving the silver leaf behind.

PHIRNI

(Also a dessert of rice and milk, this has a different texture and taste because ground rice is used.)

INGREDIENTS

5 cups (1 kg) **full cream milk**
¼ cup (50 g) **rice**

½ cup (120 g) sugar
½ tsp kewra (vetiver), optional
6 chhoti elaichi (green cardamoms) peeled and powdered
10–12 almonds, blanched and shredded
5–6 pistachios, blanched and shredded
2–3 vark (leaves of beaten silver), p 110

METHOD

1. Soak the rice in water for at least an hour. Blend fine with a little milk.

2. Place on stove a heavy-bottomed saucepan with a capacity of at least double that of the milk. Pour in the milk and bring to boil.

   Add the rice mixture and stir a few times to avoid forming lumps. Reduce heat and simmer. Stir often as ground rice tends to stick to the bottom of the pan.

3. Let the mixture cook till it becomes a well blended mass (till the grains of rice look like specks and are visible only if looked at carefully). Takes about 20–25 minutes. To test, take a spoonful of the mixture, let it cool; if it sets, it is done.

4. Add the sugar, let it dissolve; then cook for another 5–7 minutes.

5. Take the Phirni off the stove and add the cardamom and vetiver. Pour the Phirni into individual serving bowls. Cover with silver leaf, garnish with almonds and pistachios. Leave to set in a cool place and refrigerate. Serve chilled.

Note: Individual terracota bowls are very popular to set and serve Phirni in.

SHEER KHURMA

*(A simple but delicious dessert of the
kheer family, made with vermicelli.)*

INGREDIENTS

5	cups (1 kg)	**full cream milk**
50	g	roasted **sevian (vermicelli)**, broken into small pieces
50	g	sookha nariyal (dried coconut) grated
½	cup (120 g)	sugar

2 chhoti elaichi (green cardamoms)
10–12 kishmish (raisins)
¼ cup almonds, blanched and cut into 2–3 pieces each
½ tsp kewra (vetiver) essence
2–3 vark (leaves of beaten silver), p 110

METHOD

1. In a heavy-based pan, simmer the milk until it thickens to the consistency of cream.
2. Add the vermicelli, coconut, sugar, cardamom and half of the raisins and almonds. Bring to boil and then simmer for about 5 minutes. Add the vetiver.
3. Transfer to a serving bowl, garnish with silver leaf and the rest of the almonds and raisins. Serve hot. To serve cold, chill for a few hours.

MAKHANE KI KHEER

*(This is a Kheer made with lotus seeds.
In our family it is a must on Janamashtami.)*

Follow the recipe for Chawal ki Kheer (p 109), substituting rice with lotus seeds, and omitting the dates and raisins, if desired.

KIWAAMEE SEVIAN

*(This is an Eid speciality. It is easier to prepare
with the pre-roasted vermicelli now available.)*

INGREDIENTS

100	g	**sevian (vermicelli)**, broken into 3–4 pieces
¼	cup (60 g)	ghee
⅔	cup (150 g)	sugar
1	cup	water
½	tsp	kesar (saffron)
2		chhoti elaichi (green cardamom)
½	tsp	kewra (vetiver)
2		vark (leaves of beaten silver), p 110
2	tbsp	blanched and shredded almonds

METHOD

1. Heat the ghee in a large kadahi or deep saucepan, add the vermicelli and saute until an aroma emanates and it becomes slightly darker.
2. Meanwhile, heat the sugar, water, saffron and cardamom in another pan, over medium heat, stirring off and on till the sugar dissolves. Then bring to boil.
3. When the vermicelli is roasted, add the sugar syrup and the vetiver, and bring to boil. Cover and cook over low heat till the liquid is absorbed and the vermicelli are cooked through. When cooked, the strands of vermicelli should be separate, like rice in a pulao.
4. Serve hot, garnished with silver leaf and almonds.

GULAB JAMUN

*(A very simple sweet to make if you have the right kind
of khoya. Gulab jamuns are made with powdered
milk too, but if using the authentic recipe, khoya
made from cow milk is the best.)*

INGREDIENTS (MAKES ABOUT 20)

½   cup   (100 g) firmly packed **khoya (condensed milk)** p 150
6   tbsp   (45 g) **maida (refined flour)**
⅛   tsp   baking soda
Ghee for deep-frying
2   cups   (480 g) sugar
2   cups   water
2   tbsp   milk, mixed with 2 tbsp water
3–4 chhoti elaichi (green cardamoms), slightly crushed

It is very important to have a heavy-based kadahi for this, as the
gulab jamuns have to be fried over low heat, and tend to brown
before they are cooked through. The ghee should be deep enough
for the gulab jamuns to float above the base.

METHOD

1. With the heel of your palm or the base of a flat metal
   bowl, mash the khoya smooth, so that no grains remain.
   Mix in the flour and baking soda and knead into a firm
   dough. You can use a food processor too. The dough
   should be firm but pliable, and should not feel dry. If it
   does feel dry, wet your hands and work the dough
   again.

2. Shape the dough into marble-sized balls (jamuns), that
   are smooth and creaseless. The shape can be round or
   oblong.

3. Heat the ghee in the kadahi till a piece of dough tossed
   in comes up at once. Lower heat and fry a cube of bread
   till light brown (this lowers the temperature of the ghee).

4. Lift out bread and add as many jamuns as will fit in,
   without one touching the other. Keeping the heat low,
   fry these till a golden brown all over, turning if
   necessary. It is easier to stir the ghee slowly; this helps
   the jamuns turn over. Turning individual jamuns over
   may break them. (Keep the heat low as jamuns tend to
   brown very quickly).

5. Drain the jamuns out of the ghee, and fry the next lot,
   increasing the heat for a few seconds and then lowering
   it again before adding the jamuns. Keep gulab jamuns
   aside till syrup is ready.

6. Mix the sugar and water and place over low heat,
   stirring till the sugar dissolves. Make sure it does not
   boil. Increase the heat once the sugar dissolves, and then
   bring mixture come to boil.

7. Add the milk and water mixture and continue boiling
   over high heat, without stirring. Skim off any scum that
   collects on the sides of the pan. Cook till syrup thickens
   a bit (about 10 minutes). A finger dipped in slightly cold
   syrup should form a coating on it for a few seconds.

8. Take syrup off stove and cool for a minimum of half an
   hour. Strain through a fine nylon sieve or muslin cloth.

9. Add cardamom and bring syrup to boil again. Add the
   fried gulab jamuns to it and shut off heat. Let jamuns
   soak for at least half an hour before serving (they should
   double (or more) in size).

Note: You can also fry the gulab jamuns ahead of time and
   put them into the heated syrup when ready to serve.

PETHA

(A speciality of Agra, this is made from white pumpkin/ash gourd. There are two varieties of this, one dry and the other soaked in syrup. Here is the recipe for the latter.)

INGREDIENTS (MAKES ABOUT 30 PIECES)

1	kg	**safed petha (ash gourd/white pumpkin)** a large, hard one
2	tsp	chemical lime
¾	kg	(3 cups) sugar
3	cups	water
2	tbsp	milk mixed with 2 tbsp water
1	tbsp	lemon juice
3–4		chhoti elaichi (green cardamoms) peeled and crushed
1	tsp	gulab jal (rose water)

METHOD

1. Peel the pumpkin, remove the seeds and the soft, fibrous portion. Cut into large, thick slices. Prick well with a fork, all over.

2. Dissolve 1 teaspoon of chemical lime in enough water to cover the pumpkin pieces. Soak them in this water for about 2 hours. Remove from the lime water and wash well. Cut into cubes of about 3 cms/1½ in (or shape as desired). Make lime water solution with the remaining teaspoon of chemical lime. Soak the pumpkin pieces once more in the freshly made lime water for 2 hours.

3. Drain pieces and wash thoroughly, squeezing out water and rinsing again so that no trace of lime remains. Boil enough water to take in the pumpkin pieces, add the pieces to it, and cook till soft and transparent.

4. Meanwhile, fill 3 cups of water and the sugar in a pan; place over low heat, stirring till sugar dissolves. Bring to boil and then follow points 7 and 8 of the method for Gulab Jamuns (p 112).

5. Add the lemon juice and the cardamoms and cook till it reaches 'one thread' consistency—a drop pressed between the thumb and forefinger should form a thick thread when thumb and finger are separated. Skim off any foam that may collect along the sides of the pan.

6. Keep the syrup warm. When the pumpkin pieces are cooked, drain with a slotted spoon and transfer into the syrup. Simmer for a couple of minutes, take off stove, add the rose water and mix well.

7. Cool and serve.

Note: Keeps for a couple of months in an air-tight container in a refrigerator.

SHAHI TUKRA

(A very popular Mughlai dessert made of bread.)

INGREDIENTS

4		slices of a large loaf of **white bread,** with edges trimmed off
		Ghee for deep-frying
2	tbsp	(30 g) sugar
½	cup	milk
		Rabri made of ½ kg milk p 114
1	tsp	gulab jal (rose water)
½	cup	malai (clotted cream)
		Vark (leaves of beaten silver), p 110, optional
2	tbsp	blanched and slivered almonds
2	tbsp	blanched and slivered pistachios
		A few rose petals (optional)
		A few strands of kesar (saffron)

for garnish

METHOD

1. Cut dry slices of bread into half, lengthwise. Deep-fry in hot ghee, till crisp.
2. Dissolve the sugar in the milk and bring to boil. Set aside till cool enough to handle.
3. Dip the fried pieces of bread in the milk and sugar, and arrange in a serving dish, in one layer.
4. Mix the rose water in the rabri and spoon it over the fried bread pieces, to cover all of them.
5. Spoon the cream on to the centre of each piece. Garnish with silver leaf.
6. Garnish with almonds, pistachios, rose petals and saffron strands. Serve hot or chilled.

RABRI

(A milk based dessert, made by condensing milk.)

INGREDIENTS

5 cups (1 kg) **full cream milk**
½ cup (240 g) sugar
4–5 chhoti elaichi (green cardamoms)
12–15 almonds, blanched (p 150) and shredded
2 tbsp pistachios, blanched and shredded
Vark (leaves of beaten silver), p 110, optional

METHOD

1. Boil the milk in a wide, heavy-based pan or a kadahi. Add the sugar and cardamom and simmer over low heat. Do not stir too often, as a layer of cream should form over it.
2. After the layer is formed, push it away from the sides towards the centre, stir the milk below it gently to avoid scorching. Repeat the process till one-third of the volume of milk is left. The time taken will depend on the richness of the milk and the vessel. The wider the vessel and the richer the milk, the faster it will thicken.
3. When done, the colour changes to a beige-cream, and the cream that was pushed aside, collects in layers.
4. Remove from heat. When cool, transfer to a serving dish. Try to retain the shreddy effect (formed by the layers) as far as possible.
5. Garnish with silver leaf and nuts. Chill and serve.

Note: You can add condensed milk to save time, in which case, of course, the amount of sugar used must be reduced.

KULFI

(An all-time favourite, now much easier to make with the widespread availability of moulds.)

INGREDIENTS (MAKES ABOUT 8 MOULDS, THAT TAKE IN APPROXIMATELY ONE-FOURTH CUP OF MIXTURE EACH.)

5 cups (1 kg) **full cream milk**
½ cup (240 g) sugar
¼ tsp kesar (saffron)
4–5 chhoti elaichi (green cardamoms)
12–15 almonds, blanched (p 150) and shredded
2 tbsp pistachios, blanched and shredded
8 kulfi moulds
Vark (leaves of beaten silver), p 110, optional

METHOD

1. Boil the milk in a wide, heavy-based pan or kadahi and then simmer over medium heat, stirring from time to time, to avoid scorching.

2. Simmer till about half the volume of milk is left.

3. The milk will take about 30–40 minutes to thicken. When done, the colour of the milk changes to a beige-cream, and the bubbles appear mostly in the centre of the pan.

4. Add the sugar and saffron, bring to boil again, and simmer for another minute or two. Add the cardamom and turn off the heat. When cool, add the nuts, saving a few for garnishing. Mix well and pour into moulds.

5. Freeze at the lowest possible temperature. (Takes about 3–4 hours.)

6. To serve, take the mould out of the freezer and prise the kulfi out with the help of a knife, into an individual serving bowl. Garnish with the silver leaf and nuts, and serve immediately.

Note: You can add condensed milk to save time, in which case, of course, you will have to reduce the amount of sugar used. The richer the milk, the less it has to be cooked.

TIL KI BARFEE

(A barfee made of sesame seeds.
Especially good in cold winter months.)

INGREDIENTS (MAKES ABOUT 30 PIECES)

½	cup	(50 g) **safed til (sesame seeds)**
1	tbsp	(15 g) ghee
¾	cup	(150 g) khoya (p 150)
½	cup	(120 g) sugar
½	cup	water
A greased plate to set the barfee in		

METHOD

1. Roast the seeds on a griddle or frying pan till they start to splutter and take on just a suggestion of colour. Remove from the pan and set aside to cool.

2. Place a heavy-based pan, on the stove. Put in the ghee and khoya and saute till it appears to be of a uniform consistency and looks slightly fried. Take off the heat, add the roasted sesame seeds, leave to cool.

3. In another pan, warm the sugar and water together over low heat, stirring a few times till the sugar dissolves. Make sure not to let it boil before the sugar dissolves. Once the sugar dissolves, let the syrup boil over high heat till it thickens. (A drop of syrup on a cold surface or in a cup of cold water, sets at once, into a firm, but not hard ball, p 109).

4. Mix immediately into the cooled khoya mixture, stirring vigorously to blend well. As you mix it in, it will begin to set, so it is essential to blend it in as fast as you can.

5. Transfer on to the greased plate, pat to level, and leave to cool and set.

6. Cut into pieces of desired size, using a sharp knife. Arrange in a serving dish and serve. Can be stored in an airtight container for 8–10 days or more.

BEEJ KI BARFEE: Substitute the same quantity of magaz (melon seeds) for the til (sesame seeds).

KHUS KI KATLI: Substitute the same quantity of khus khus (poppy seeds) for the til (sesame seeds).

NARIYAL KI BARFEE/GOLE KI BARFEE: Substitute the same quantity of kassa hua nariyal (grated coconut) for the til (sesame seeds).

MAKHANE KI KATLI: Substitute the same volume of roasted and pounded makhana (lotus seeds) for the til (sesame seeds).

CHIRONJI PAAK: Substitute the same quantity of chironji (sunflower seeds) for the til (sesame seeds).

BADAAM KI BARFEE

(A barfee that is extremely popular and equally easy to make. This was taught to me by Anila Bhabhi.)

INGREDIENTS (MAKES ABOUT 24 PIECES)

250 g **almonds**, blanched
240 g (1 cup) sugar
240 g (1 cup) milk
Vark (leaves of beaten silver), p 113, optional
A greased plate to set the barfee in
A greased rolling pin

METHOD

1. Finely blend the almonds and milk using a blender, or grind the nuts on a stone with the milk.

2. Put the paste in a heavy-bottomed kadahi and add the sugar.

3. Place the vessel over low heat and stir until the sugar dissolves. Then bring to boil.

4. Continue stirring over medium heat, till the mixture leaves the sides of the pan, and becomes a dough-like paste.

5. Once it gathers up together into a mass, remove from heat and cool for a while. When cool enough to handle, roll it on to the greased plate, with the greased rolling

pin. It must be rolled before it cools completely. Do not roll while it is too hot, as it is sticky when hot.

6. Roll to ½ cm/ (⅛ in) thickness. Cover with silver leaves and leaf to cool.

7. When cold, cut the barfee into diamond-shaped pieces, and transfer to a serving dish and serve.

BESAN KI BARFEE

(A barfee made from chickpea/gram flour and khoya.)

INGREDIENTS (MAKES ABOUT 30 PIECES)

½ cup (60 g) **besan (chickpea/gram flour)**
2 tbsp (30 g) ghee
½ cup (100 g) khoya (p 150)
½ cup (120 g) sugar
½ cup water
¼ tsp powdered elaichi (cardamom)
A greased plate to set the barfee in

METHOD

1. In a kadahi, stir-fry the ghee and chickpea flour over low heat, till the flour looks crumbly and darkens a little. (Cook over low heat and stir constantly so that the chickpea flour is cooked through and does not darken before that.)

2. Take pan off heat and transfer flour into another vessel. Put the khoya into the pan and stir till it takes on a uniform consistency and looks a bit fried.

3. Add the fried chickpea flour to the khoya, and mix well to blend together. Add the cardamom powder.

4. In another pan place the sugar and water together, and warm over low heat stirring a few times till the sugar

dissolves. Do not let it boil before the sugar dissolves. Once sugar dissolves, increase the heat and bring to boil and cook syrup till thick. A drop on a cold surface or in a cup of cold water, sets at once into a firm, but not hard ball (p 109).

5. Mix the sugar syrup immediately into the cooled khoya mixture, stirring vigorously and quickly, to blend well. It must be mixed as fast as possible as it begins to set even while being mixed.

6. Transfer on to the greased plate and pat to level. Leave to cool and set.

7. Cut into pieces of desired size, using a sharp knife. Arrange on a serving dish and serve.

8. The barfee can be stored in an airtight container for about a month.

GUNJIYA

(A fried stuffed sweet made mostly at festival time.)

INGREDIENTS (MAKES ABOUT 20)

Dough:
2 cups (240 g) **maida (refined flour)**
¼ cup (60 g) ghee
Cold water to mix

Filling:
½ cup packed (100 g) **khoya** (p 150)
½ cup (120 g) sugar
½ tsp powdered chhoti elaichi (green cardamom)
1 tbsp finely chopped almonds
Ghee for deep-frying

METHOD

1. Rub one-fourth cup ghee into the flour and knead into a stiff dough with water. Leave to rest for at least half an hour.

2. For the filling, saute the khoya over medium heat till it looks slightly fried (that is, until the excess moisture evaporates). Take off the heat, and when cool, mix in the sugar, cardamom and almonds.

3. Shape the filling into ovals about 2½ cm/1 in length and ½ cm/¼ in thickness.

4. Make balls of the dough and roll out into ¼ cm/ ⅛ in thick rounds.

5. Take a round, wet the edges with water and place a piece of filling over one half. Fold the other half over and press the edges together to seal. Either cut off the edge with a fancy cutter, or make a design by pinching and twisting all along the sealed edge. Make up all the gunjiyas in this way.

6. Heat the ghee in a kadahi. To check if the ghee is hot enough put a piece of dough in it. If it comes up at once, add as many gunjiyas as fit in comfortably. Turn them over and lower the heat to medium. Fry till golden brown on all sides (takes about 15 minutes). Lift out and leave to drain on absorbent paper.

7. Fry the rest, increasing the heat for a few seconds before adding the next lot. Can be eaten hot or at room temperature, and can be stored in airtight containers, as they last for a couple of months.

BESAN KE LADDOO

*(Laddoos are a favourite with most of us.
This one is made from gram flour, and was
taught to me by my friend Pushpa Gupta,
who is an expert at making them.)*

INGREDIENTS (MAKES 12–14)

2 cups (240 g) **besan (chickpea/gram flour)***
½ cup (150 g) ghee
¾ cup (180 g) powdered sugar**
¼ tsp powdered chhoti elaichi (green cardamom)
Some blanched and slivered almonds and pistachios to decorate,
    if desired

METHOD

1. In a kadahi, melt the ghee and add the chickpea flour.

2. Stir-fry over low heat. It takes about 30 minutes for the flour to get cooked through and it gets a pasty look when done. The colour should be a light brown/ochre.

3. Shut off the heat and leave the mixture to cool completely. If it does not cool entirely, it becomes moist when sugar is added.

4. Add the sugar and cardamom and mix well by rubbing it with your open palm against the base of the bowl. Rub till blended thoroughly.

5. Shape into tight, hard balls, pressing hard at every stage. At the final stage, keep it pressed a little longer, so that the surface become smooth (when the ghee comes in contact with body heat, it melts and smoothens the mixture).

6. Decorate the top of each with almonds and pistachios, if desired.

7. Can be stored in airtight containers for 4–6 weeks.

Note: * Some people prefer to use chickpea flour which is a little coarsely ground.

** Ideally, sugar is substituted by karara, which is crystallised sugar syrup, powdered when cool.

GAJAR KA HALWA

*(A popular winter dessert throughout north India,
this is made of carrots and milk or khoya. Several
people serve it with ice-cream, rabri or clotted cream.)*

INGREDIENTS

1 kg **carrots**
1 cup (200 g) khoya (p 150)
½ cup (125 g) sugar
1 tsp powdered choti elaichi (green cardamom)
5–6 almonds, blanched and shredded
8–10 kishmish (raisins)
¼ cup (60 g) ghee
3–4 vark (leaves of beaten silver), p 110 for garnish

METHOD

1. Peel and wash the carrots before grating them. Discard any hard insides.

2. In a heavy-based pan, place the carrots with one-forth cup of water, cover and cook over low heat till tender. The water helps to start the cooking process, after which the carrots will cook in their own juice.

3. When the carrots are cooked, crumble three-fourth of the khoya and add. Cook the two together, till well blended. Add the sugar and continue stirring, till the carrots have a slightly glossy look and the moisture has evaporated.

4. Add the cardamom and ghee and half the almonds and raisins. Saute till the ghee separates (approx 5 minutes).

5. Transfer to a serving dish. Crush the rest of the khoya and sprinkle. Garnish with silver leaf and the remaining almonds and raisins.

SOOJEE KA HALWA

(A commonly made halwa, this makes a good breakfast as well as a dessert.)

INGREDIENTS

1	cup	(120 g) **soojee (semolina)**
1	cup	(240 g) sugar
4	cups	water
6	tbsp	(90 g) ghee
¼	tsp	powdered elaichi (green cardamom)
1	tbsp	blanched and shredded almonds, for garnish

METHOD

1. In a deep, heavy-based saucepan, melt the ghee, add the semolina and stir-fry over medium or low heat, depending on how often you stir it.

2. At the same time, in another (long-handled) pan, dissolve the sugar in the water over low heat and simmer till required. A long-handled pan is needed because while pouring the sugar solution into the semolina mixture, the steam could burn your hand.

3. When the semolina is fried enough it will turn light brown, look glossy and not stick together very much. Add the sugar solution and cardamom and bring to boil. Simmer till the liquid is absorbed, stirring off and on. Takes about 5 minutes.

4. Serve hot, garnished with the almonds.

MOONG KI DAAL KA HALWA

(This is a halwa which takes a lot of patience to make, so try this only if you have it!)

INGREDIENTS

½	cup	(90 g) **dhuli moong ki daal (split green gram),** soaked in water for 5–6 hrs
½	cup	(120 g) ghee
½	cup	(120 g) sugar
½	cup	(120 g) milk
1	cup	(240 g) water
¼	tsp	powdered chhoti elaichi (green cardamom)
2	tbsp	slivered and roasted almonds
2	vark	(leaves of beaten silver), p 110, optional

(ghee, sugar, milk, water) mixed together

METHOD

1. Wash the lentils and rub till all the husk is removed. Grind coarsely in a food processor or on a grinding stone. (Grind till slightly more coarse than the texture of fine sand.)

2. Take a kadahi with at least 3 times the capacity of the quantity of halwa to be prepared. Mix the ghee and lentils and place over low heat.

3. Stir-fry over low heat till well fried. Initially, you will have to stir continuously, as it tends to stick to the bottom of the pan. It is necessary to keep the heat low, so that the lentils cook through, and the halwa does not taste raw.

4. Continue stir-frying (over low or medium heat) till it browns and the fat separates. At first it will tend to stick together, but will soon separate and begin to look fried.

5. Meanwhile, heat the milk mixture and bring to boil. Keep hot till lentils are fried completely. Add boiled milk mixture to fried lentils and stir well to blend together. (It will sizzle and bubble, before settling down to a simmer).

119

6. Cook over low heat till liquid is absorbed, and stir-fry once again till fat separates. The mixture will first get a pasty consistency, then will collect together, and as you go on, will start breaking up, before fat separates.

7. Mix in the cardamom powder and half the almonds. Transfer to a serving dish, decorate with silver leaf and the rest of the almonds. Serve hot.

JALEBI

(Available in almost all parts of India, a popular combination is jalebies dunked in hot milk! Making jalebies may seem very daunting, but is surprisingly simple.)

INGREDIENTS (MAKES ABOUT 20)

½ cup (60 g) **maida (refined flour)**
¼ cup (50 g) **dahi (yogurt)** preferably sour
$\frac{1}{8}$ tsp baking soda, if required
Ghee for deep-frying
A square piece of cloth with a small hole in it, or a thick polythene bag for piping out the jalebies

Syrup:

1½ cups (360 g) sugar
½ cups water

METHOD

1. Mix the flour and yogurt, to form a thick, smooth paste (dropping consistency), adding water if necessary.

2. Cover and leave to ferment for 6–7 hours. (The texture should be spongy and bubbles should appear along the edges.)

3. Make the sugar syrup by dissolving sugar in water over low heat, then cook over high heat till slightly thick (when lifted with a spoon and poured back into the pan, it should fall in a thin, smooth stream, like honey, or, a cooled drop of it pressed between the thumb and forefinger and pulled apart, should form a suggestion of a thread). Set aside till you fry the jalebies.

4. Take a shallow heavy-bottomed pan and heat the ghee till a drop of batter tossed in comes up at once. If (and only if) the texture of the batter is not as described in step 2, add the baking soda (try to avoid using it) and fill the plastic bag with the batter. Twist the opening to seal the bag. Snip one lower corner of the bag to make a small hole, through which you can pipe out the jalebies (the smaller the hole, the thinner the jalebies.)

5. Hold the bag over the hot ghee in the pan and pipe out swirls (like whirlpools), of the desired size into it. Make as many such rounds as will fit in comfortably. Lower the heat to medium and turn the jalebies over and fry till light brown on both sides.

6. Using a draining spoon lift out the fried jalebies; make sure you allow ghee to drain out. Put jalebies into the syrup and leave for a minute or so. Take out of syrup and serve. You will have to adjust the heat of the ghee as you continue frying the rest of the jalebies, increasing or decreasing the heat as required. The jalebies should be fried crisp.

Note: If you want to make the jalebies ahead of time, fry and dip them for a while in syrup. Then take them out and store. Re-heat syrup just before serving and dip jalebies into it, for about a minute.

SANTRE KI KHEER

*(Kheer made with peeled orange segments.
Especially popular in Varanasi, where they seem
to use oranges in several sweet and savoury dishes.)*

INGREDIENTS

5   cups (1 kg) **full cream milk**
½   cup   (240 g) sugar
4–5 chhoti elaichi (green cardamoms)
3   large oranges, with segments peeled and broken upunevenly
12–15 almonds, blanched (p 150), and shredded
2   tbsp pistachios, blanched and shredded
Vark (leaves of beaten silver), p 110, optional

METHOD

1. Bring the milk to boil in a wide, heavy-based pan; add the sugar and cardamom and simmer over low heat. Stir often enough to avoid scorching.

2. Simmer till mixture is thick. Time taken will depend on the richness of the milk and your vessel. The wider the vessel, the faster the milk will thicken.

3. When thick (like thick cream) and colour darkens a little, shut off heat. Cool and add pieces of orange. Mix well, chill and serve garnished with the silver leaf, almonds and pistachios.

MALPUA

*(I call these Indian pancakes dipped in syrup.
Quite a festive dish in many areas, and a hot
favourite on a rainy day in some families!)*

INGREDIENTS

1   cup   (120 g) **maida (refined flour)**
½   cup   (100 g) **dahi (yogurt)**
¼   tsp   baking soda, if required
2   tbsp khoya, grated (or 2 tbsp whole milk powder)
2   tsp   saunf (fennel seeds) coarsely powdered
2   chhoti elaichi (green cardamoms), coarsely powdered
Ghee for pan frying
1   cup   (240 g) sugar
1   cup   water
Vark (leaves of beaten silver), p 110, optional
¼   cup   almonds, blanched (p 150) and shredded

METHOD

1. Mix the flour and yogurt with some water to make a smooth paste of pouring consistency. Add khoya, powdered fennel seeds and powdered cardamom; set aside to ferment for 5–6 hours. If making within an hour, add the baking soda.

2. Meanwhile, dissolve the sugar in the water over low heat; when dissolved, increase heat for about 5 minutes; keep warm. Skim off any bubbles or residue that may gather along the sides of the pan.

3. When ready to serve, check to see that the batter is a little spongy. If it is not, add the baking soda. Heat enough ghee in frying pan to cover base. Over high heat, pour about 2 tablespoons of batter on to frying pan and spread with back of ladle to make a thin flat pancake.

4. Lower heat and cook till the edges are browned and begin to rise. Flip over and cook on other side too, till brown.

5. Remove from pan, dip into syrup and transfer to a serving dish. Pour some more syrup over it. Garnish with the silver leaf (if using it) and the nuts.

ﾒﾆ🙲ﾆ🙲ﾆ🙲

NIMISH/DAULAT KI CHAAT/MALAYEE

*(A royal dessert, made very rarely at home,
this is especially popular in Lucknow and Agra.
In Agra it is called Solah Maza, because the
vendors there claim to add 16 spices to it!)*

INGREDIENTS

10 cups (2 kg) **full cream milk**
1 cup (240 g) sugar
½ tsp powdered samudri jhaag (cuttle bones) or baking soda
½ tsp tightly packed kesar (saffron)
4 chhoti elaichi (green cardamoms), powdered
A few shredded almonds
¼ tsp powdered cardamoms ⎫ for garnish
¼ tsp powdered cinnamon ⎭

METHOD

1. In a wide saucepan or kadahi, mix all the ingredients and bring to boil, stirring to dissolve the sugar. Lower heat and simmer, stirring now and then to avoid scorching. Simmer till about one-third has evaporated. The wider the vessel, the faster the milk will thicken.

2. When cool transfer into a broad dish (like a paraat). Cover with a thin muslin cloth and place it outside overnight so that it can soak in the dew. This is the traditional method of making the dish. Alternatively, place it in the refrigerator for 12 hours.

3. Next morning, skim off the cream from the top of the milk, leaving behind the milk, if any. Whip the cream with beater or in food processor. Transfer to serving dish immediately and serve garnished with ground spices and almonds.

ﾒﾆ🙲ﾆ🙲ﾆ🙲

ZARDA/MEETHE CHAWAL

*(As the name suggests, this is sweet rice. Besides being
served as a dessert, it is sometimes made at festivals.
For Basant Panchami it is made with a lot of kesar
(saffron) in it, so that it is yellow, the colour of basant.
In some homes children are sent off to take their
exams after being given a spoonful of this and dahi.)*

INGREDIENTS

1 cup (210 g) **sela chawal (parboiled rice)**, picked, washed and soaked for about an hour
1 tsp yellow colouring, optional
2–3 laung (cloves)
4 chhoti elaichi (green cardamoms)
1¼ cup (300 g) sugar
A large pinch of kesar (saffron) soaked in 1 tbsp of warm milk
4 cups water
10–12 raisins
5 almonds shredded
¼ cup (60 g) ghee
Dough to seal dish and a little fat to grease the lid

METHOD

1. Bring the water to boil and add the rice after draining out the water; add also the yellow colouring, cloves and cardamom. When it boils, lower heat and simmer till rice is almost cooked (about 12 minutes).

2. Drain rice, rinse twice in cold water and leave in a colander to drain.

122

3. In a heavy-based pan heat the ghee, fry the raisins and almonds and saute till they change colour. Remove nuts and raisins and set aside. Add the rice to the same ghee and mix well.

4. Grease the edges of the lid. Roll a string of dough and grease it slightly. Stick the dough along the edges of the pan.

5. Lower heat, remove half the rice and sprinkle half the sugar over it. Then layer the rest of the rice and sugar over it, and sprinkle over with the tablespoonful of saffron milk. Seal with lid and dough and place pan on griddle over low heat for about half an hour.

6. Break seal and serve garnished with raisins and nuts.

ANARSE KI GOLI

(This dish is made and sent by mothers to their married daughters around the time of the festival of Teej.)

INGREDIENTS

1	cup	(210 g) **rice flour**
¼	cup	(60 g) sugar, powdered
¼	tsp	baking soda
2	tbsp	(30 g) ghee
2	tbsp	safed til (white sesame seeds)
2	tbsp	dahi (yogurt)
		Ghee to deep-fry

METHOD

1. Rub 2 tablespoons ghee into the rice flour. Mix in the sugar, sesame seeds and yogurt and knead into a soft dough with a little water. Rest dough for 15–20 minutes.

2. Shape dough into walnut-sized balls.

3. Heat the ghee till a little piece of dough dropped in comes up at once. Put in as many balls as fit in comfortably. Lower heat to medium and fry till brown and cooked through.

4. Serve hot, or cool to room temperature and store in airtight containers.

ANDE KA HALWA

(A halwa made of eggs, milk and sugar, which is very popular among the Muslim of U.P.)

INGREDIENTS

4		**eggs**, with yolks and whites separated
1	cup	(240 g) sugar
1	cup	(200 g) milk
2	tbsp	nariyal ka burada (dessicated coconut)
¼	cup	(60 g) ghee
1	tsp	powdered elaichi (cardamom)
2	tbsp	shredded almonds

METHOD

1. Beat the egg yolks and sugar together till creamy. Add the milk, beating all the time till well mixed.

2. Beat the egg whites till fairly stiff, and mix into the milk and yolk mixture.

3. Heat the ghee in a heavy-based saucepan and add the milk mixture and stir-fry over low heat. Add the coconut and continue cooking over low heat till mixture becomes slightly granulated.

4. Add the cardamom powder, mix well and serve hot, garnished with the shredded almonds.

Snacks

Snacks are always welcome in any cuisine. Most snacks in India are multi-purpose, and can be served for the main meals (breakfast, lunch or dinner), cocktails and at tea time as well. They can be had on their own or eaten with a side dish or with chutney. The accompaniment also depends on when the snack is being served, e.g. Khasta Kachauri can be served by itself at tea or cocktails. When served with a meal it has Aloo Rasedaar to. go with it.

Many snacks can be made and stored for later use but some have to be made fresh. There are several sweet snacks, like barfee, peda, rasgullas, etc., which are also served as desserts.

ALOO KI TIKKI

*(A favourite chaat item with
almost everyone, this can be made
with as much filling as one desires.)*

INGREDIENTS (MAKES 6–8)

500 g (2–3 large) **potatoes,** boiled in their jackets, cooled and peeled
1 slice bread, crust removed
Salt to taste
¼ tsp kali mirch (powdered black pepper)

Filling:
¾ cup (120 gms) dhuli moong daal (husked green gram), soaked in water for 3–4 hours
2 tbsp (30 g) ghee

1 tsp jeera (cumin seeds)
⅛ tsp heeng (asafoetida)
½ tsp garam masala I (p 148)
1 tsp chilli powder
2 tsp dhania (coriander powder)
Salt to taste
1½ tsp amchoor (mango powder)
Ghee for pan frying

METHOD

1. Grind the lentils coarsely, either in a food processor or on a grinding stone.

2. Heat the 2 tablespoons of ghee and add the cumin seeds and asafoetida. When they start to splutter, add the lentils and the rest of the ingredients for the filling.

3. Saute over low heat till mixture is well fried. It will stop sticking to the pan, when done. Take mixture off heat and leave to cool.

4. Grate the potatoes along with the bread, add the salt and pepper and mash well with the heel of the palm or a rounded bowl, till smooth. Knead to make like pliable dough.

5. Grease your palms and shape potato mixture into round balls 5 cms/2 in in diameter. Take a ball, press to flatten a little, and pinch about ½ in of the edge all around, leaving the centre thicker. Place a heap of filling in centre. Bring edges together, covering the filling completely and seal.

6. Smoothen ball a little between palms and flatten to form a pattie, taking care not to tear the potato coating.

7. Heat enough ghee in a heavy-based frying pan to form a thin layer. Fry tikkis over low heat, first on one side and then the other, till crisp and brown. You will have to keep adding ghee a little at a time, when required. The longer you cook them, the more ghee you will need to add and the crisper they will get.

8. Serve hot with green chutney (p 134) or with Sonth ki Chutney (p 134).

BHALLA, AGRA STYLE

(Aloo ki Tikkis are called bhallas in Agra. A favourite with Brijan Bhabhi who introduced me to them.)

INGREDIENTS

The potato mixture is the same as that for Aloo ki Tikki (p 124)

Filling:

Diced boiled potatoes
Chopped cashew nuts
Kishmish (raisins)
Chopped coriander
Green chillies
Finely chopped ginger
A generous amount of ghee for frying

METHOD

1. Make the tikkis as for Aloo ki Tikki (p 124), substituting the filling with the one given above.

2. Heat a generous layer of ghee in a frying pan and fry a tikki till golden brown and crisp on both sides. The side that is frying must be almost covered in ghee.

3. Fry all the tikkis and set aside. Before serving, break the tikkis by pressing with the finger tips and fry again on both sides. Serve with green chutney (p 134) or with Sonth ki Chutney (p 134).

DAHI KE KABAB

(As the name suggests, these are made with yogurt. This is especially popular in eastern U.P. and was taught to me by Pushpa Bhalla from Varanasi.)

INGREDIENTS

2½ cups (500 g) **dahi (yogurt)** made from full cream milk and refrigerated for at least 6 hours
¼ cup (30 g) **besan (chickpea/gram flour),** dry roasted over low heat till slightly dark
1 tbsp finely chopped hara dhania (coriander leaves)
1 tsp finely chopped green chilli (or to taste)
2 tbsp finely chopped onions
Salt to taste
1 tsp roasted and powdered jeera (cumin seeds)
Oil/ghee for pan-frying

METHOD

1. Line a colander with muslin. Place colander in a pan. Place the yogurt in the colander to drain out the water into the pan. Takes 3–4 hours.

2. Mix in the rest of the ingredients in the yogurt except the oil/ghee, and chill for an hour (this makes it easier to handle).

3. Shape the mixture into flat rounds (like patties) and pan-fry over medium heat till brown on both sides. Keeping the patties refrigerated helps. To brown on the other side, turn them over gently with a spatula, as they are soft.

4. Serve hot with green chutney (p 134).

125

KHASTA KACHAURI

*(A very popular snack all over U.P. Holi and
Diwali are occasions when this is a must.)*

Ingredients (Makes about 15–20)

2   cups   (240 g) **maida (refined flour)**
¼   cup   (60 g) ghee
Salt to taste
Cold water to mix
Oil for deep-frying

Filling:

¾   cup   (120 g) **dhuli urad daal (husked black gram),** soaked in
                water for 3–4 hours
2   tbsp   (30 g) oil
1   tsp   jeera (cumin seeds)
⅛   tsp   heeng (asafoetida)
¾   tsp   garam masala I (p 148)
¾   tsp   chilli powder
2   tbsp   powdered saunf (fennel seeds)
2   tsp   dhania (coriander powder)
Salt to taste
1½ tsp   amchoor (mango powder)

Method

1. Grind the lentils coarsely, either in a food processor or
   on a stone.

2. Heat the 2 tablespoons of oil and add the cumin seeds
   and asafoetida. When they begin to splutter, add the
   lentils and the rest of the ingredients which make up the
   filling. Saute over low heat till mixture is well fried. It
   will stop sticking to the pan when done. Take mixture
   off heat and leave to cool.

3. Dough: Mix in the flour and salt. Add the ghee to the
   flour. Make it into a crumbly mixture with the tips of
   your fingers.

4. Add enough water, to make it into a stiffish dough (it
   should not yield easily when a finger is pressed into it).
   Cover and leave to rest for at least 15–20 minutes.

5. Make marble-sized balls of the lentil mixture (called
   pithee) wetting your hands as and when necessary to
   prevent the mixture from sticking to them. Cover with
   a cloth till ready to fill.

6. Make about 20 smooth balls from the dough. Roll them
   out till ½ cm/¼ in thick (about 5 cms/2 in diameter).

7. Take one piece of round dough and pinch about 1 cm/
   ½ in of the edge all around, leaving the centre thicker.
   Dampen the pressed edges, place a ball of filling in the
   centre, and bring wet edges together, covering filling
   completely. Press together to seal.

8. Place this piece in your palm and with the heal of the
   other palm, press gently in the centre (to break the ball
   of filling inside). Flatten a bit with palm first, then roll
   lightly into a round, about ½ cm/¼ in thick. The
   kachauris are now ready to fry.

9. Heat the oil in a kadahi. When a piece of dough
   dropped in the oil comes up at once, put in as many
   kachauris as can fit in; turn over immediately and
   lower heat to medium.

10. Fry kachauris till evenly golden, reducing heat from
    medium to low. Takes about 10 minutes for one side
    and 6–7 minutes for the other. Remove from oil, drain
    and place on absorbent paper. Serve hot.

Note: Temperature for frying has to be adjusted from time
      to time. Increase heat every time you put in a fresh
      lot. Heat may have to be increased for sometime in
      between too, if you feel the oil is not hot enough.
      When a kachauri is first put in, it should make a
      sizzling sound, and come up at once. If it sinks to the

bottom, it means the oil is not hot enough. Store kachauris in airtight containers.

⋇⋇⋇⋇⋇⋇⋇

SAMOSA

(An item that needs no introduction and one of the most popular Indian foods that has made inroads into the international market.)

INGREDIENTS (MAKES ABOUT 20)

2 cups (240 g) **maida (refined flour),** sifted
Salt to taste
2 tbsp oil
Cold water to knead
Use only half the quantity of Sookhe Aloo (p 25) or Sookhe Matar on (p 38) for filling.
Oil for deep-frying

METHOD

1. Using the ingredients to make the covering, knead into a firm but pliable dough (a finger pressed lightly into it should not go in easily). Leave the dough to rest for about 15 minutes.

2. Shape the dough into 8–10 smooth balls. Roll them into thin rounds, about 15 cm/6 in in diameter, and cut into halves.

3. Take one half, wet the edges and fold the straight edge at the centre to bring the two halves together, overlapping a bit to form into a triangular case.

4. Press portion that overlap, and fill case with potato mixture, leaving a margin of 1 cm/½ in all around. Press edges together to seal the samosa. Repeat till all pieces are used up, keeping those done covered with a damp cloth.

5. Heat the oil in a kadahi till a piece of dough dropped in it comes up immediately. Add as many samosas as will fit in comfortably. Lower heat to medium.

6. Fry until golden brown on both sides. Increase heat before adding next lot and then lower again.

7. Serve hot, with a chutney.

Note: The filling and size can vary according to taste. Some popular fillings: lentils as for Aloo ki Tikki (p 124), minced meat as for Keema Matar (p 55), etc.

⋇⋇⋇⋇⋇⋇⋇

PAAPRI

(Even though these can be bought easily in the market, paapris are quite easy to make and store for ready use. They keep for almost a month if stored well in airtight containers.)

INGREDIENTS (MAKES 80–100)

2 cups (240 g) **maida (refined flour)**
2 tbsp (30 g) oil
¼ tsp salt
Water to knead the dough
Oil for deep-frying

METHOD

1. Mix the salt and oil into the flour and knead into a stiff dough with the water. Rest covered, for at least half an hour.

2. Roll out dough till it is ¼ cm/$\frac{1}{8}$ in thick, and cut out into 3 cms/1¼ in rounds with a cutter.

3. Heat the oil till a piece of dough dropped in comes up at once. Then add as many rounds as fit in comfortably. Lower heat to medium. Fry paapris till golden brown on

both sides. Some will puff up. These can be used for Gole Gappas (p 128) and the rest for Paapri Chaat (p 128).

4. Lift out of oil and drain on absorbent paper; repeat with rest of dough, increasing heat for a few seconds before adding a fresh lot.

Note: These can be stored in an airtight container.

SOOJEE KE GOLE GAPPE: Make puffed paapris as above, substituting 1½ cup semolina and ½ cup refined flour for 2 cups of refined flour in the recipe above.

JAL JEERA/GOLE GAPPE KA PAANI

(This is a spicy drink which is an appetiser and a digestive. And as the name suggests it, is also the liquid filling used in Gole Gappas.)

INGREDIENTS (MAKES ABOUT 8 CUPS)

1 cup **sonth (ginger powder) chutney** (p 134)
2 cups (125 g) firmly packed pudina (mint leaves)
1 cup (75 g) firmly packed hara dhania (coriander leaves)
6–7 green chillies (or according to taste)
2 tbsp roasted and powdered jeera (cumin seeds)
Salt to taste
1 tsp chilli powder
8 cups water

METHOD

Mix all the ingredients together, chill and serve.

GOLE GAPPE

(This is just in case you do not know the sequence for the serving of Gole Gappas!)

INGREDIENTS

24 **puffed paapri** (p 127)
1 cup boiled and diced **potatoes**
1 cup boiled **channa (chickpeas)**
Jal jeera/gole gappe ka paani (p 128)
Sonth ki chutney (ginger powder), p 134, optional

HOW TO EAT (FOR THOSE WHO HAVE NEVER EATEN THESE!)

Tap a small hole in the centre of the thinner side of the puffed paapri, and fill with a little potato, chickpea and ginger powder chutney, if so desired; then fill with the spiced water and put the whole poori into your mouth in one go!

PAAPRI CHAAT

(An introduction to making it at home, especially for guests from overseas who will not risk eating out.)

INGREDIENTS

24 flat **paapris**
1 cup boiled and diced **potatoes**
½ cup boiled **kabuli channa (chickpeas)**
1 cup (200 g) **dahi (yogurt)** mixed with water to make into desired consistency
½ cup Sonth ki Chutney (ginger powder) (p 134) mixed with water to a pouring consistency
Hara dhania chutney (coriander leaves chutney) (p 134) mixed with water to a pouring consistency, optional
Chaat masala (p 149)

Chilli powder
Very thinly sliced fresh ginger } for garnish
Hara dhania (coriander leaves)

METHOD

1. Dip the paapris into the yogurt mixture and arrange in a flat serving dish, close to each other.
2. Sprinkle the potatoes and the chickpeas over them and then sprinkle ginger powder chutney (and green chutney, if desired) in a thin layer.
3. Sprinkle the chaat masala, chilli powder and then the sliced ginger and coriander leaves and serve.

GOLE GAPPE KI CHAAT

(Gole gappas filled with potatoes, yogurt and ginger powder chutney.)

INGREDIENTS

The same as Paapri Chaat (p 128), using puffed paapris instead.

METHOD

1. Break a hole in the paapris and fill them with the potatoes and chickpeas.
2. Then fill them with the yogurt and ginger powder.
3. Sprinkle the chaat masala, chilli powder, sliced ginger and coriander leaves and serve.

MATHI

(Few would venture to make these at home, but I can assure you, the home-made ones are far tastier than the ones that can be bought. And more so when they are freshly made.)

INGREDIENTS (MAKES 24)

1	cup	(120 g) **maida (refined flour)**
1	cup	(120 g) **soojee (semolina)**
½	tsp	ajwain (thymol seeds)
1	tsp	salt
¼	cup	(60 g) ghee

Cold water to mix
Oil for deep-frying

METHOD

1. Mix the thymol seeds, salt and flour together and rub the ghee in lightly so that the mixture resembles breadcrumbs.
2. Knead into a stiff dough with cold water (stiff enough to require a little force to press your finger in).
3. Cover dough and set to rest in a cool place for at least 15 minutes.
4. Roll out dough into ¼ cm/¹/₈ in thick rounds, about 8 cms/3 in in diameter, and prick these with a fork all over the surface, to prevent them from puffing up while frying.
5. Heat the oil in a kadahi till a piece of dough dropped in, rises to the top at once. Then, put in as many mathis as will fit in comfortably. Turn once, and lower heat to medium.
6. Fry mathis till light brown on both sides. Lift out and place on absorbent paper. Fry the rest similarly, increasing heat before adding a fresh lot.

129

7. Cool and store in an airtight container.

Note: You can make these entirely with refined flour or with 3 parts semolina and one part refined flour. The combination can vary according to taste.

≈≈≈≈≈≈≈

PAKORA

(This is the most irresistible snack in my reckoning, and there are a large variety of them too.)

Almost any vegetable can be used to make pakodas. These can also be made with fish and chicken, not to mention lentils. Here I have dealt with only a few basic recipes and leave the rest to your imagination and ability to innovate.

INGREDIENTS

Batter for about 250 g vegetables:

1 cup (120 g) **besan (chickpea/gram flour)**
2 tsp salt
½ tsp haldi (turmeric)
½ tsp chilli powder
1 tsp amchoor (mango powder)
Water (approx 2 cups)
125 g onions, sliced into thin rounds
125 g potatoes, sliced into thin rounds
Oil for deep-frying

METHOD

1. With the ingredients for the batter make a batter of pouring consistency (when lifted in a spoon and poured, it should fall in a continuous, smooth stream). Adjust the water as required.

2. Mix the onions and potatoes into batter.

3. Heat the oil in a kadahi till some batter dropped into the oil comes up at once. Now scoop the pieces of the vegetables out of the batter and drop them into the hot oil.

4. Fry over medium heat, to very light brown. Remove from oil with slotted spoon and set aside. Continue till all the onions and potatoes are used up.

5. When ready to serve, heat oil again and fry pakoras over high heat till golden brown. Remove from oil, drain on absorbent paper, and serve with green chutney (p 134).

Some ideas for pakoras:

• Slices of kaddu (pumpkin)
• Palak (spinach) leaves
• Flowerets of cauliflower
• Slices of baingan (brinjal)
• Mix some desired spices into the Mangauri mixture (p 151) after beating it light. Drop teaspoonfuls into the hot oil and fry twice, and serve. These are called Moong ki Daal ki Pakori (green gram). You can add some fenugreek leaves to it.
• Whole green chillies

≈≈≈≈≈≈≈

MANGAUDE

*(A version of pakodas, this is a speciality of Agra.
The difference lies in the fact that instead of chickpea flour, the batter is made of soaked and ground green gram.)*

INGREDIENTS

1 cup (180 g) **dhuli moong (husked green gram)** soaked in water for 4–6 hrs
Salt to taste
½ tsp haldi (turmeric)
½ tsp chilli powder

1 tsp   amchoor (mango powder)
Water
125 g   onions, sliced into thin rounds
125 g   potatoes, sliced into thin rounds
Oil for deep-frying

METHOD

1. Drain the water from the lentils. Grind lentils very fine, either in a blender or on a stone.
2. Add enough water to make into a batter of thick, pouring consistency; add the salt, turmeric, chilli powder and mango powder. Mix well.
3. Proceed to fry the Mangaudas like the Pakodas (p 130), substituting this batter for the chickpea flour batter.

༄༅༄༅༄༅༄

MOONG DAAL KE CHOPS

*(Cutlets made from green gram. A delicacy that
will leave your guest wondering!)*

INGREDIENTS (MAKES ABOUT 12)

1 cup   (180 g) **dhuli moong (husked green gram),** soaked in water for 3–4 hrs
1 cup   (200 g) **dahi (yogurt)**
2 tbsp (30 g) ghee
1 tsp   jeera (cumin seeds)
Salt to taste
1 tsp   chilli powder
½ tsp   garam masala I (p 148)
Ghee to pan-fry
Separated and peeled segments of 1 orange ⎫ mix
1 tbsp kishmish (raisins)   ⎪ together
2 tbsp chopped hara dhania (coriander leaves) ⎬ for
2 tsp   chopped green chillies or to taste   ⎪ filling
Salt to taste   ⎭

METHOD

1. Drain the lentils and set aside. Heat the 2 tablespoons of ghee in a kadahi and add the cumin seeds. When they splutter add the lentils and salt. Saute over medium heat till tender but whole. Takes about 5 minutes. Remove from heat and cool.
2. Hang one-fourth cup of the yogurt in a muslin cloth or sieve till the water drains out. (Takes about half an hour.) Mix this with the filling mixture and set aside.
3. Grind the lentils in a food processor or on a stone to make a dough of fine consistency. Avoid adding water.
4. Mix the salt, chilli powder and garam masala into the ground lentils. Add the rest of the yogurt and enough water to make into a soft pliable dough.
5. Divide this into about 12 portions and shape each into round balls.
6. Take one at a time; flatten it between your palms and pinch about 1 cm/½ in of the edge all around, leaving the centre thicker. Place a little of the filling in the centre and bring the edges together, covering the filling completely. Press together to seal and smoothen by rolling between your palms. Press to flatten into round patties about ½ cm/¼ in thick.
7. Heat enough ghee in a heavy-based frying pan to form a thin layer. Fry patties over low heat, first on one side and then the other, till crisp and brown. Add ghee as and when required.
8. Serve hot with green chutney (p 134) or with Sonth ki Chutney (p 134).

༄༅༄༅༄༅༄

PHAL KI CHAAT

*(Fruit chaat—a mixture of fruit spiced
with masala and lemon.)*

INGREDIENTS

A mixture of fruit of your choice, peeled and diced
Chaat masala (p 149)
Sour lime juice
Chilli powder
Roasted and powdered jeera (cumin seeds)
Salt
Finely chopped green chillies
Chopped hara dhania (coriander leaves)

METHOD

Mix the diced fruit together, adding spices depending on how
strong you want it to taste, and serve.

Note: Some like to add ginger too.

SHAKARKANDI KI CHAAT: Boil, peel and cube the shakarkandi (sweet potato), and mix with the above spices.

ALOO KI CHAAT: Boil, peel and cube the potato and mix
with the above spices.

ALOO-MATAR KI CHAAT: Use boiled and fried potatoes
and boiled peas and mix with the above spices.

Relishes

These include chutneys and kass (grated vegetables) of various kinds. This is a regular accompaniment to an Indian meal, and more so in U.P. Chutneys change according to the season, and are best had within 3–4 days (refrigerated during the summer months) of their being made.

CACHOOMBER

(A tangy salad which goes especially well with biryani or a meat dish.)

INGREDIENTS

1	cup	(200 g) **tomatoes,** de-seeded and diced small
1	cup	(200 g) **cucumbers,** diced small to match the tomatoes
1	cup	(200 g) **onions,** diced small

Salt to taste
¼ tsp kali mirch (black pepper)
2 tsp jeera (cumin seeds) roasted and powdered
2 tbsp hara dhania (coriander leaves) chopped
2 tsp green chillies finely chopped (or to taste)
¼ tsp chilli powder
1 tbsp lemon/lime juice

METHOD

Mix all the ingredients together and serve.

KARAUNDE KI CHUTNEY

(A sauted chutney made with Carissa carandas and green chilli, which can be refrigerated for 3–4 days. This has a very short-lived season. One of my favourite combinations with this is Dhuli Urad ki Daal p 17 and Rote p 89.)

INGREDIENTS

1½ cups (200 g) **karaunda (Carissa carandas)**
2 tbsp sarson ka tel (mustard oil)
1 tsp jeera (cumin seeds)
½ tsp kalonji (onion seeds)
¼ tsp heeng (asafoetida)
1 tsp saunf (fennel seeds)
Salt to taste
2 tbsp thickly chopped green chillies

METHOD

1. Wash and cut the *Carissa carandas* lengthwise into halves and remove the seeds imbedded in both halves. (They make the dish very bitter if not removed.)

2. Heat the oil in a heavy-based pan, and when the strong fragrance of mustard oil fills the air, add the cumin seeds, onion seeds, asafoetida and fennel seeds.

3. When the seeds splutter, add the green chillies, *Carissa carandas* and salt, and stir-fry over high heat till vegetables look glossy.

4. Lower heat, cover and cook till tender. Serve hot or cold, as desired.

SONTH KI CHUTNEY

*(It is useful to make and keep this in the refrigerator
as it can be used for many dishes. It also lasts a long time.)*

INGREDIENTS

½	cup	(100 g) **imli (tamarind)** tightly packed, soaked in warm water for at least half an hour
¾	cup	(150 gms) **gur (jaggery)** broken up
2	tsp	salt
1	tsp	powdered kala namak (black rock salt)
½	tsp	garam masala I (p 148)
1	tsp	powdered sonth (dry ginger)
¼	tsp	kali mirch (powdered black pepper)
¼	tsp	chilli powder
1	tsp	chaat masala (p 149)
2	tbsp	raisins
		Sliced bananas

METHOD

1. Strain the tamarind through a sieve, adding water to make it easier.
2. Add enough water to the pulp to make it of pouring consistency.
3. Mix in the rest of the ingredients except the bananas and bring to boil. Lower heat and simmer, stirring occasionally, till it thickens a bit, and pours off a spoon in a smooth stream. Cool, add the bananas and serve.

HARA DHANIA CHUTNEY

*(A must at every table, especially with
vegetarian food; and a relish to accompany
kababs for the non-vegetarians.)*

INGREDIENTS

2	cups	(100 g) **hara dhania (coriander leaves)** cleaned and plucked
¼	cup	(40 g) chopped **green chillies,** or according to taste
2	tsp	salt
1	tbsp	nimbu (sour lime) juice

METHOD

Grind the coriander leaves and green chillies to a fine paste either in a food processor or on a grinding stone. Add the salt and lime juice, mix well and serve.

Note: Lime juice is generally substituted with raw mango when in season.

TIL ALOO KI CHUTNEY

*(A hot, tangy sesame-flavoured preparation that goes
well with pooris. Padma Chachiji, whose speciality it is,
was always requested to make it!)*

INGREDIENTS

500	g	**potatoes,** boiled, peeled and cut into 2½ cm/1 in cubes
¼	cup	**kala til (black sesame seeds),** soaked in water for 3–4 hours
10–12		green chillies (or according to taste), chopped not too fine
¼	cup	(60 g) sarson ka tel (mustard oil)
2	tbsp	salt
¼	cup	nimbu (sour lime) juice

METHOD

1. Strain the sesame seeds and grind coarsely.
2. Heat the oil in a heavy-based pan and add the ground sesame seeds and saute for a few seconds.
3. Add the green chillies and stir-fry 2–3 times; then add the potatoes and salt.
4. Mix well and stir-fry over high heat, till potatoes are coated with the sesame seeds. Lower heat, cover and cook for 3–4 minutes. Remove from stove and add the lime juice. This can be served hot or cold. It is better not to re-heat it, once the lime juice has been added.

PUDINE KI CHUTNEY

(The ever-refreshing mint made into a tangy relish to accompany many a meal!)

INGREDIENTS

100 g		fresh **pudina (mint leaves and tender stalks)**
1	cup	(125 g) **onions** coarsely chopped
1	tsp	roasted jeera (cumin seeds)
Salt to taste		
2	tbsp	chopped green chillies
2	tsp	sugar
¼	cup	(50 g) dahi (yogurt), beaten smooth

METHOD

1. Chop the tender stalks and the mint leaves roughly.
2. Grind all the ingredients together, except the yogurt, to form a smooth paste.
3. Mix the yogurt into the chutney and serve.

MOOLI KA KASS

(A combination of grated radish and lemon, extremely popular in some homes, when radish is in season.)

INGREDIENTS

250 g		**safed mooli (white radish)**
1	tbsp	chopped green chillies
1	tbsp	tender leaves of radish, very finely chopped
1	tsp	jeera (cumin seeds), roasted and powdered
Salt to taste		
2	tsp	lemon juice

METHOD

1. Peel/scrape the outer skin of the radish and grate.
2. Mix all the ingredients, and serve.

PYAAZ KA LACHCHA

(Spiced onion which goes well with a variety of foods.)

INGREDIENTS

2	large	(250 g) **onions,** peeled and sliced thin, lengthwise
Salt to taste		
2	tsp	lemon juice
1	tbsp	chopped hara dhania (coriander leaves)
1	tsp	finely chopped green chillies

METHOD

Mix all the ingredients together and transfer to a serving dish.

PYAAZ-PUDINE KA LACHCHA: Add ¼ cup finely chopped pudina (mint leaves) to the Pyaaz ka Lachcha (above).

ADRAK KA KASS

(A relish made from fresh grated ginger and lemon.)

INGREDIENTS

1 cup   (200 g) fresh **green ginger,** shredded
1 tsp   salt
2 tsp   lemon juice

METHOD

1. Scrape the skin off the ginger and wash well.
2. Slice ginger thinly along width, then slice further into shreds as thin as possible.
3. Add the salt and lemon juice and mix well. If ginger is tender it will turn a light pink as soon as lemon juice is added.

Note: This keeps well for 2–3 days in the refrigerator, but is best made fresh.

DANA METHI KI CHUTNEY

(This chutney is made by cooking various ingredients together. A ready mix is now available for sale in some places, to be cooked in plenty of water. Especially good with Bedvin/Aloo p 96.)

INGREDIENTS

1 cup   (50 g) loosely packed **sabut amchoor (dried mango)**
¾ cup   (50 g) loosely packed kachri (p 8)
¼ cup   (15 g) sabut dhania (coriander seeds)
2 tbsp   (15 g) saunf (fennel seeds)
¼ cup   (25 g) methi dana (fenugreek seeds)
1 tbsp   haldi (turmeric)
2 tbsp   (10 g) chilli powder
2 tbsp   salt
½ tsp   heeng (asafoetida)
Approx 3 cups water

METHOD

1. In a heavy-based saucepan, bring the water to boil and add all the ingredients.
2. Bring once more to boil; then simmer till all the spices are soft, and a very thick gravy is formed. Add more water if required.
3. This can be made and stored in a refrigerator for a couple of weeks.

Pickles

In the past, pickle-making was quite a social activity. Neighbours and friends got together, brought their own ingredients with them, and made their pickles while gossiping. The ingredients have to be picked and cleaned of stones and mud. In my experience it is well worth buying the ingredients from a source that may be a little more expensive, but is clean and provides better quality goods. Today, fewer housewives make pickles at home, and do so more out of necessity than as a social event. As children, my sisters and I were always roped in to help with the preparing of the ingredients for the pickles, and we always tried to disappear when we saw the first signs of pickle-making!

Do not compromise on the quality of ingredients; avoid turning pickle-making into a chore. Good quality products will make the experience enjoyable and the end product much tastier too!

Another point to note is that, though sunning is an important aspect of making pickles, it does not follow that you cannot make pickles or that your pickles will spoil if there is no sun. The sun helps mature the pickles with its heat. Without sunshine the pickle will only take a little longer to mature. In cold countries where the sun is not very strong, it helps to keep the jar of pickle near a heater.

Here are some points to help you preserve your pickles:

1. The utensils should all be clean and dry and the storage jar sterilised.

2. The ingredients should be clean and of good quality.

3. The pickle should be always covered with oil or lemon juice, as the case may be, except for the dry pickles, to ensure that it does not spoil.

4. Pickles should be stored in a dry and clean place.

5. The jar should be airtight and whenever you take some pickle out, do so with a clean and dry spoon, and keep the jar clean.

If you adhere to all these rules, your pickles should last you a year or longer.

LAL MIRCH KA BENARSI ACHAAR

*(A speciality of Varanasi, made
with the large red peppers
available in winter.)*

INGREDIENTS

50–60	(1 kg)	**taazi moti lal mirch (pimentos)**
1¾ cup	(250 g)	amchoor (mango powder)
2½ cup	(250 g)	rai (mustard seeds) powdered
1¼ cup	(125 g)	methi dana (fenugreek seeds) powdered
1 cup	(125 g)	saunf (fennel seeds) powdered
1½ tsp	(5–6 g)	heeng (asafoetida) as strength of flavour varies, add to taste
1 cup	(180 g)	salt
½ cup	(40 g)	haldi (turmeric)
4 cups	(1 kg)	sarson ka tel (mustard oil)

A sterilised container with a lid

METHOD

1. Remove the stalks of the pimentos cutting around base of stalk, thus creating an opening to fill the peppers.

2. Mix together everything except the oil and red peppers. Add ¼ cup of the oil and rub into mixture. Stuff mixture into pimentos, pressing the filling in firmly so that each is tightly stuffed.

3. Dip each pimento into the oil and place in the container, one by one. Pour the remaining oil over to cover the pimentos. Sun for about a week.

KATHAL KA ACHAAR

*(Quite a typical pickle of the U.P.
area, this is made of jackfruit.
The recipe I share with you
is my mother-in-law's.)*

INGREDIENTS

3	kg	**kathal (jackfruit)** peeled and cut into chunks* (about 2¼ kg remains after peeling)
¼	cup	salt for the water
1¼	cup	(250 g) salt
1	cup	(75 g) haldi (turmeric)
2½	cups	(250 g) rai (mustard seeds) powdered
1	cup	(90 g) lal mirch (red chilli) coarsely ground
2	tbsp	(10 g) kalonji (onion seeds)
2	tsp	heeng (asafoetida)
2	kg	sarson ka tel (mustard oil)

METHOD

1. In a large saucepan, boil enough water to take in the jackfruit. Add ¼ cup salt to it. When it boils, add the jackfruit and bring to boil again. Then, shut off heat, drain out water and leave in a colander for the water to dry up. You might have to pat it dry.

2. When cool and dry, mix in the 1¼ cup salt, mustard powder, chilli powder, onion seeds and asafoetida. Mix well (your hand is the most effective for this!).

3. Keep thus for 3–4 days in a covered saucepan, stirring once a day, till it gets moist. Pack this tightly into a sterilised jar. Heat the oil till the aroma is very strong and starts to smart the eyes. Cool to room temperature and pour over the jackfruit. The oil should come above jackfruit mixture.

4. Leave pickle to mature for another 2–3 days before serving. Like with all pickles, see that it stays covered with oil to ensure that it lasts through the year.

* The chunks are usually big enough so that the seeds are imbedded in them. In some places you can request the vegetable vendor to peel and cut it for you. If you have to cut it yourself, keep your palms greased as jackfruits are very sticky when cut.

HARI MIRCH KA ACHAAR

*(A simple pickle made with the normal
green chillies used in everyday cooking.)*

INGREDIENTS

250 g		**green chillies** (slightly plump and light ones, not the tight and thin ones)
¼	cup	(50 g) salt
¼	cup	(25 g) rai (mustard seeds) powdered
1	cup	lemon juice
A sterilised jar		

METHOD

1. Wash and wipe the green chillies and slit them to make space for a filling.

2. Mix the salt and mustard and fill into the green chillies.

3. Place chillies in the jar and pour the lemon juice over them. Sun for 3–4 days, before eating.

❊❊❊❊❊

HARI MIRCH AUR NIMBU KA ACHAAR

(This pickle is made of large green peppers and lemon juice. I learnt this receipe from my mother-in-law, who was very proud of her pickles and distributed them generously!)

INGREDIENTS

1	kg	large **green peppers (capsicum),** washed and wiped dry
8–10	**nimbu (sour limes),** cut into small pieces	
4	cups	lemon juice
1½	cups	(300 g) salt
¾	cup	(75 g) saunf (fennel seeds), powdered coarsely
¾	cup	(75 g) rai (mustard seeds) powdered
½	cup	(40 g) haldi (turmeric)
2	tbsp	(10 g) kalonji (onion seeds)
¼	cup	(50 g) methi daana (fenugreek seeds)
1	tbsp	heeng (asafoetida)
1	cup	(240 g) vegetable oil

} roasted and powdered fine

METHOD

1. Slit the capsicums lengthwise on one side, snipping a little on the base of the stem (to ease filling).

2. Mix together ¾ cup salt, the powdered fennel and mustard seeds, turmeric, onion seeds, fenugreek seeds and asafoetida. Mix in ¼ cup each of lemon juice and oil.

3. Fill capsicums with spice mixture by pressing in firmly. Mix the lemon pieces into the rest of the salt. Fill a sterilised airtight jar with alternate layers of capsicums and lemons, pressing tightly to pack.

4. Pour remaining lemon juice over capsicums and lemons and leave thus for 3–4 days.

5. After 3–4 days, heat the rest of the oil, cool to room temperature and pour into jar. This pickle can be served right away if you like the capsicum crunchy. If preferred soft, wait 10–15 days before serving. Keep capsicums covered with oil, to prevent them from spoiling.

❊❊❊❊❊

AAM KA ACHAAR I

(Mango pickle made with oil that has been heated and cooled. The subtle difference between this and the pickle described next is quite obvious when the pickle is eaten.)

INGREDIENTS

5	kg	**raw mangoes,** cut into pieces of desired size
2	kg	sarson ka tel (mustard oil)
1	tbsp	heeng (asafoetida)
3	cups	(600 g) salt
1¼	cup	(100 g) haldi (turmeric)
1¼	cup	(100 g) lal mirch (red chilli) coarsely ground
4	cups	(100 g) loosely packed, sabut lal mirch (whole, dried red chillies), optional
2	cups	(200 g) saunf (fennel seeds), coarsely ground
1½	cup	(200 g) methi dana (fenugreek seeds), coarsely ground
1½	cup	(125 g) kalonji (onion seeds)

METHOD

1. Heat the oil till the aroma is strong and begins to smart your eyes.

2. Add the asafoetida to the oil; then add the turmeric, coarsely ground red chillies, whole red chillies, fennel seeds, fenugreek seeds and onion seeds and mix well.

3. Take saucepan off heat and mix in the mango pieces and salt.

4. When mixture is cool, pack into a sterilised jar, and store. This pickle can be served after a couple of days. Keep pieces in jar covered with a layer of oil while in storage, to prevent spoiling.

AAM KA ACHAAR II

*(This is made with unheated mustard oil and whole spices.
I prefer this pickle to the one described earlier!)*

INGREDIENTS

5	kg	**raw mangoes,** washed, wiped clean, and cut into pieces of desired size pieces
1½	cup	(200 g) methi dana (fenugreek seeds)
1¼	cup	(100 g) lal mirch (red chillies) coarsely ground
1½	cup	(125g) kalonji (onion seeds)
2	cup	(200 g) saunf (fennel seeds)
¼	cup	sabut kali mirch (peppercorns)
1¼	cup	(100 g) haldi (turmeric)
3	cups	(600 g) salt
4	cups	(100 g) loosely packed, whole, dried red chillies
3	kg	sarson ka tel (mustard oil)

A sterlised airtight jar

METHOD

1. Add about a cup of oil to the spice mixture and mix well.

2. Sprinkle a little of this mixture into the jar. Put some pieces of mango into the spice mixture and rub well to coat mango pieces with mixture. Put mango pieces in a layer over the mixture. Cover this layer with some more spice mixture. Repeat till mango pieces and spices are

used up. The final layer must be of spices (sprinkle whatever is left over the surface).

3. Cover jar with lid and place in the sun for 2–3 days, shaking it 2–3 times a day to mix well.

4. On the fourth day, add the rest of the oil to cover contents of jar, adding more if contents are not covered. Sun for another 3–4 days, then store. By now, it is ready to serve, though it gets even more tender after a month or so.

AAM KI CHUTNEY

*(A simple sweet and sour pickle made with grated
mangoes and sugar, and matured in the sun.
The alternative is to cook the sugar to a syrup,
but the traditional and convenient way is to
sun it—provided you have enough sun!)*

INGREDIENTS

1	kg	**raw mangoes,** peeled and grated
4	cups	(1 kg) sugar, or according to taste
¾	cup	(150 g) salt
¼	cup	(20 g) chilli powder
1	tbsp	sabut kali mirch (peppercorns)
2		tej patta (bay leaves)
1	tsp	heeng (asafoetida) } powdered
1	tbsp	laung (cloves)

An airtight sterilised jar

METHOD

1. In a steel or a glass bowl, mix in the grated mango and sugar. Tie with a piece of muslin or thin cloth and keep in the sun, stirring twice a day for about 4 days.

2. Mix in the salt, chilli powder, peppercorns and powdered garam masala and continue sunning till the sugar dissolves. (It may take 4 days to a week, depending on how strong the sun is.)
3. Transfer into a sterilised jar and store.

KABULI CHANNA AUR AAM KA ACHAAR

(An interesting combination of chickpeas and grated mangoes, which I learnt from Aruna Bhabhi.)

INGREDIENTS

¾ kg **kabuli channa (chickpeas),** soaked overnight in water with ¼ cup salt added to it
2 kg **raw mangoes,** peeled and grated
1¼ cup (250 g) salt
½ cup (40 g) haldi (turmeric)
1 tbsp heeng (asafoetida)
4 cups (1 kg) sarson ka tel (mustard oil)
A sterilised jar

METHOD

1. Remove the chickpeas from the water and spread out on a piece of cloth to dry. Discard the water.
2. When the chickpeas dry out, mix in the rest of the ingredients, transfer into jar and sun for 3–4 days. It is ready to serve after this.

AAM KA SOOKHA ACHAAR

(An oil-less pickle which not only tastes good, but is convenient for packed lunches too. I learnt this from Alka whose grandmother packed many dinners for us with this over the years!)

INGREDIENTS

5 kg **raw mangoes,** cut into pieces of desired size, with stones removed
3 cups (600 g) salt
1½ cup (200 g) methi dana (fenugreek seeds) coarsely ground
1¼ cup (100 g) lal mirch (red chillies) coarsely ground
1¼ cup (125 g) kalonji (onion seeds)
2 cup (200 g) saunf (fennel seeds) coarsely ground
1¼ cup (100 g) haldi (turmeric)
A sterilised jar

METHOD

1. Mix the salt into the mangoes and keep overnight in a steel or a glass bowl.
2. The following day, squeeze liquid out of mangoes, and set aside till ready to use. Spread mangoes out in the sun to dry (this may take 2–3 days, depending on how strong the sun is).
3. Mix the rest of the ingredients into liquid set aside and then into the dried mangoes. Transfer into sterilised jar and sun for 5–6 days.

NIMBU KA ACHAAR GARAM MASALEWALA

*(Spicey pickled sour lime stays good for years,
and sometimes dries out over time. It is a
good cure for flatulence or nausea.)*

INGREDIENTS

1   kg   **nimbu (sour limes),** washed and wiped dry
1¼ cup   (250 g) salt

Powder together:

¼   cup   roasted jeera (cumin seeds)
¼   cup   (60 g) sugar
2   tbsp   sonth (dried ginger)
2   tbsp   ajwain (thymol seeds) roasted
1   tbsp   badi elaichi (black cardamom) seeds
1   tbsp   laung (cloves)
1   tbsp   dalchini (cinnamon)
2–3 tej patta (bay leaves)
¼   cup   (50 g) kala namak (black rock salt)
1   tbsp   sabut kali mirch (peppercorns)
½   a jaiphal (nutmeg)
6–7 blades of javitri (mace)
2   tsp   heeng (asafoetida) roasted

METHOD

1. Make cuts at right angles to each other along the length of the limes. Make sure to leave them joined at just the ends, so that they do not fall apart.

2. Pack as tightly as possible, the mixed spices into space created in lemons.

3. Place limes in jar and sprinkle any left over spice mixture over the top. Sun for about a month, shaking the jar 2–3 times a day, to mix well.

4. Leave to mature another 15 days or so, before serving.

Note: This is a pickle without oil. The lime juice and salt are the main preservatives. It keeps well for years, and continues to dry with age, but does not spoil. It also gets darker, so do not worry about changes in colour.

NIMBU KA SAADA ACHAAR

*(A simple pickle of sour limes, which can
also be made with lemons (gulguls). Lemons
take longer to mature and become tender.)*

INGREDIENTS

1   kg   **nimbu (sour limes),** washed, wiped dry and cut into quarters
1¼ cup   (250 g) salt
1   cup   (25 g) sabut lal mirch (whole, dried red chilli)
1   tsp   heeng (asafoetida)
¼   cup   (60 g) powdered sugar (optional)
A sterilised jar

METHOD

1. Mix all the ingredients together, rubbing them well into the pieces of limes.

2. Transfer into the jar and sun for a month or so.

Note: You could add some sliced ginger, if so desired.

BHINDI KA ACHAAR

*(I learnt this in Agra. A unique and tasty pickle,
it stays good only if covered with vinegar.)*

INGREDIENTS

1 kg   tender and green **bhindi (ladies' fingers)** of uniform size, washed and wiped dry

Mix together:

½ cup   (100 g) salt
1 tbsp   haldi (turmeric)
¼ cup   dhania (coriander powder)
2 tbsp   chilli powder
2 tbsp   jeera (cumin seeds) roasted and powdered
5 cups   (1200 g) vinegar mixed with 2 tbsp salt
A sterilised jar
Some string

METHOD

1. Cut off the top of the ladies' fingers and slit length-wise on one side, to make an opening.
2. Add a little vinegar into the ingredients mixed together, to dampen. Stuff into the ladies' fingers and tie each with a string, to keep the filling intact.
3. Layer the ladies' fingers in jar, pour vinegar over them to cover, and sun for 3–4 days. Let them mature for a week before serving.

KARELE KA ACHAAR

*(Made of bitter gourd, this is a delicious pickle.
Make sure the vegetables stay covered with
the lemon juice to avoid spoiling.)*

INGREDIENTS

1 kg   **karela (bitter gourd)** of uniform size
2 tbsp   salt

Mix together for masala

¾ cup   (150 g) salt
1 tbsp   haldi (turmeric)
1 tbsp   sonth (ginger powder)
¼ cup   (40 g) chilli powder
¼ cup   ajwain (thymol seeds) roasted and powdered
2 tbsp   saunf (fennel seeds) roasted and coarsely pounded
2 cups   lemon juice
A sterilised jar
Some string

METHOD

1. Scrape off the rough surface of the bitter gourd, slit lengthwise on one side, rub all over with salt and set aside for 3–4 hours.
2. Squeeze bitter gourds to rid them of the juices, scoop out seeds, wash and squeeze again.
3. Mix a little bit of the lemon juice into the masala to dampen it, then stuff filling firmly into the bitter gourds and tie each one to secure filling.
4. Place stuffed bitter gourds neatly in sterilised jar and pour enough lemon juice to cover.
5. Sun for 3–4 days and mature for a week before serving.

SEM ALOO KA ACHAAR

(This is made with potatoes and broad beans, preferably the lighter ones. A seasonal pickle, it keeps for only 2–3 weeks. This is a basic recipe and can be used for pickling different vegetables.)

INGREDIENTS

1	kg	**potatoes,** boiled and diced
1	kg	**sem (broad beans),** washed
1	tbsp	turmeric powder
¼	cup	(45 g) salt
½	cup	(40 g) rai (mustard seeds) powdered
2	tsp	chilli powder
1	cup	(240 g) sarson ka tel (mustard oil)

A sterilised jar

METHOD

1. Fill a pan with enough water to cook the beans. Add 1 teaspoon turmeric and set to boil. When it comes to boil, add the beans, blanch for a minute, then drain and leave in a colander for all the water to dry out. Spread beans out on cloth, to ensure that they dry out.

2. String beans and split them apart.

3. Mix all the ingredients together and place in the jar. Sun for 3–4 days, before serving. This has a shelf life of 3–4 week'.

Note: You can make the following pickles in the same manner:

GOBHI GAJAR KA ACHAAR: Combine cauliflower, carrots and shelled peas, blanch and add the same masalas. This is a winter pickle.

KAMRAKH KA ACHAAR: Chop kamrakh (star fruit) and proceed as above without blanching.

ALOO KA ACHAAR: Made only with boiled potatoes.

Some Popular Beverages

The beverages in this section are typical of the U.P. region. Most of them are everyday drinks in homes, but there are also some places in various towns where they are known to be especially good. Besides these, there are also sherbets of various flavours, which one rarely ventures to make at home now, but are extremely refreshing in the summer months. In many case, the bottled drink has replaced old favourites—a pity as these beverages are natural and refreshing.

MEETHI LASSI

INGREDIENTS (MAKES 2 GLASSES)

1	cup	(200 g) **dahi (plain yogurt)**
1	cup	crushed ice
¼	cup	(60 g) sugar (or to taste)
2	tsp	gulab jal (rose water)

METHOD

Blend ingredients in a blender. Fill in tall glasses and serve. The flavour can be varied according to taste. Many people like it topped with a layer of clotted cream.

NAMKEEN LASSI

INGREDIENTS (MAKES 2 GLASSES)

1	cup	(200 g) **dahi (plain yogurt)**
1	cup	crushed ice
1	tsp	salt (or to taste)
⅛	tsp	black pepper
1	tsp	jeera (cumin seeds) roasted and powdered

METHOD

Blend ingredients in a blender. Fill in tall glasses and serve. You can add chopped coriander leaves or other flavours, if you so desire. This too can be served topped with a layer of clotted cream.

AMIYA KA PANNA

INGREDIENTS (MAKES 5–6 GLASSES)

500	g	**kairi/amiya (green mangoes)**
½	cup	(120 g) sugar
2	tsp	salt
2	tsp	kala namak (black rock salt)
2	tsp	jeera (cumin seeds) roasted and powdered
2	tbsp	pudina (mint leaves) finely chopped
2	cups	water

METHOD

1. Boil the mangoes till they are soft inside, and the skin is discoloured.

2. When cool enough to handle, remove skin and squeeze pulp out of the mangoes.

3. Add all the dry ingredients to the pulp. Add 2 cups of water and blend.

4. Pour into glasses and serve with ice.

THANDAI

(I call this a very 'Holi' drink, because one associates thandai with bhang and thus with the festival of Holi! It is also had at other times, though. Holi implies the beginning of summer, and this is a drink that can be had right through the hot summer months.)

INGREDIENTS

¼   cup   (25 g) **khus khus (poppy seeds)**
½   cup   (40 g) magaz (melon seeds) dried and peeled
¼   cup   (25 g) blanched almonds
2   tbsp   saunf (fennel seeds)
2   tbsp   dried red rose petals
1½ tsp   sabut kali mirch (peppercorns)
1   cup   water
½   cup   (120 g) milk
½   cup   (120 g) sugar
A few rose petals, for garnishing

METHOD

1. Soak the poppy seeds, melon seeds, fennel seeds, rose petals and peppercorns in the water for 2–3 hours.

2. Finely blend the almonds, milk and sugar together in a blender.

3. Blend or grind the soaked ingredients very fine and strain through a cloth, adding water if necessary.

4. Mix the milk and strained mixture together and pour over crushed ice. Serve garnished with the rose petals.

KANJI

(A spicy and tangy appetiser, made with ground mustard seeds. The one made from carrots is the most popular, but other vegetables can also be used. This is a seasonal drink enjoyed on cold winter afternoons, while you sit in the warm sun.)

INGREDIENTS

250 g   **kaali gajar (carrots,** preferably the dark variety)
6   cups   water
3   tbsp   rai (mustard seeds) powdered
2   tbsp   salt

METHOD

1. Peel and cut the carrots to finger-size or 7 cm/3 in length.

2. Boil the water and add the carrots to it. When water boils again, shut off heat and leave to cool.

3. Add the salt and ground mustard, transfer into jar with lid. Mature in the sun for about 3–4 days. Take out of sun once taste of mustard is strong enough.

4. Serve before meals with the pieces of carrot in it or on the side. (The carrots make a good cocktail snack.)

Note: Potatoes can be used instead of carrots. These should, of course, be cooked till almost tender. Alternatively, they can be boiled separately and added to the boiled water later. Fried Moong Daal Pakories (p 130), can also be substituted, in which case the water must be boiled separately, and the pakories added as soon as the heat is shut off.

AAM RASS

(A popular seasonal drink made from fresh, ripe mangoes, this can be had at any time of the day or with a meal.)

INGREDIENTS (MAKES 4 GLASSES)

1	kg	fresh, **ripe mangoes**
1	cup	(250 g) sugar, or to taste
1	cup	(240 g) cold milk
Crushed ice		

METHOD

1. Peel and chop the mangoes and blend in a food processor together with the sugar. Alternatively, squeeze out juice from mangoes, by hand, and dissolve sugar in it. If squeezed with hand, the juice might have to be strained.

2. Mix in the milk and pour into glasses quarter-filled with crushed ice.

Note: The proportion of milk added can be varied to taste.

Basic Recipes

This chapter is devoted to recipes for masalas and other items which are used for further cooking.

MASALAS

It is important to remember that masalas are best powdered as and when required. This is conveniently done if you have a coffee grinder at hand. Most people, of course, prefer to make their combinations and store them for ready use. This is certainly the more practical way out and so, I list below, the recipes for the different kinds of masalas. These too, vary from house to house. There are also several packaged masalas available. Using these is the easiest way out. Nevertheless, for the enterprising person, I have here a few of the popular masalas to be made and kept. They can be adjusted to suit your taste, if you so desire. I can assure you that it is worth the effort to make them!

GARAM MASALA I

(This is a basic combination of spices which has the ingredients used in almost all recipes.)

INGREDIENTS

150 g jeera (cumin seeds)
50 g badi elaichi (black cardamoms), seeds only, (wt before peeling)
25 g dalchini (cinnamon)
25 g laung (cloves)
25 g sabut kali mirch (peppercorns)
4 tej patta (bay leaves)

METHOD

Sun all ingredients or place them over an oven (so that the gentle heat works on them, while you have something baking), to rid them of any moisture. Then grind to a powder in a food processor, or, with a mortar and pestle. Store in an airtight jar.

GARAM MASALA II

(Another version of garam masala, this is distinctive of the area.)

INGREDIENTS

150 g jeera (cumin seeds)
25 g badi elaichi (black cardamoms), seeds only (wt before peeling)
20 g chhoti elaichi (green cardamom)
15 g dalchini (cinnamon)
25 g laung (cloves)
25 g sabut kali mirch (black peppercorns)
4 tej patta (bay leaves)
1 jaiphal (nutmeg)
8–10 blades javitri (mace)

METHOD

Follow the same method as described for Garam Masala I.

GARAM MASALA III

*(Used mostly in the cooking of meat,
but can, of course, be mixed and matched
with vegetables according to taste.)*

INGREDIENTS

50	g	badi elaichi (black cardamoms), seeds only, (wt before peeling)
25	g	sabut kali mirch (peppercorns)
25	g	laung (cloves)
100	g	dhania (coriander seeds), roasted
100	g	roasted jeera (cumin seeds)
50	g	khus khus (poppy seeds), roasted

METHOD

Follow the same method as described for Garam Masala I (p 148).

༺་ཥ༈་ཥ༈་ཥ༈་ཥ༈

CHAAT KA MASALA

(The combination of spices can be increased or decreased according to taste. Packets of these can be bought ready-made, but for your own special flavour, go right ahead and make it!)

INGREDIENTS

100	g	(1½ cups) sabut dhania (coriander seeds)
200	g	(2 cups) jeera (cumin seeds)
75	g	(¾ cup) ajwain (thymol seeds)
150	g	(1 cup + 2 tbsp) amchoor (mango powder)
10	g	(2 tbsp) garam masala I (p 148)
300	g	(1½ cups) powdered kala namak (black rock salt)
20	g	(2 tbsp) kali mirch (powdered black pepper)

40	g	(¼ cup) nimbu ka sat (citric acid)
50	g	(½ cup) dried and powdered pudina (mint) leaves

METHOD

1. Roast the coriander, cumin and thymol seeds in a heavy-based pan till dark brown. Remove from pan and leave to cool.
2. Put all the ingredients together and powder fine, in a processor or with a mortar and pestle.
3. Store in an airtight jar.

༺་ཥ༈་ཥ༈་ཥ༈་ཥ༈

PANCH PHORAN KA MASALA

(A combination of five different kinds of spices, mixed and kept whole, and used to temper some vegetables or lentils as suggested by my friend Minni. Especially good for bitter gourd, round gourd, etc. And try it with Bengal gram for a flavour of Bengal in Allahabad!)

INGREDIENTS

25	g	jeera (cumin seeds)
25	g	sarson (mustard seeds)
25	g	methi dana (fenugreek seeds)
25	g	saunf (fennel seeds)
25	g	kalonji (onion seeds)

METHOD

Mix the ingredients together and store in an airtight container.

༺་ཥ༈་ཥ༈་ཥ༈་ཥ༈

BLANCHED ALMONDS

Bring water to a boil, put almonds in it and shut off heat. Leave for 15–20 minutes, drain water and peel.

KHOYA

(Khoya is actually condensed milk. It is used a lot in Indian dishes, especially sweets. Making khoya literally involves cooking the milk till only the solids remain.)

Points about khoya:

1. It can be bought in the market.
2. Dhaap ka Khoya, is smooth and slightly darker in colour. It is used to make gulab jamuns, barfees, etc.
3. Daanedaar Khoya is used to make kalakand, halwa, etc.
4. A kg of milk yields 250 g of Khoya.

INGREDIENTS

1 kg full cream milk
A kadahi which has a capacity of at least four times the quantity of khoya to be made

METHOD

1. Bring the milk to boil in the kadahi and then simmer over low heat.
2. Stir to avoid scorching till the milk thickens and collects together in a solid mass.

GHEE

(Also called clarified butter, as the procedure entails clarifying.)

Place 2 cups (500 g) unsalted butter in a pan over low heat. When it melts, increase heat till butter begins to foam, stir once and lower heat. Simmer till solids settle to bottom (and turn light brown) and liquid on top is transparent. Takes 30–40 minutes, though time depends on water content in the butter. Drain the transparent liquid through a fine muslin into a clean jar, while it is still warm. Make sure the sediment is not disturbed. The solids can be discarded, though in some homes they add semolina or wheat flour to it and make it into savoury dish or a sweet like a halwa.

PANEER

(More a favourite in Punjabi households, paneer is gradually becoming popular in U.P. too. I always prefer making it at home, because it tastes the best.)

INGREDIENTS (MAKES 150 G/5 OZ)

5 cups (1 kg) full cream milk
2 tbsp nimbu sour lime juice or 1 tsp citric acid dissolved in ¼ cup water

METHOD

Boil the milk, lower heat and add lime juice or citric acid water solution, stirring till milk begins to curdle. When the whey is clear, stop adding the solution, shut off heat and leave for about 5 minutes. Drain curdled milk through a cloth or colander and leave to set for an hour or so. The

whey left behind is very nutritious and can be used for gravies, rice, lentils, etc.

URAD DAAL KI BADI

(Dried and stored, these are made from black gram.)

INGREDIENTS (MAKES ABOUT 1½–2 KG)

6   cups (1 kg) **dhuli urad ki daal (split black gram)** soaked for 5–6 hours

1½ tsp (5–6 g) heeng (asafoetida) strength of flavour varies, so use according to taste

6   tbsp (30 g) lal mirch (red chillies) coarsely ground

Thin cloth on which you will make the badis and leave to dry

METHOD

1. Rub the lentils and wash off skin. Grind to a fine paste on a grinding stone or in a food processor. Leave to ferment till light and airy. Takes 6–7 hours in warm weather and 10–12 hours in cold weather.

2. Soak the asafoetida in a little water to dissolve.

3. Beat the ground lentils till fluffy, and add the asafoetida and chilli powder to it.

4. Badis—keep a bowl of water handy, as you might have to wet your hands every time you take in a fresh lot of batter. Dip your hand in water, and drop the equivalent of about 2 tablespoonfuls of batter, at a time, on to the cloth till all the batter is used.

5. The badis have to be left to dry out in the sun. When the top seems quite dry, try to pull off a badi. If it comes clean off the cloth, turn the cloth over, so that the under-side is exposed to the sun—the badis will now be under the cloth (this is why it is necessary to have a thin cloth).

6. Only 1–2 days of drying will still be required. When dry, pull all the badis off the cloth, pack them in polythene bags, seal and store.

Note: Drying time will depend on the temperature and dryness of the atmosphere. You will have to judge that for yourself. To be absolutely sure, break a badi to check that it is dry inside. If not completely dry, they will spoil soon. Some people add grated ash gourd and other spices to the mixture.

MANGAURI/MOONG DAAL KI BADI

(These badis are made from green gram.)

INGREDIENTS (MAKES ABOUT 1½ KG)

6   cups (1 kg) **dhuli hui moong ki daal (split green gram)**

1½ tsp (5–6 g) heeng (asafoetida) strength varies, so use to taste

2   tbsp (10 g) lal mirch (red chillies) coarsely ground

¼   cup (30 g) jeera (cumin seeds), pounded coarsely

Select a place to spread a thin cloth, on which you will shape the badis and leave till dry.

METHOD

Proceed as for Urad Daal ki Badi folding in the spices after beating the lentils till fluffy. But drop equivalent of 2 teaspoonfuls of batter instead of tablespoonfuls.

Festival Foods

All over India, every one looks forward to festivals and the celebrations associated with them. U.P. too has its favourite festivals when special foods are cooked and different kinds of rituals are performed. I will touch on only the most important ones for their typical food: Holi, Janmashtami, Diwali and Eid.

HOLI

Holi is the festival of colour. It signifies the end of winter and the onset of summer. The change of season from that day on is remarkable, and intriguing. Even a few days before Holi, the weather is still quite cool and the thought of playing with water-based colour makes one shudder! Often, it is only on the day before Holi that there is a sudden increase in temperature. The sun gets so hot, that the water thrown brings a welcome respite. As people visit each other on this day, food is an important part of the festival.

The traditional food items made during this festival are:

GUNJIYA: p 117. served as a sweet snack when people visit.

KHASTA KACHAURI: p 126, a savoury snack.

SOOKHE KOFTE: p 70. also a Kayasth delicacy.

BHAANG KI PAKORI: p 130, various pakoras to the batter of which bhang (cannabis) is added. The cannabis leaves are ground to a paste, strained through a fine muslin and added, so that its presence is not obvious and people can be fooled into having it.

PAAPRI: p 127, a savoury snack made of besan (chickpea/gram flour) which is quite labourious to make. For this reason it is often bought (like most things are today).

THANDAI: p 146, a must for this occasion, when it is spiked with bhang like the pakoras.

KULFI: p 114, also spiked with bhang in many homes.

MATHI: p 129.

BHUNI KALEJI: p 64, made in Kayasth homes at Holi.

JANMASHATAMI

Celebrating the birth of the god Krishna, people fast all day and generally eat at midnight. In many homes such as mine, the fast is broken at about 3 p.m., because it is not easy for everyone to fast all day! The fast is traditionally broken with only specific, non-cereal foods, which are called Phalahaar. For instance, Singhare ka Aata made from dried singhara (water chestnuts), and Kootoo ka Aata and Senda Namak for salt. The ingredients that are taboo are, ordinary salt, turmeric, garam masala and coriander. Here is a simple menu for this occasion:

MENU FOR JANAMASHTAMI

- Kootoo ke Dahi Bade
- Aloo Rasedaar Vratwale
- Arbi ki Sabzi
- Kaddu ki Pakori/Aloo ki Pakori
- Kootoo ke Paranthe/Poori
- Makhane ki Kheer (p 111)

KOOTOO KE DAHI BADE

(Since lentils are taboo, flour made of water chestnuts provides an excellent alternative.)

INGREDIENTS

Batter:

1	cup	(120 g) **kootoo ka aata**
1	cup	(120 g) **singhare ka aata (water chestnuts flour)**
¼	kg	**arbi (colacasia)** boiled, peeled and mashed
1	tsp	senda namak (rock salt)

Water to make the batter
Oil for frying

Sauce:

2½	cups	(500 g) **dahi (yogurt)** beaten smooth
2	tsp	senda namak (rock salt) powdered
2	tsp	jeera (cumin seeds) roasted and powdered
½	tsp	chilli powder
1	tsp	kala namak (black rock salt)
1	tbsp	hara dhania (coriander leaves) choppped
¼	tsp	kali mirch (black pepper) powdered

METHOD

Make dough as for Kootoo ke Paranthe (p 160), adding enough water to make it of dropping consistency. Fry like pakories in Dahi ki Pakories (p 32). Follow the rest of the recipe, making the yogurt sauce with the ingredients listed. Alternatively, the pakories can be made using only kootoo ka aata, by making it into a paste of dropping consistency and frying into pakories.

ALOO RASEDAAR VRATWALE

(Potatoes are always permitted, whatever the taboos.)

INGREDIENTS

500	g	**potatoes,** chopped into small pieces
¼	cup	(60 g) ghee
1	tsp	jeera (cumin seeds)
1	tbsp	finely shredded ginger
½	cup	(100 g) yogurt
½	tsp	sonth (ginger powder)
2	tsp	senda namak (rock salt) powdered
½	tsp	chilli powder

METHOD

1. Heat the ghee, add the cumin seeds and when they begin to splutter add the yogurt and stir-fry till the ghee separates.

2. Add the ginger powder, salt and chilli powder and stir a few times, till well mixed. Then add the potatoes and turn over high heat, till they look slightly fried.

3. Add about 2 cups water and bring to boil. Simmer uncovered for about 15 minutes, till tender. Serve hot with pokories made of kootoo ka aata.

ARBI KI SABZI

Similar to Aloo Rasedaar Vratwale (p 153). Substitute colacasia for the potatoes and the thymol seeds for cumin seeds. If you want a dry preparation, do not add water.

ALOO KI PAKORI

*(Made like ordinary pakories,
substituting permissable ingredients
for chickpea flour and salt.)*

INGREDIENTS

Batter:

1   cup   (120 g) **kootoo ka aata**
2   tsp   senda namak (rock salt)
½   tsp   chilli powder
Water (approx 2 cups)
250 g   **potatoes** peeled and chopped into slices of desired size
Ghee for deep-frying

METHOD

Follow the method for Pakories (p 130), using the ingredients listed above.

KOOTOO KE PARANTHE/
KOOTOO KI POORI

(The staple bread eaten during a fast or vrat.)

INGREDIENTS

1   cup   (120 g) **kootoo ka aata**
1   cup   (120 g) **singhare ka aata (water chestnut flour)**
¼   kg   **arbi (colacasia)** boiled, peeled and mashed
1   tsp   senda namak (rock salt)
Water to knead dough
Ghee for frying the paranthas
Dry flour for dusting

METHOD

1. Mix the two types of flour and the colacasia and knead with the water into a soft and pliable dough, as for Rote (p 89). Colacasia is added to bind the dough, and can be adjusted according to the desired consistency.

2. Cover dough and leave to rest for at least 30 minutes and proceed to make paranthas as for Saada Paranthas (p 93), or Poories (p 96).

MAKHANE KI KHEER: p 111.

CHIRONJI PAAK: p 116.

BEEJ KI BARFEE: p 115.

GOLE KI BARFEE: p 115.

DIWALI

As we all know Diwali signifies the return of Ram from exile. His return to Ayodhya is celebrated with lights, crackers and new clothes. Gifts and sweets are exchanged. Today, many of the traditional sweets are replaced with chocolates and pastries. Fortunately, there are still several homes where traditions are kept going. Let's have a look then, at these traditional food items.

The traditional items served are:

GUNJIYA: p 117.

KHASTA KACHAURI: p 126.

SAMOSAS: p 127.

BARFEE: pp 115–16.

MENU FOR DIWALI

- Aloo Rasedaar (p 37)
- Jimikand Ki Sabzi (p 39)
- Ghutti Hui Gobhi (p 31)
- Dahi Ki Pakori (p 32)
- Dana Methi Ki Chutney (p 136)
- Bedvin/Poorie (p 96)
- Chawal Ki Kheer (p 109)

MUTHIA KI SABZI

(I learnt this from Snehjiji in Agra. This is a typical delicacy and is a must in their home on Diwali.)

INGREDIENTS

250 g	(about 2 cups) **potatoes,** peeled and diced
250 g	**phool gobhi (cauliflower)** cut small
100 g	(about ¾ cup) **gajar (carrots),** diced small
100 g	(5–6) small **baingans (bringals),** slit
250 g	(½ cup) **green peas,** shelled
½ cup	**mooli (radish)** peeled and diced
2–3	sabut lal mirch (whole, dried red chillies)
2 cups	(480 g) **sarson ka tel (mustard oil)**
250 g	tomatoes, grated
1	ripe banana, peeled and chopped into chunks
¼ cup	(60 g) ghee
¼ tsp	heeng (asafoetida)
½ cup	(100 g) dahi (yogurt)
2 tbsp	finely chopped ginger
2 tsp	finely chopped green chilli (or to taste)
¼ cup	hara dhania (coriander leaves) chopped fine
1 tsp	garam masala, soaked in water for about 5 minutes
4 tsp	salt
2 tbsp	lemon juice

Muthia:

250 g	**methi (fenugreek leaves)** 3 cups after chopping
1 tsp	salt
1 tsp	ajwain (thymol seeds)
½ tsp	heeng (asafoetida)
1 tsp	chilli powder
2 tsp	dhania (coriander powder)
1 tsp	jeera (cumin seeds)
¾ cup	(90 g) besan (chickpea/gram flour)
2 tbsp	sarson ka tel (mustard oil)
¼ cup	(50 g) dahi (yogurt)

Soak together in water

1 tbsp dhania (coriander powder)
1 tsp haldi (turmeric)
1 tsp jeera (cumin seeds)
1 tsp chilli powder

METHOD

1. Heat the mustard oil and deep-fry over high heat, the potatoes, cauliflower, carrots, brinjal, peas, radish and whole red chilli and set aside.

2. Pinch off the fenugreek leaves, discarding the stems all together and chop fine.

3. Mix the muthia ingredients into a firm dough, and shape into small rounds.

4. Deep-fry muthias and set aside.

5. Heat the ghee and add the ¼ teaspoon asafoetida and soaked masala. Now add the tomatoes and stir-fry till fat separates.

6. Add the yogurt and stir-fry till fat separates again. Add to this all the vegetables that have been fried, the banana, chopped ginger, green chillies, coriander leaves and garam masala.

7. Mix well and add enough water to just about cover the vegetables (approx 4 cups); bring to boil and then simmer for 15 minutes, or until vegetables are cooked through.

8. Add the muthia and simmer for 5 minutes; add the lemon juice and serve.

156

BHAAJAA

(Another winter preparation of mixed vegetables, predominantly green, which is made in our house the day after Diwali—Govardhan Pooja. This has a bit of a Rajasthani touch to it, which is that, instead of Muthia, Gatte are added in.)

INGREDIENTS

400–500 g	**palak (spinach greens),** chopped fine
200 g	**mooli ka patta (radish leaves),** the tender ones, chopped fine
200 g	tender **leaves of cauliflower,** chopped fine (best got from a vegetable garden or farm)
125 g	**baingan (brinjal),** diced small
125 g	**parwal, (gherkin),** peeled and cut into small pieces
250 g	**tori (ridge gourd),** peeled and diced
250 g	**mooli (radish)** scraped and diced
250 g	**gajar (carrots)** scraped and diced
500 g	**peas,** shelled
250 g	**phool gobhi (cauliflower)** chopped fine
125 g	**sem (broad beans),** strung and chopped
500 g	**kaddu (pumpkin)** cut into small pieces
250 g	**potatoes,** peeled and diced
250 g	**ghiya (bottle gourd),** peeled and diced
½ cup	(120 g) ghee
2 tsp	jeera (cumin seeds)
1 tsp	heeng (asafoetida)
2 tbsp	chopped ginger
2 tbsp	chopped green chillies
2 tbsp	dhania (coriander powder)
1 tsp	haldi (turmeric)
2 tsp	chilli powder
1 tsp	garam masala I (p 148)

Salt to taste
500 g chopped tomatoes
Gatte made from 2 cups chickpea/gram flour (p 157)

METHOD

1. In a large, heavy-based saucepan, heat the ghee and add the cumin seeds and asafoetida. When the cumin seeds splutter, add the ginger and green chillies and stir a few times.

2. Add the coriander, turmeric, chilli powder, garam masala and salt. When the mixture darkens a bit, add the spinach, radish and cauliflower leaves and stir-fry a few times; then lower heat and simmer for about 15 minutes.

3. Add the brinjal, gherkin, ridge gourd, radish, carrots, peas, cauliflower, broad beans, pumpkin, potatoes and bottle gourd. Stir to mix well. Cover and simmer over low heat till vegetables are cooked well.

4. Add the gatte (recipe given below) and simmer for another 10 minutes; then add the tomatoes and simmer till well blended. Add this water or fresh water in case the vegetables dry out too much. The consistency should be damp and moist but not liquid.

2. Rub the ghee into the flour with the tips of your fingers till crumbly. Now add water and knead to a stiff dough. Knead till the dough becomes smooth and glossy and comes off clean from the kneading surface. Cover and set aside for about 15 minutes.

3. Fill a pan with 4 cups of water and place on the stove. While the water is heating, shape the dough into cylindrical rods of about 1 cms (½ in) diameter, and long enough to fit comfortably in the pan in which the water is boiling, without touching its sides. When the water boils, add these and simmer till they come up and are covered with small light coloured bubbles. Lift out of water and set aside to cool. Do not throw away the water.

4. When cool, slice cylinders into about 1 cm/½ in thick discs, which are called gatte.

5. Deep-fry gatte over high heat to golden-brown, and transfer to absorbent paper before adding to the Bhaajaa.

GATTE

INGREDIENTS

2 cups (240 g) **besan (chickpea/gram flour)**
3 tbsp (45 g) ghee
Salt to taste
¼ tsp chilli powder
¼ tsp haldi (tumeric)
Water to knead
Oil to deep-fry

METHOD

1. Sieve the flour and add the salt, chilli and turmeric powder.

EID

This festival is celebrated twice a year. On one occasion meat is distributed and on the other, sevian or sweets are distributed. There are a few dishes made especially on these occasions:

SHAHI KORMA

(A rich, elaborate dish made of boneless mutton/lamb—a dish for special occasions.)

INGREDIENTS

500 g	**meat,** boneless, wt after de-boning	
1 cup	(250 g) onions, chopped and boiled	
5–6	cloves garlic, finely chopped	
1 tsp	ginger, finely chopped	
2 tsp	roasted jeera (cumin seeds)	
1 tbsp	roasted dhania (coriander seeds)	
2 tbsp	poppy seeds (khus khus), soak in water, roast and dry grind	ground to a paste
6–8	almonds, blanched (p 150)	
2 tbsp	magaz (melon seeds), soaked in water	
¼ tsp	kesar (saffron)	
½ cup	(100 g) dahi (yogurt)	

Salt to taste
½ tsp   chilli powder
¼ cup   (60 g) ghee
2   laung (cloves)
2   chhoti elaichi (green cardamoms)
1   tej patta (bay leaf)
4   sabut kali mirch (peppercorns)
2   laung (cloves)

1/8 tsp	roughly broken dalchini (cinnamon)	powdered
1/8 tsp	grated jaiphal (nutmeg)	
½ tsp	kala jeera (black cumin seeds)	
½ cup	finely sliced onions	

½ cup   (120 g) oil
¼ cup   cream
2–3 vark (leaves of beaten silver), for garnish
1 tbsp   slivered, roasted almonds

METHOD

1. Mix together, the meat, ground paste, yogurt, salt and chilli powder and marinate for 3–4 hours.
2. Heat the ghee and add the 2 cloves, cardamoms, bay leaf and peppercorns. When slightly darkened, add the meat mixture and stir-fry over high heat for about 1 minute. Cover and simmer over low heat for about half an hour.
3. Meanwhile, fry the sliced onions in the ¼ cup oil over low heat, till brown and crisp. Drain on absorbent paper, and grind to a paste with a few drops of water.
4. Uncover the meat and continue cooking till tender and fat separates.
5. Mix the ground spices, fried onion paste and cream into the meat preparation and serve hot, garnished with the silver leaf and almonds.

SHORBA-E-PULAO: p 107.

BHUNI KALEJI: p 64.

GURDA KAPOORA

(A speciality which everyone may not have a taste for, but those who do, just love it!)

INGREDIENTS

500 g   **gurda, kapoora (kidneys, sweetbreads),** cleaned and skinned
½ tsp   ginger paste
½ tsp   garlic paste
½ cup   (125 g) grated onions

½	tsp	chilli powder
¼	cup	(50 g) dahi (yogurt)
¼	tsp	garam masala III (p 149)
2	tsp	salt
2	tbsp	(30 g) oil
2	tbsp	hara dhania (coriander leaves) and lemon wedges, for garnish

METHOD

1. Wash meat and mix with ginger, garlic, onions, chilli powder, yogurt, garam masala and salt.

2. Heat the oil and add the onions and saute till golden brown. Add the kidneys and sweetbreads and saute till oil separates. Add ¼ cup water and cook till soft. Saute till oil separates again.

3. Serve garnished with the coriander leaves and lemon wedges on the side.

MAGAZ MASALA: p 65.

SHEER KHURMA: p 111.

Index

Index

162